C0-AUD-264

WHAT I THINK

WHAT I THINK

by

ADLAI E. STEVENSON

GREENWOOD PRESS, PUBLISHERS
WESTPORT, CONNECTICUT

0735459

Library of Congress Cataloging in Publication Data

Stevenson, Adlai Ewing, 1900-1965.
    What I think.

    Selected speeches and articles written after the
Presidential campaign of 1952.
    Reprint of the ed. published by Harper, New York.
    1. United States--Politics and government--1953-
1961--Collected works. 2. World politics--1945-
--Collected works. I. Title.
[E742.5.S752 1974]   320.9'73'0921   74-12647
ISBN 0-8371-7738-3

"My Faith in Democratic Capitalism" is reprinted by
special permission from the October 1955 issue of
Fortune Magazine, © 1955 Time, Inc. "This I Believe"
is reprinted from *This I Believe* by permission of Simon
& Schuster, Inc., Copyright 1954 by Help, Inc.

Copyright 1954, 1955, 1956 by R. Keith Kane

*All rights in this book are reserved. No part of the book may
be used or reproduced in any manner whatsoever without
written permission except in the case of brief quotations
embodied in critical articles and reviews.*

Originally published in 1956 by Harper & Brothers Publishers,
New York

Reprinted with the permission of Harper & Row Publishers, Inc.

Reprinted in 1974 by Greenwood Press,
a division of Williamhouse-Regency Inc.

Library of Congress Catalog Card Number 74-12647

ISBN 0-8371-7738-3

Printed in the United States of America

Dedication

To those thoughtful friends, here and abroad,
who have shared with me their understanding
of the great age in which we live.

Publisher's Note

This book, consisting of selected speeches and articles written by Adlai E. Stevenson since the Presidential campaign of 1952, has been edited to omit repetition, purely local references, and ephemeral matter no longer of interest. Speeches and articles such as these, which relate to changing events and issues, require that the reader bear in mind the circumstances prevailing at the time and the context in which they were prepared.

Contents

Publisher's Note   vi

Introduction   ix

I **The Great Partners: Business, Labor, Farmers and Government**

My Faith in Democratic Capitalism   3

America, the Economic Colossus   18

For the Farmer: Remedies, Not Miracles   30

The Crisis in Agriculture   38

The Legacy of Philip Murray   43

The American Vision   47

II **Democrats and Republicans**

Campaign Mythology and the Public Weal   59

Crusades, Communism, and Corruption   64

The Congressional Campaign Begins   72

Kansas—A Kind of Prophecy   76

A Truth Beyond Politics   82

Rapier versus Ax: A Constructive Opposition   84

The Congressional Campaign Ends   88

The Challenge to Political Maturity   96

On Giving Government Back to the People   105

III **The Common Welfare**

Farewell Report to the Citizens of Illinois   117

Medicine and Public Policy   124

0735459   ~~66314~~

Public Lands, Public Interest, and Republican
    Promises   133
Education, a National Cause   140

IV *First Principles*

This I Believe   151
Free Speech: A Duty   153
Faith, Knowledge, and Peace   157
The Reputation of the Government   164
A New Year's Message   170
The Educated Citizen   172
Women, Husbands, and History   182

V *America and the World*

Traveler's Report   193
War, Weakness, and Ourselves   200
Israel and the Arabs: Ancient Glory and New
    Opportunity   210
The Formosa Crisis: A Peaceful Solution   215
Partnership and Independence   225
The Road Away from Revolution   232

Introduction

FOLLOWING THE Presidential campaign of 1952, a selection of my campaign speeches was published in book form here and abroad.[1] With that first excursion into inadvertent authorship —the words had been intended for the ears, not the eyes, of my audience—I assumed that I would be quit of what Walt Whitman once called "the glad, clear sound of one's own voice."

But since then the Godkin Lectures which I delivered at Harvard in March, 1954, have also been widely published.[2] Articles of mine, moreover, have appeared in magazines and newspapers. And now the patient public is to be afflicted with yet another selection of my writings which take off where the 1952 campaign ended and carry on to the latter months of 1955.

It would seem clear from this record that authorship, like age, creeps up on a man. I am, it would seem, finding my own voice ever gladder and clearer and from being an involuntary author am well on the way to becoming a compulsive one. Perhaps, therefore, a word of explanation is in order to give the context of this book and to suggest why I have felt obliged in the last three years to say so much.

The determining fact in my mind after the elections of 1952 was that I remained—and would remain for some time—the "titular head" of the Democratic party. In our country this role is a very ambiguous one. The titular leader has no clear and defined authority within his party. He has no party office, no staff, no funds, nor is there any system of consultation whereby he may be advised of party policy and through which he may help to shape that policy. There are no devices such as the

[1] United States—*Major Campaign Speeches of Adlai E. Stevenson,* Random House, 1953.
[2] United States—*Call to Greatness,* Harper & Brothers, 1954.

British have developed through which he can communicate directly and responsibly with the leaders of the party in power. Yet he is generally deemed the leading spokesman of his party. And he has—or so it seemed to me—an obligation to help wipe out the inevitable deficit accumulated by his party during a losing campaign, and also to do what he can to revive, reorganize, and rebuild the party.

Taking account of these things, I concluded to try to play my part as best I could and with some degree of planned consistency, until the shadows that await defeated candidates and titular leaders enveloped me. I enlisted a small, informal group of experts in various fields to review and critically evaluate our major public policies, most of which were of Democratic origin. I also resolved to travel extensively in order to enlarge my knowledge of the problems of a world in which the United States has such preponderant power, and, therefore, responsibility. And, finally, there was the necessity of earning some money and maintaining a personal staff.

This was the background to my attempts to fulfill in some measure the responsibilities I inherited from the campaign of 1952. In speeches, articles, and lectures I expressed my view of the contemporary scene. I attempted from time to time to put before the people considered assessments of the administration's policies. And in the mid-term elections of 1954 I played an active and rewarding part in the campaign from Alaska to the Atlantic.

Whether all this added up to responsible political leadership, I do not know. What I do know is that it added up to a staggering amount of writing and speaking, and it is from fragments thereof, selected by the publisher's editors, that the present volume has been put together.

Given this context, it should not surprise anyone to discover that this is primarily a book of criticism. If "the duty of a loyal opposition is to oppose" I cannot see how one can offer effective opposition without giving reasons for it and these reasons are, of course, criticisms. Yet I very well know that in many minds political "criticism" has today become an ugly word. It has become almost *lèse-majesté*. And it conjures up pictures of insidious radicals hacking away at the very foundations of the American way of life. It suggests nonconformity and non-conformity suggests disloyalty and disloyalty suggests treason, and before we know where we are, this process has all but identified the critic with the saboteur and turned political criticism into an un-American activity instead of democracy's greatest safeguard.

The irony of this position—so often held by people who would regard themselves as most respectably conservative—is that it is nowhere more ardently embraced than in Moscow or Peiping. There the critic really is a conspirator and criticism is genuinely an un-Russian or un-Chinese activity. In fact, if I were asked to choose a single principle which underlines more than any other the difference between the Communist and the free philosophy of government, I would be inclined to single out this issue of criticism, which we in the West not only tolerate but esteem. But for the Communists there is one infallibly correct or "objective" method of conducting politics, science, literature, the economy, foreign affairs, love affairs, plumbing, and chess. This one orthodoxy is determined by the Marxist-Leninist world view which, in its turn, is luminously clear to the leaders who happen at the moment to be maintaining themselves at the top of the hierarchy. At all subordinate levels, the only duty is to conform, and the regime continues—infallible, intolerant, and intolerable.

There is nothing new, of course, about compulsory conformity. It has long, frighteningly long, antecedents. Tribal society and archaic civilization and the great Asian cultures—in other words, the overwhelming mass of mankind in time and space—have also believed in a fixed social order, guided by those in authority, which individual men and women are expected not to criticize but to accept. Since the beginning of time, governments have been mainly engaged in kicking people around. The astonishing achievement in modern times in the Western world is the idea that the citizen should do the kicking. So when a large segment of our fellow citizens in this empirical nation develop a strong distrust of criticism, they are reverting to one of humanity's oldest and most deeply rooted instincts. They are abandoning an attitude of mind which one society and one only has managed to evolve—our own free society. And they are suppressing an attitude toward authority and its exercise which has been as characteristically American as baseball.

Here in the West our traditional attitude is that criticism is neither a menace nor an aberration. It is an essential principle of social development. The reason for this is, I suppose, that no civilization has ever had so haunting a sense of an ultimate order of goodness and rationality which can be known and achieved. We even take the Utopian goal of a perfect society seriously. Our attitude toward criticism springs, I believe, from our unique belief in man. We believe that in every human being is implanted reason and the capacity to search for and recognize the truth. But we also believe that this divine spark, this godlike reason, is in tough competition with other needs and drives in the human psyche, including the drive for power. Everyone has it in him to reach for truth and discover it. Similarly, everyone has it in him to distort truth and subject it to his own often dubious ends. The gifts are delivered impartially. Governors and governed are equally equipped and equally vulnerable—the only difference being that the temptations to misuse power are greater for those in positions of power, and likewise their obligations not to mislead their sovereign, the people, are also greater.

How, then, in the face of all these risks and hazards, can truth be advanced and a better order of things achieved? Is not the answer to refuse no man his part in the search and to believe that, if the search is honest, out of all the questioning and searching, the fuller, better answer will emerge? "Great is the truth and will prevail!"—provided no arbitrary limits are set to the probings and searchings of the human mind. That such a process implies criticism is obvious. Criticism is simply the method by which existing ideas and institutions are submitted to the test of principles, ideas, ideals, and possibilities. Criticism, in its fairest and most honest form, is the attempt to test whether what is, might not be better.

This sense of man's balanced greatness and fallibility in the search for truth has made ours a profoundly questing civilization. The Greeks gave us the Promethean myth: of man challenging not impiously but rationally the eternal gods. They laid the foundations of all ordered inquiry in the Socratic method,

xii

the method of advancing upon truth by constant critical questioning and by the rejection of the irrational and illogical as the inquiry proceeds. The Jews gave us the extraordinary figure of Job who, virtually alone of all the figures of antique religion, insisted upon questioning "God's ways with man." Our modern world found its voice in Goethe's Faust, to whom no social order was finally satisfying. And it has always seemed to me singularly appropriate that one of the great symbolic occurrences in our American political history was that honest, fierce, and dignified exchange of criticism known as the Lincoln-Douglas debates in my home state of Illinois.

The tradition of critical inquiry and discussion informs our entire civilization. Our scientific progress is based upon a final belief in rational order coupled with trial and error in establishing that order. At its finest, our religious tolerance is based not on a denial of a spiritual order but upon the belief that man's dignity demands that he should make his own search and find, through freedom to know and to see, the truth which he has it in him to find. And in the field to which fate seems particularly to have assigned me—the field of politics—I claim that our political institutions reflect, profoundly and dynamically, the critical view of life. As Walter Bagehot said: "It was government by discussion that broke the bond of ages and set free the originality of mankind."

We believe that it is better to discuss a question even without settling it than to settle a question without discussing it. And to conduct the discussion the party system has sprung up, based upon the premise that no one political organization has a monopoly of truth and reason. (The totalitarian principle is the exact opposite—that all truth lies in the single party.) The fact that no one planned the party system—that it arose both in Britain and America spontaneously from the conflict of ideas, not of men—suggests how natural an expression it is of fundamental attitudes in the Western mind. The party in power, not possessing infallibly all the answers and being exposed, moreover, to the pressing temptations of power, requires the constant check of critical opposition. Equally, the opposition, mindful that it must be able in due season to take over government, should shun irresponsible criticism.

In this manner, the critical tension between the parties tends to keep both closer to the line of responsibility and honest policy making. The critical dialogue between them is the means of enlightenment to both. The administration in power and the opposition alike are essential to the healthy functioning of the political system. In no other society has the problem of power been so ambitiously, yet subtly, resolved. Self-criticism and self-examination are, as I have said before, the indispensable and not-so-secret weapons of democracy.

But in thus asserting the role of criticism in our public life, I have to make one reservation. The function of criticism as the means of defining virtue and advancing the general welfare can be realized only if its purpose is honest. Scientific research contributes nothing to the advancement of learning if a scientist knowingly falsifies his finds to advance his career or to satisfy "the Party line." Religious freedom is weakened by prophetic frauds and cheap exploiters of emotionalism. Above all, in politics, criticism divorced from honest and constructive purpose ceases to be a proper instrument of democracy. Criticism, not as an instrument of inquiry and reform, but as an instrument of power, quickly degenerates into the techniques of deceit and smear.

The fact that the totalitarians have made the most blatant use of such techniques should not blind us to the fact that their malevolent appearance is not unknown among the democracies. When, for example, in the elections of 1951 some British Labour party candidates cried that Churchill was a warmonger, they were using not criticism but calumny to maintain themselves in office. Yet that was good clean fun compared to the long campaign waged in this country in late years by some Republican partisans to discredit the intelligence, the honesty, even the loyalty, of Democratic leaders in order to capture or keep public office. But such criticism, which is calculated to obscure facts and drown reason in a tide of passion, debases the democratic process and bears no relationship to legitimate criticism which appeals to facts and reason.

Nor are we unfamiliar with critical doubletalk and that cynical partisanship that views public policy as good or bad not on its merit but according to the party or organization that puts it forward. There comes to mind just now, for example,

xiv

the daily denunciation of the "New Deal" by people who not only propose no changes but publicly applaud social security, slum clearance, minimum wages, or what not. In the same pattern some of us have in recent years heard the epithet "appeasement" loud and clear for proposals which later and under different political auspices are acclaimed as shrewd blows for peace and inspired diplomatic initiatives.

This matter goes deeper than the feuds of parties or the day-to-day tactics of political campaigning. If criticism is distorted into calumny, mud slinging, and doubletalk, or if at the other extreme criticism is silenced in a reverential hush, it is not simply this or that party or this or that political figure that must suffer. It is the Republic itself.

No one can suppose that America, in spite of its great achievements and visible well-being, has yet reached the Beatific Vision. No one can suppose the system so perfect that, as a Duke of Cambridge once remarked, "any change in whatever direction for whatever reason is strongly to be deprecated." Since there *is* constant need for change and constant room for improvement, since there is scope for better and wider horizons in our daily life, I would ask by what other mechanism they can be achieved if the spirit of constructive criticism is stifled or abused.

That "a nation without means of reform is without means of survival" is as true today as it was in the time of Burke; yet no reforms have ever been accomplished in free society without full, searching, and vigorous criticism. At all times, such criticism has been resented. At all times, the attempt has been made to discount it by attacking and vilifying the motives of the critics. But democracy has never been saved either by slander or silence. Today, when mass literacy, mass communication, and a contracting ownership of press and radio make conformity the easy option, it is all the more imperative to enliven the attitude of questioning based upon honest concern for the general welfare and upon respect for the honesty of other people's critical approach.

For, paradoxical thought it may seem, free criticism can flourish only in a society where mutual trust is strong. The spirit of criticism shrivels when citizens distrust their neighbors and the give and take of confidence gives place to the silence of suspicion. The neighborliness, the charity, the very goodness of a society, can best be measured by the freedom with which men may honestly speak their minds. Criticism is therefore not only an instrument of free society. It is its symbol and hallmark as well.

This is what I *think*; and there follows some of what I've *said* during the past three years. If what I've *said* falls short of what I *think*, well, ". . . a man's reach should exceed his grasp, or what's a heaven for?"

Libertyville, Illinois
October 15, 1955

ONE

The Great Partners: Business, Labor, Farmers and Government

My Faith in Democratic Capitalism

I AM INVITED by the editors of *Fortune* to look forward with them toward 1980 and to join in the suggestion of goals for American achievement during the next quarter-century. The ultimate goals are, of course, very clear: peace, freedom for ourselves as individuals, and a realization of man's place in a meaningful scheme of things. But it is to a narrower focus that I am asked to address myself; namely, the future of the relationship between two great forces in America's structure—the force of business and industry on the one hand, and on the other, the force of government, particularly the federal government.

If it is expected that comment on this subject by one sometimes close to government—particularly a Democrat!—must inevitably be antagonistic and critical, and slanted against "Big Business," I promise disappointment. I think of this relationship between business and government as essentially one of cooperation between two institutional forces wholly dependent upon each other. If there were but one twenty-five-year goal to fix upon in this area it would be, for me, to stop the talk about a basic antagonism between American business and government, and replace such nonsense with a recognition of the common purposes and obligations of these two cornerstones of democratic capitalism.

We all make the mistake of thinking about institutions, such as business and government, as ends in themselves. Most of the friction between businessmen and bureaucrats in this country has arisen from their constantly having to remind each other that neither government nor business is an end in itself, that they both are only institutional means to the ends of individual purpose; and that whether the relationship between

Originally published in Fortune, *October, 1955.*

them is "good" or "bad" is measurable solely in terms of how the relationship pays off in the lives and satisfactions of 165 million people, or, more broadly, of all humanity.

I find the measure of the strength of this relationship in the fact that the past quarter-century has seen in America the most extraordinary growth any nation or civilization has ever experienced. Our rise in population has been largely a function of our increased prosperity and productivity; our millions of new mouths to feed are better fed than fewer mouths were only twenty-five years ago. The possessions of a modest family today exceed those of a "prosperous" one in 1930. While the population of some unhappy countries rises against the most dreadful counterpressures and in spite of wishes that it could be restrained, our numbers increase out of a sense that we can well afford such increase. An important part of the example we show the world is the fact that we are the nation of the most powerful consumers on earth.

It was not always so. It was not so twenty-five years ago. It is a curious thing that the two institutional forces in the democratic capitalistic society that contributed most directly to this emergence of the powerful consumer during this quarter-century seemed to snarl at each other every step of their common way. The bounding prosperity of postwar America has been due in large measure to processes in which government and business have in effect played complementary and co-operative roles. The New Deal legislation of the thirties helped to provide a "built-in" consumer demand that business could then work to satisfy, and the increase of 70 per cent in the scale of the American economy between 1939 and 1944 was achieved by the closest co-operation between government and industry in America's war effort.

Yet, in spite of this practical realization of common interests and common goals, it became part of the ritual of New Deal politics to castigate a business system that has always been recognized by Americans as the only permanent source of the jobs and consumer purchasing power which "the government" was trying to restore. And in the meantime the businessmen, who rose from prostration to record-breaking prosperity through satisfying a multibillion consumer demand that was stimulated and buttressed by New Deal legislation, became the bitterest critics of this New Deal legislation.

I know the arguments that business *might* have recovered even faster in the later thirties if it hadn't been for government "regimentation" (also referred to as "drift") and "exercise of arbitrary power" (also referred to as "indecisiveness"). If those arguments ever needed answer they have it in the decision of the present "businessman's government" in Washington not to curtail the federal programs that underwrite consumer purchasing power but to enlarge them. Nor in current talk of "getting government out of business" does there appear to be much recognition that government is in business to the tune of about $15 billion worth of military orders each year and is therefore playing, whatever the theory of the matter, a decisive part in keeping demand steady through the whole economy.

One of the future goals for American government and American business must surely be a fuller recognition that the maintenance of demand in the interests of the consumer— which is one of the few things everybody in this country is—is basic to both.

A broader aspect of the common purpose of business and government in America emerges from recognition of the new and tremendous sense of commonality that has come over this nation in the past twenty-five years. The individual no longer stands alone. His smallest community is larger, and more diverse in its services. His light and power come no longer from his own windmill or from some small local utility company, but usually from a vast network. His bank is strongly interconnected with its fellows, and his deposits are insured. The same news reaches him and his neighbors, and faster than it ever did before. An incredible linkage of wires and roads and co-operative enterprises, public and private, has taken isolation (and now isolationism) from all but the remotest homes in America.

In ways we hardly realize, this commonality brings inevitable interweavings of the functions of business and government. When the services of even two people are joined there are decisions of "governing" to be made; and when thousands and then millions invest or work together in a common business enterprise, their dealings together become more and more like the relationships we call government. What we used to think of as the "decentralized decision-making of the market place" has given way to various processes of large-scale private institutional decision-making remarkably like that of government in both its methods and its results. We constantly see in such things as labor unions, corporations, and trade associations, and in the "bargaining" that goes on between them, a reflection of the private institutional needs for "government."

As a people we are doing world-shaking and history-making things today—partly as the result of individual genius, but perhaps even more because we have learned of the powers of individuals working together. A brilliant professor turned businessman, Beardsley Ruml (who reformed the nation's thinking on how to collect the income tax and has more recently been trying to perform an equal miracle on our notion of the federal budget), has declared that the greatest economic discovery of the twentieth century so far is the realization that the wisely directed actions of all of us, *as a whole,* can compensate for the aberrations or misfortunes of a few. A. J. Toynbee suggests that three hundred years from now the twentieth century will be remembered, not for its wars, not for its conquests of distance and disease, not even for the splitting of the atom—but for "having been the first age, since the dawn of civilization, some five or six thousand years back, in which people dared to think it practicable to make the benefits of civilization available for the whole human race." I hope the judgment of this great historian comes true. My instincts tell me it will.

It was in America that the first practical stirrings of this great idea began. We must bring the idea to such perfection that it will save the very civilization it has awakened. Another goal, then, for 1980 America—so that we may disprove George Orwell's terrifying prediction for 1984—is that this process of our growing commonality must and will be everywhere recognized and acknowledged, *not so that it can be senselessly accelerated, but so that it can be wisely guided and controlled.* I hold no belief in economic determinism; I bow to Shakespeare, not Marx, when I declare that there is a tide in the affairs of men, and that we had better acknowledge it.

This new sense of commonality is not without its dangers.

6

Security, whether economic, political, or social, has become an individual and national obsession. I wonder if we fully realize the relationship between this yearning for security and the problem of maintaining our civil liberties. Security doesn't come free. Sometimes its price—or the price some would charge for it—is conformity and groupthink, and so it becomes part of the future joint obligation of the forces of business and government to respect, yes and protect, those elements of individuality that commonality threatens.

It is not true that the individual rolls around today like a kernel of grain between the upper and nether millstones of Big Government and Big Business—but there is a danger here that is great enough to warrant our keeping such a picture always in mind. Even as we become increasingly vigilant in our battle against the debilitating force of Communism we must be aware of another enemy that creeps upon us even more quietly and insidiously: the army of mass mediocrity, with banners flying.

Democracy's literature is full of warnings against the overpowering of the individual by the agencies of government and business. A hundred years ago John Stuart Mill deplored society's encroachments on the individual. John Ruskin prophesied the destruction of aesthetics by the industrial revolution. Lord Acton used some of his careful, rationed counsel to warn that democracy's flaw might prove to be—despite its protestations of the state's sublimation to the individual—a lack of moral criteria. Learned, sensitive, eloquent, these eminent Victorians voiced their concern that progress in the arts of statecraft and industry might make its intended beneficiaries its victims. Perhaps our survival in the face of these unhappy prophecies shows how wrong they were. Surely the individual is still today not *wholly* fenced in, except by the Kremlin, which Mill did not happen to be thinking of. As for the destruction of aesthetics, it turns out that in some ways—in modern design, in support of artistic efforts—industry is one of the best friends aesthetics has in the modern world.

Yet we know, from warnings that are more sensed than seen or heard, that all is not well with our status as individuals. Consciously or unconsciously, we are erecting battlements against our own accomplishments. Man in the individual sense today is not man's only adversary. We are concerned, too, about a strange, not wholly definable force in which there are at least the identifiable elements of "government" and "technology" and "massiveness" in this age of mass population, mass education, mass communications—yes, and mass manipulation. Indeed it seems that at mid-twentieth century, mass manipulation is a greater danger to the individual than was economic exploitation in the nineteenth century; that we are in greater danger of becoming robots than slaves. Surely it is part of the challenge of this next quarter-century that industry and government and the society they both support must find new and better ways of restoring scope to that strange eccentric, the individual.

Nostalgia won't help. We shall never dis-invent the airplane, which sets down the evil of Communism in our back yard instead of leaving it to fester outside our notice five thousand miles away. We shall never recover the quiet privacy the individual had before the telephone, the hand camera, and the microphone. We shall not relock the atom. A small fraction of our citizens have already come out flatly for government by lie detector. Some businesses maintain, in the name of security, "black lists" that in effect can deprive a man of the right to work without inquiry, due process, or even hope of ultimate redress. I can't help suspecting that some social scientists and even psychiatrists would love to find a combination of electronic devices by which every citizen could be measured for the slightest personal or social aberrations from some assigned "norm," and I suspect they will get it from our onrushing technologists. On this kind of assault on the individual I stand precisely where Calvin Coolidge stood on sin: I am agin it. I propose to keep on being agin it.

But we shall have to learn the art of coexistence with many strange things in the future, some of them perhaps even stranger than Communism. Technology, while adding daily to our physical ease, throws daily another loop of fine wire around our souls. It contributes hugely to our mobility, which we must not confuse with freedom. The extensions of our senses, which we find so fascinating, are not adding to the discrimina-

8

tion of our minds, since we need increasingly to take the reading of a needle on a dial to discover whether we think something is good or bad, or right or wrong.

Deepest pride in the accomplishments of America's inventive genius is no warrant for congratulating ourselves on any best-of-all-possible-worlds. Materially we can—and will—do better still. But spiritually, morally, and politically, I don't think we are doing so well. Both industry and government are contributing enormously to the almost unbelievable advance of technology in America—but both must become increasingly aware of their moral and spiritual responsibilities. The representative of a great manufacturing concern, speaking about the phenomenon we call automation, concluded: "I don't think it is the part, nor can it be the part, of industry to try to plan the social aspects of this thing." It seems to me, to the contrary, that industry is eventually, with government, going to have to do its full share of thinking about the sociology as well as the economics of such things as automation and the split atom. The more realistic and broad-gauge view is suggested by David Sarnoff's comment, in an earlier article in this *Fortune* series, that "if freedom is lost, if the dignity of man is destroyed, advances on the material plane will not be 'progress' but a foundation for a new savagery."

There is increasing realization that one of the biggest problems of these next twenty-five years will be what we are going to do with "the new leisure" which it appears will develop as one of the fruits of the new technology. As people learn how to live longer after their service in the regular work force is done, as machines and "feedbacks" and push buttons take on more and more of the job of production, as the inevitably shortened work week materializes—with these things there comes a whole host of new adjustments to be made. No one need fear the long-range effects of machines replacing men, but the adjustment is going to require responsible and thoughtful administration, and the new leisure will mean new happiness only if care is taken not to confuse leisure with just plain having nothing to do.

It is inevitable that government in America will be called upon during this next quarter-century to meet the social implications of these ever more rapid technological advances, and I see no reason why American industry should not participate fully and freely in this enterprise. There seems to me no escape from this obligation. It just will not do to leave all worrying about our souls to the educators, the clergy, and the philosophers. The men to whom mass America tunes its ear today are businessmen—indeed, they seem to have more influence on youth than the schools, more influence on the devout than the clergy, more influence on the wicked than the thought of perdition. With this prestige goes a responsibility that can be given no artificial boundaries.

I shall not attempt to suggest a particular role for industry in the transforming of technology's dark threats into bright promises. Part of this role will undoubtedly lie in an increased laying aside of great funds to foster education in all fields, not confining such funds to the sciences or to what is of immediate or "practical" significance. The day of the great individual philanthropist is nearly over, and industry must step into this breach. Even as I write this there comes to my desk a list of fifty research memoranda being prepared as part of a joint project of a large private corporation and a branch of the federal government. Would that just one of the fifty memoranda related to the heart of industrial progress—instead of all of them to its hands and feet and muscle! Adolf A. Berle, Jr., suggests in his recent book a broader emergent concept of the corporation as an instrument of social leadership and responsibility, chargeable with a stewardship as broad as all the implications of its economic effects. This, it seems to me, must be the direction of our progress.

It could be hoped that one of the dividends of a "businessman's government" might be a merging of the thinking *both* in business and in government about economic and human affairs. And yet there has been quite a lot of talk from high government spokesmen about being "conservative" in economic affairs and "liberal" in human affairs. I don't know how this works where something like unemployment or social security is involved. Are those "economic" or "human" affairs?

If there is value in a definition of "conservatism" that would cross economic-human and business-government lines (and even Republican-Democratic lines), may I reiterate what Thomas Carlyle said a hundred years ago: the conservatism that *really* conserves is that which lops off the dead branch to save the living tree. Our American economy has fewer dead branches than that of any other nation, I am sure; but that we shall need pruning and spraying and the application of new fertilizers and growth regulators in the future as in the past, I have no doubt. Should it perhaps be part of our purpose in these years ahead to recognize that the process of conservation must be a joint government and business responsibility, and that division of function between "human" and "economic" is unrealistic in today's complex society?

I hope this quarter-century will see a frank recognition that every new frontier in American progress has been, and will always be, opened up by the *joint* enterprise of business and government. Great respect for the concept of the "rugged individualist" (usually incorporated) is no warrant for the illusion that modern America was *created* by businessmen—any more than it was by Senators or the Founding Fathers. Before colonial America could emerge from its colonialism, and a few cities could become interconnected with a subsistence agriculture and the tinkering sheds of a few ingenious Yankees, the federal government had to assert its power. Before America could become a great industrial nation the federal government had to assert its power over territory in terms of a U.S. Army that would explore and protect; in terms of a federal treasury that would regulate and expand the national credit; and in many other terms of a state that would hold title to the whole public domain until private entrepreneurs could slowly, on terms adjudged to be for the public benefit, take over vital business and industrial procedures. There were very few businessmen (and no government officials) in the Conestoga wagons that toiled across the West only a little more than a century ago; their time and place and function came later.

No; business did not create America or the American way. The American way was created in a complex collaboration whereby the federal government offered to individuals the best soil and nurture for enlightened capitalism ever devised—and the individuals took it on the generous terms offered.

11

Nor is this interdependence of government and business reflected only in historical vignettes. We accept today as one of our great principles that operation of industry is a properly private function. Yet so long as technology burgeons, the interrelationships between government and industry will continue to grow more complex, not less. Where technology disemploys workers, government will be asked to help. It must help. Where it creates surpluses, government will be asked to help. It must help.

There is no reason to be afraid of growing complexity; indeed our option is to deal cheerfully and courageously with growing complexity—or to go over the authoritarian abyss. I see no reason why the need to confront complexity is more ominous merely because it may require new formulas of private-public co-operation.

A fascinating future relationship between government and business, for example, will occur when Alaska is truly "opened." Before business and industry can begin to pour Alaska's resources into the mainstream of the world's commercial life, millions of dollars' worth of trunk and access roads will have to be built, and someone will have to complete the geological mapping of 586,400 square miles of territory so that private mining companies will have some notion of what, where, and how great the mineral treasure of Alaska really is —facts unknown today. Shall we organize a purely private Alaskan Corporation of America to take all these risks? Or may it be necessary to accept some subvention from the federal government to get things going? Regardless of our preachments we may be sure it will be the latter, as in large part it already has been.

In spite of resounding keynote speeches and business-convention oratory, it is an obvious fact that this pattern of co-operation between government and private enterprise runs through our economy from end to end. One of the most pervasive of all influences is without doubt the tariff—that massive governmental intervention that is generally left off the standard anathema list of many businessmen. Much of the work of the Atomic Energy Commission is undertaken through the agency of private corporations. Business in the Northwest has certainly not been retarded by cheap public power. And just how much of the newspaper and magazine industry is carried by the taxpayer through the government's massive subsidy of second-class mail?

There will be a testing of a good deal of unthinking talk when it comes time to consider translating into action the Hoover Commission's recommendations for liquidating the structure of government lending agencies. It seems a conservative prognosis that these recommendations will be loudly honored for their expression of the sacrosanct and sound principle of the least-government-possible and that it will then be more quietly decided that most of these agencies (with perhaps a little exterior redecoration) come within the least-possible limits.

I am not suggesting that American business and industry owe either an unpaid debt or any attitude of servile gratitude to the federal government. The creative record of American capitalism is altogether too strong and dignified in its own right to call for subservience to any other force. What I am suggesting, however, is that there could be a good deal more realism and quite a lot less nonsense in the recognition by the business community of the interdependence, if you will, of the two essential democratic capitalistic institutions of business and government. We are past the point of adolescence in a relationship where it once was perhaps understandable that those who profited in largest sum from the operation of our system of things might still clamor about the federal government as a childishly operated nuisance, which hampers business, which intrudes, which confiscates or expropriates profits, and in a thousand ways spoils all the fun and is constantly threatening to "socialize" all America by creeping. It seems to me an essential element of our present maturity to recognize that the relationships between the two institutions do not consist exclusively of government's recourseless taxation or browbeating of business.

We too rarely realize how very great and needless a strain is placed on this relationship just by the verbal violence that is indulged in in describing its elements. "Economic royalists" was an unfair and unfortunate epithet. To call the TVA "Communism," or rural electrification "Socialism"—the list of such clichés is long—is a kind of nonsense that insults the facts and serves only evil. It is an important goal for America-1980 that what is publicly said or reported regarding such things be better adjusted to what is generally true. This will require, among other things, an enormous improvement in the standards and practices of American journalism.

Before leaving the subject of the interaction of government and industry, I should speak of a vital area in which failure to formulate joint and consistent policies can have the effect not simply of weakening the domestic economy but of imperiling America's position of leadership in the free world. I refer, of course, to those tariff, trade, and custom practices that hamper and addle world commerce to the disadvantage of the whole Western world, ourselves included. As a goal for the future, to be achieved many years sooner than distant 1980, I would certainly hope for relaxed restrictions on world commerce—a relaxation not just on tariffs—to the end of freer and freer trade among the nations. Policies that were appropriate only in the day when it was accurate to speak of "our infant industries" can lead to social, political, and economic misfortune in our industrial manhood. And insofar as the need for capital and technical assistance in the less developed areas has become perhaps the greatest limiting factor on expanding world trade, I would hope, too, for new and courageous action by public and private agencies in this field as well. On tariff reductions the government (under Democratic administrations, at least) has led the way since 1934 and earlier. In providing capital and technical "know-how" for world development, it is the government that has made the start. Business must educate its members to follow.

But perhaps the most urgent problem that will be set before government and business alike by pressures generated beyond America's frontier will prove to be the issue of disarmament. We cannot deny that the overwhelming desire of our own people and of all the world's peoples is to be rid of the nightmare of atomic war. There are some signs that the Communists are feeling this enormous pressure of popular longing for peace. It is not inconceivable that in the next decade we shall

14

be required to take the lead in dismantling a part of our vast military structure of preparedness. The impact upon the national economy of falling expenditures for arms will be profound and it will take the best efforts and the concerted efforts of government and business to see that the transition from a large measure of military spending to an overwhelmingly civilian economy is accomplished without a downward spiral and grave dislocation in the whole economic system. Neither government nor business can manage that alone. It would be well if its implications were examined jointly—and soon.

Perhaps most of what I have mentioned here comes together in a suggestion that we might profitably think in terms of a doctrine of "separation of powers" in this area of business and government relations—a separation resembling the constitutional differentiation between the executive, the legislative, and the judicial in government itself. This is a formula for "checks and balances," and yet essentially for co-ordination and co-operative functioning toward common goals. The future of government and business does not consist in *either one* having ambitions to take over the functions of the other. It is an essential goal for the future to keep their separation jealously guarded.

Government in America has *always* regarded the operation of industry as a purely private function. To return to an earlier example, even the newest-biggest of all governmental agencies, born in the early days of the Atomic Age and the Fair Deal— the AEC—operates its vast, complex, "monopolistic," and largely secret domain through private industrial contractors. But business has yet to show a comparably broad and tolerant understanding of the legitimate domain of government. In fact, some sections of the business community could not do better than follow, in this regard, Dr. Johnson's advice, and clear their minds of cant and prejudiced misinformation, not to say the downright nonsense about "governmental dictatorship," and, of course, "creeping Socialism" that all too often, as a species of businessmen's groupthink, takes the place of responsible consideration of the proper functions of government in free society.

This idea of a different kind of "separation of powers" does not require being against "businessmen in government." Not at all. But it does suggest that when businessmen, like anyone else, are being selected for government posts, it should be because of their talents for the job of government and for no other reason. To the extent that "businessmen in government" means the introduction into government of the ideals and practices of efficiency for which American business is justly famous —and to the degree that it also means adding to government councils an intimate understanding of industry and commerce —to that extent and degree this is all to the good and none should object. The case is very different, though, wherever a businessman brings with him to government any ideas other than a completely objective and independent concept of the public good.

An intelligent businessman, now a member of the current administration, said before he reached his present public eminence: "Commercial interests are not the same as national interests." How right he was, and is. Although commercial interests and national interests can and usually do walk a certain distance hand in hand, no full identity between them can ever be forced, and any attempt to force it would be apt to end in misery, or disaser, or both—and for both.

Over the years, the federal government, in Republican and Democratic administrations, enacted the Sherman and the Clayton acts to prevent concentrations of power in plutocratic hands, and no wiser or more beneficial legislation has ever been enacted in America—for business. In Europe, where these laws are incomprehensible, and a cozy hand-in-glove-ism between governments and industries has its expression in the cartel system, we see many brilliant accomplishments. But we do *not* see any properly significant diffusion downward of the profits and benefits of the industrial system, which, in this country, constitutes our most effective safeguard against radical infection in any large masses of our public.

It was governmental intervention, beginning about fifty years ago, that broke up the trusts. If American business had remained in the image of the "oil trust," the "steel trust," the "sugar trust," the "whiskey trust," America as we know it today would never have come into existence, and the leadership of the modern world would almost certainly reside elsewhere—

doubtless in a totally Prussianized or Communized Europe, with the British Isles reduced to the status of a tourist resort, and America still a giant agricultural bumpkin among the nations.

Events took a very different turn. We are not yet fully grown up to our responsibilities of world leadership, and we groan understandably under the burdens placed upon us. But despite two hideous wars, the history of the twentieth century is by no means so tragic—yet—as it might be, and the vast area of hope still alive in the world lies squarely here, with us. The past interactions between American government and American business, brawling and ill-natured though they were, have been a major determinant of the shape and course of the modern Western world. Given an improved respect and understanding between these properly separated forces in America, I can look forward to the next twenty-five years with confidence, and think of all the Western world, potentially, as a land of hope and glory, Mother of the Free.

"What is past," says the inscription in front of the National Archives Building in Washington, "is prologue." To this I say amen.

America, the Economic Colossus

A COUNTRY that is large, strong, and rich in material blessings in a world that is much less favored—that is the position of the United States in the world at large. What, first of all, does this mean?

As the plane I came here on today rose above Chicago and its neighboring cities, I saw from its windows the mills which produce twenty-five million tons of steel each year—seven million tons more than is produced in the Ruhr, core of Western Germany's industrial might and the greatest steel-producing center in Europe.

Beyond the great industrial girdle of Chicago I looked down on what is to me one of the great sights of the earth—the corn belt, the richest farming country in the world, rolling away to the horizons in geometric patterns of green pastures, black earth, and brown oceans of ripening corn. I saw the neat, trim farmhouses and silos of mid-America, the cattle and the hogs, the barns which house tractors, corn pickers, combines, and all the other machines which every year increase the embarrassment of riches we call the "farm problem."

Do you know what I thought about most as this spectacle of wealth and beauty unfolded beneath me? I thought first of the Soviet farm officials who have recently seen this, too. And I wondered if they came to understand while they were here not only the technology of our productive agriculture, but also that it is the product of free men and that, being rooted in human freedom it can neither be achieved nor long maintained in any other condition. And my other thought was of people. Having visited much of the world, I recalled how densely

From the Great Issues lecture, University of Texas, September 28, 1955. The general title for the series of lectures in which Mr. Stevenson was asked to participate was "The American Dollar, for Peace or for Power."

crowded most of the good places are, and I thanked Providence that our problem is too much, not too little.

Then came the vast expanse of the Great Plains, so well named, where a whim of the weather may increase or decrease the wheat yield by more than enough to supply all of Britain's wheat needs for a whole year—and the English, I should add, must import 130 million bushels of wheat every year, 10,000 tons every day.

From that silent, majestic drama of nature I turned for a moment to our staggering statistics of production. We produce, for example, half of the world's cotton (a significant portion of it right here in Texas) and almost half of the world's electric power. Our national income during the 1950's equaled the national incomes of Britain, Germany, France, Canada, and Japan combined.

These figures merely suggest the material dimensions of America, the economic colossus. In terms of sheer material potency and well-being, we are without equal or precedent. Nor need there be any sense of guilt over this happy result; our living standards have not been gained by impoverishing others. Even back in the disagreeable old days before "Geneva," not even the Communists seriously claimed that! While material well-being may not be the first and is certainly not the only requisite for happiness, it surely helps. Man does not live by bread alone, but neither can he live without it. And nations who would help others must first have helped themselves.

Yet we know that nations, like men, have trouble wearing riches and power with grace. Indifference and arrogance have too often been the handmaidens of success. We are familiar with the temptation to attribute one's own accomplishments to virtue, and the misfortunes of others to a lack of diligence, brains, or piety. Early in the present century, a prominent American industrialist stated that the interests of the workingmen would be protected, not, to use his term, by the "agitators," but "by the Christian gentlemen to whom God in his wisdom has entrusted the property interests of this country." He was not the first to confuse the prestige and power which go with the ownership of wealth with omniscience, virtue, and even divinity. Rich nations have made the same mistake. His-

19

tory in the end has always proved them wrong. In the meantime they have not had or deserved the affection of the less fortunate.

We must not repeat this error. Humility and modesty, not pride or arrogance, must be the badges of our greatness. I do not think we are an arrogant or an immodest people, and certainly we have been a generous people. Let us so remain.

And now, having humbly acknowledged our debts and modestly cheered our successes, let us ask: How did our economic power come about? How have we used it? How shall we use it?

A glance at our economic history will disclose that we have never been the isolated, self-reliant, and self-sufficient nation that some of our shriller patriots picture us. While most thoughtful people realize that "going it alone" is insane egotism in the modern world, many don't realize that we didn't exactly make it all on our own in our glorious past.

There is no need to remind the reader that it was the demand for cotton for the Lancashire mills that opened a great industry in Texas, and that without foreign trade our prosperity would be but a shadow of its present rotund self.

But though I stress our economy's interdependence with that of other peoples lest we forget it, our present tremendous industrial strength is due largely to devices of our own creation. Some are technological inventions—the telegraph, telephone, electric light, airplane, and so on indefinitely. Others are devices for increasing production and improving distribution— the assembly line, mass merchandising, modern transportation, for example.

I think of Eli Whitney, a most interesting Connecticut Yankee, as symbolizing much of this history of America's ingenuity and enterprise. In 1798 he contracted to supply 10,000 muskets to the United States government in two years. Impossible! cried skilled gunsmiths. Not at all, replied Whitney. And he proceeded to do so.

By 1801, Jefferson could write to Madison, marveling that Whitney had "invented molds and machines for making all the pieces of his locks so exactly equal that, take 100 locks to pieces and mingle their pieces, and the 100 locks may be put together by taking pieces which come to hand." And so the system of manufacturing standardized interchangeable parts through a division of labor and the use of machines came into existence, to be followed by the assembly-line techniques of mass production which men like Henry Ford later applied with such huge success to industry in general.

But Whitney could not have visualized what was to flow from his inspired genius. Since the success of his armory, individual human skills, whether manual or mental, have become steadily less important to the actual work of producing goods. Machines took over. Organization took over. Routine took over. And they continue to take over with a frightening speed as we move into the age of automation—an age in which accounting and even the administration or direction of work is increasingly usurped by electronic brains.

Eli Whitney was most certainly a "rugged individualist" in the sense in which that phrase is commonly used. But the America which Whitney foreshadowed and helped create was to require new meaning for this phrase. It became an America in which industrial individualism meant less and less as the old-style craftsman was replaced by a machine. In this new America the shoemaker, the ironmonger, the gunsmith, the miller, the butcher, the merchant, was with increasing frequency not an individual but a corporation whose "personality" was a legal fiction. (Indeed, it would seem that our industrial genius flourished not so much from the "rugged individualism" in which we have been wont to take such pride, but in almost the very opposite—in planning and administering vast organizations in which the individual plays a limited role.)

As time went on these corporations grew in size. They also grew in effectiveness and in vigor. We owe much to their development. There was also a price. From the abuses of unregulated and aggressive enterprises came anti-trust laws, militant labor unions, measures to protect and succor the small man. Here arose many of the great issues that have divided our two major political parties and given to them their distinctive features through the last eighty years.

And out of the debates of our political parties, through two major depressions and two world wars, out of corporate risk-taking and enterprise, out of the interaction of science and industry, labor and agriculture, out of our universities and public

21

forums, out of all this creative ferment has emerged this giant of power and complexity, this marvel of vital flexible organization, which is America, the Economic Colossus of today.

If men and women as individuals have contributed greatly to this development, so have they, too, through their common agencies of government. At the time when we ourselves were an underdeveloped nation and suffering from a shortage of private capital, not only investors abroad but our state and national governments supplied indispensable help and stimulus to businessmen. Ever since, our governments have undertaken or stimulated a wide variety of economic activities. Between the Panama Canal and the Alaska Railway, both public enterprises, the government has hundreds of enterprises and some of them, like the Tennessee Valley Authority, have become models for the modern world. The proper test of the propriety of these activities, not always an easy one to apply, is whether the government can do a thing more efficiently and effectively than private enterprise or whether it does something that private enterprise cannot or will not do at all. We rely as a rule on private enterprise, not because it is sacred, but because it is more efficient and effective, and because the business of government is government, and not business.

I am persuaded that we Americans, since 1900, have not searched altogether in vain for means of reconciling individual freedom and this highly organized and impersonal industrial society. It seems to me that we are finding the answers by replacing the old concept of freedom *versus* organization with a new concept of freedom *through* organization. Government, according to our new working conception, may and indeed must play a positive role in our economy in order to make sure that advancing technology is the servant, not the master of our people.

In other words, we have formed a unique partnership between governmental and private enterprise, a mixed economy which is the despair of doctrinaire reactionaries as it is of doctrinaire radicals—including the Communist leaders who have been freely predicting the collapse of capitalism for a long time. It is an arrangement which has thus far proved remarkably responsive to our vast and varied and constantly shifting needs.

Slowly, sometimes painfully, most of us have come to realize that mass production implies mass consumption, and that mass consumption in a free economy requires mass purchasing power. This in turn requires that our total national income, in dollars, be so distributed as to be quickly effective in the market place. It is bad economics for too high a proportion of our total income to go into too few hands—another instance, I think, of the fact that in our society social justice and economic well-being go hand in hand and that there can be no fruitful coexistence between prosperity and selfishness.

To achieve a market whose demand keeps pace with an ever-expanding supply, we have used the power of representative government in several creative ways. Through graduated income taxes, through public works, through encouragement of labor unions and collective bargaining, through slum clearance and public housing, through the protection of the public domain, through expansion of foreign trade, through the policy of equal treatment for the farmer—through these and other public measures we have helped to make our way to our present power and abundance, our present impressive and always dangerous eminence as the economic colossus of the twentieth century.

Now how have we *used* our abundance? How have we worn our crown, how have we waved our scepter—imperiously and acquisitively, or humbly and generously? Here I think the record—the record of late years—is best of all.

We have—at least most of us—abandoned the illusions of isolationism, whose disastrous consequences following World War I we all know. (Although I can't overlook that many bitter and myopic authors of that policy long enjoyed public favor.) Latterly many of us have been inclined to resent the burdens which world leadership imposes on us. We've been irritable and impatient and sometimes dangerously wrong as we strove to organize the free world against the Communist threat. But in general we have realized in effective action that our individual liberties as well as our national security require strong allies and our vigorous participation in all the affairs of the world in which we live. We have, in short, accepted the international obligations which our strength imposes upon us. We have decided wisely, I think, to use our economic power for peace, and peace, we have come to realize from the experience of two global wars, is indivisible in an interdependent world.

The cost to us has been enormous; and be it said to America's everlasting credit that we have asked nothing in return that we have not wished for all people—peace, security, and well-being. While the record in Asia is less comforting, our foreign policy achievements, in short, are impressive and they disclose, *on the whole*, a generosity, a practicality, a concern for human values, and a respect for other peoples worthy of our great blessings, and our colossal economic potency. And meanwhile *we* Americans have also prospered, man for man, as never before.

Quite an achievement, indeed, in the past twenty years, and I say "on the whole," because we have not been without error. We have often obscured the purity of our purpose and created many false impressions of America—that it was selfish, acquisitive, irritable, erratic, belligerent, and dangerous. And, of course, we have left no uncertainty about our preference for our way of doing things, whether applicable or not. Not long ago loud and influential voices in this country were denouncing aid for Britain because it had a Socialist government. The noisy controversy about sending wheat to starving India because it was neutral was overheard in Asia. Our debates have not been without serious proposals to use economic coercion. Our preoccupation with military co-operation has disturbed many newly independent and suspicious peoples. And some of us have lectured our friends very freely on the error of their economic ways.

Indeed, from our fertile fields or possibly from our less fertile minds, we seem to produce two kinds of economics. One is a highly refined, triple-distilled product which is roughly 200 proof *laissez faire*. This is bottled exclusively for export. We never drink it at home. For home consumption we have a much milder drink, a mixture of many ingredients, which isn't so easily described but doesn't give such a shock to the system as we prescribe for others whose systems are much weaker.

We should be careful and discriminating in all the advice we give. We should be especially careful in giving advice that we would not think of following ourselves. Most of all, we ought

24

66314

to avoid giving counsel which we don't follow when it damages those who take us at our word. Unhappily, I can easily illustrate what I mean.

During the last few years we have heard a lot of talk about trade and not aid. Repeatedly our friends abroad have been told to rely on trade and not handouts. Trade, it was said, marks the only path to prosperity that is both self-respecting and reasonably permanent. And "trade not aid," a phrase that was coined abroad, is precisely what these foreign countries want too.

But the gap between our professions and our performance has been widening. As our friends have expanded their trade with us—as they have enlarged their American markets—we have raised tariffs or imposed quotas, or simply refused to buy. These actions have not yet been especially important in the dollar volume of the trade they have affected, but collectively they have served notice on our friends as to just what may happen if they are successful in developing large exports to this country.

The Secretary of Commerce, crowned last year as the favorite friend of free enterprise by the National Association of Manufacturers, has been quoted as saying that we should avoid the embarrassment of rejecting low bids on government contracts from abroad by giving notice that we won't accept them in the first place. I think the gentleman is correct. If our government has changed its mind on "trade not aid" and is opposed to both trade and aid, then it should say so. Such a policy might be inconsistent, selfish, shortsighted, and equally damaging to ourselves and to our friends, but at least it would not be transparently deceptive.

In saying all this I am not proposing that we adopt free trade tomorrow, or that we take any precipitous step which would cause serious dislocations of the American economy. I do think, however, we should recognize once and for all that we are the great creditor nation of the world, and that if we are to sell our goods abroad, whether they be farm surpluses or automobiles, we must permit foreign producers to sell in our market to earn the dollars to buy our products. Once we face this fact squarely and act accordingly, *as producers* we will find more purchasers for our goods and we will sell more;

as consumers, we will be able to buy what we need more cheaply; and *as a nation* we will have a far stronger moral position in our international dealings. To paraphrase a familiar remark, and I hope improve it: What is good for the whole free world is good for the U.S.A.

A well-considered and carefully administered program of economic and technical assistance to underdeveloped areas should also be a fixed part of the policy of a developed and prosperous country. Others have assumed this responsibility through the United Nations and the Colombo Plan of the British Commonwealth. This is a time of revolution in the underdeveloped areas of the world. I have called it "the revolution of rising expectations" because countless people are becoming aware of the modern world and demanding more of the good things of life. We will not enjoy our own well-being so long as they hunger. Perhaps we will not be allowed to enjoy it *if* they hunger.

In many places friendly people in Asia, Africa, and Latin America are making vigorous efforts to help themselves—struggling to escape the vise of poverty, ignorance, and disorder. In some countries the progress is already apparent. In others, it is certain to come. But we can help to make progress both faster and far more certain. It is the margin that can make the difference between hope and hopelessness—for people with new visions of distant goals—poor people, overcrowded, underfed, illiterate, and aware.

The future of mankind will be gravely affected by the outcome of this revolution. If the uncommitted third of the world ends in the Communist camp, freedom (and that means us) will have suffered a staggering blow. We can help these countries to help themselves and fulfill their aspirations in a framework of growing democracy and freedom. It would be the worst of all ironies if we, the richest land in the world, should stand on the sidelines and watch this fateful struggle go against us by default.

But we must not think of this aid only as saving these countries from Communism. This is important, to be sure. It is more important for the countries concerned than for us. I doubt if any of them wish to fall within the Soviet orbit; none, I am sure, are staying out merely as a favor to the United States. We should justify our aid on the grounds of compassion and the sense of common humanity which make people at least a little different from animals. Idealism in modern times has not always been fashionable. Unless something can be justified by hardheaded self-interest, it is said to have no chance. But let us remember that kindness and idealism may be practical too, and, practical or not, they stand well in the eyes of God.

There are constant complaints about these heresies from men who say that in aiding the less fortunate lands we are giving away our substance and playing a sucker's game of global Santa Claus. From them will continue to come demands that technical and economic aid be stopped altogether. I wonder if even they have really missed the minor fraction of our national income—a fraction of one per cent—that we have spent on aid to underdeveloped countries since the war. I doubt it.

(Parenthetically, and speaking as a politician, I have never been able to understand this attack on Santa Claus. The attackers imply that he is softheaded and subversive, that there is nothing worse than playing Santa Claus. But surely this can't be good politics. Most of us remember Santa as a good fellow and a very welcome visitor. As a Democrat, I want to speak up for him.)

But there is little point in talking about *how* we shall use our material might unless we have it to use. So the most indispensable obligation of a rich and fortunate country to its neighbors is to see that its own prosperity remains on a solid foundation. This is an obligation, I need hardly remind you, which is of paramount importance to Americans themselves. We do not want another depression or a recession or even one of these things called a rolling readjustment. By whatever name, these things are a grievous misfortune, and nothing has been so important in modern economic policy as our efforts to conquer the business cycle of boom and bust.

But our economic stability is also vitally important for our friends abroad. Depressions begin in the big countries, not the small ones. The small country has little choice but to grin and bear it—or anyway to bear it. In countries like those of Central and South America, Malaya, Indonesia, parts of Africa and the Middle East which sell us raw materials, it strikes with redoubled force.

At the present time, we are very prosperous. We are indeed riding—as we are regularly told—on the crest of the greatest boom in our history.

I am not a prophet of gloom. I am not a prophet of any kind whatever. Nonetheless I groaned the other day when a leading politician said with glee: "Everything is booming but the guns." I wish people would take less interest in booms and more in stability—in making good conditions last. For nearly everyone agrees that there are serious flaws in the present situation. Farmers are not sharing at all in the good times. Their prices continue to fall while prices to consumers do not and the profits of manufacturers rise to unprecedented levels. In the past, such a trend has been an ominous warning of trouble ahead.

In the past year automobile sales have been sustained not by the current income and purchasing power of the people but by an unparalleled expansion of installment buying. Consumer debt in the first six months of this year increased $2.4 billions, or 11 per cent. House buying has been kept up by a similar expansion in mortgage loans; mortgages on homes during the first half year rose by nearly $7 billion as compared with $9.6 billion in all of 1954—and 1954 was a year of record increase. We have had more speculation on Wall Street this year than at any time since 1929. The National City Bank of New York in its September letter referred to "crazy credit" and observed: "A sensible optimism is an essential to prosperity. Optimism running to an uncontrolled excess has been our historical path to disaster."

Let us keep in mind that prosperity has two dimensions: one is its level and the other is its durability. I wish we might hear more talk for a time about this second dimension, because it is durability that will determine just how great we are.

Wealth has always had its responsibilities. This is so of individuals; life has rarely, and history never, been kind to those who refused to shoulder them. The case of nations is far more grave. The nation has in trust the well-being of its citizens. The great and powerful state has, in addition, custody of the welfare of other peoples. If wise and kind, it can be a good friend. If reckless or callous, it can damage or destroy.

28

History will measure the American performance, not by the treasure we pile up, but by the uses to which we put it. We will fulfill our destiny as a nation, not by materialism but by magnanimity. For the highest purpose of man and state in the truly peaceful world we have never known is to serve, not just our selfish aims, but the cause of mankind—for "above all nations is humanity."

So, at the end, when all our achievements have been cheered and all our debts have been acknowledged, our proper mood becomes a sober pride, a kind of solemn joy and self-respect in the recognition that "to whom much has been given, of him much shall be required."

We are left, I think, with a renewed understanding that the essence of our material power is a moral commitment whose maintenance against hostile outside pressures, and against our own inward corruption by the very power we wield, is our greatest mission as a people.

0735459

For the Farmer:
Remedies, Not Miracles

OUR MINDS and hearts lie in the shadow of the sad misfortune that has befallen our President. And our anxiety and sympathy are not bounded by party lines. Rising above division of feeling on any public issue is our common hope that his health will be restored as quickly, as fully as possible.

It is not that there is now reason or even justification for stopping debate or stilling disagreement about the problems that face the nation. But it is a time for thinking of the broader aspects of the differences there are, of what ties us together as a party, what distinguishes us from our political opponents, what it is in the issues we face that should be emphasized.

The Republican party, it is said, was born here in Wisconsin, at Ripon, a century ago. But it was only a few days later that it was also born in Illinois in my home town of Bloomington, at a meeting at which Abraham Lincoln made his famous "lost speech." (Now it's a fact that I usually disclose only to Republican audiences that my own great-grandfather was largely responsible for calling that first Republican meeting in Illinois. But if, as his descendant, I am charged with any responsibility for the Republican party, I hasten to point out that from those two earliest meetings, in your state and mine, there sprang a party which rallied around a great moral issue, brought Lincoln to power, and rendered our nation a profound service in its darkest hour.)

But, except in name, this original Republican party did not long survive its first great leader. While Lincoln's party was essentially the party of a single, compelling moral idea, under

From an address at the Democratic State Convention, Green Bay, Wisconsin, October 7, 1955.

his successors it became essentially the party of a single economic interest—and so, with deviations to be sure, it has continued to this day.

The Republican party has stood traditionally for an isolationist foreign policy, high tariffs, and other business subsidies. It has opposed most efforts of government to regulate business abuses, to conserve natural resources, to assure the growth of co-operatives, the development of cheap power, and the growth of organized labor.

The Democratic party, on the other hand, has grown from many different groups and interests. Our party members have been mostly working people, farmers, small businessmen, and professional people. There has been no dominance by any single interest, and if there ever is it will be a sorry day, in my opinion, for the Democratic party and the U.S.A.

Because of the nature of the Democratic party, the shaping of party policy has always been a process of reconciling discordant and often contradictory interests. The result has been an extraordinary record of accomplishment, of doing things for the first time, of serving no special interest but the general welfare.

This has meant to the nation—to all the people—just in recent years:

The Securities and Exchange Commission to protect the public's interest in honest stocks and bonds.

The Federal Deposit Insurance Corporation to protect bank deposits.

The Agricultural Adjustment Administration which saved many a farmer in days that are gone but not forgotten.

The Wagner Act to assist labor organization and collective bargaining.

Social Security to bring dignity to millions of lives.

The Tennessee Valley Authority which has become a model of regional development for all the world.

The Federal Housing Administration and the various programs of slum clearance.

The Rural Electrification Administration which has wired American farms through farmer co-operatives.

The Truman-Acheson foreign policy of arresting Communist expansion and giving new hope to free nations.

31

The Marshall Plan which saved the day for freedom in western Europe.

The reciprocal trade acts whereby the free economy of the world is strengthened.

The leadership of the United States in the development of the United Nations.

All these, including licking the greatest depression and winning the greatest war, were American accomplishments under Democratic administrations—under, if you please, a political direction inspired not by one interest, but many.

From such differences in composition, in basic philosophy, and in past accomplishment emerge the political issues which confront us now as we approach another election year.

On the edge of Wisconsin's north woods frontier, an outsider is sharply aware of our heritage of land and water, and forest and wildlife.

But there is an ominously different policy of non-conservation or anti-conservation in Washington these days—an indifference that is alarming to many who seek to preserve our wildlife resources.

The Soil Conservation Service has had its effectiveness cut drastically by reorganization.

Bills passed by the Republican Eighty-third Congress, advertised as attempts to "free" the Menominee Indians of Wisconsin and the Klamath Indians of Oregon, seem better designed to free the Indians from their timberlands and their inheritance.

These developments are disquieting. Soil and water and vegetation and wildlife are important not so much for themselves but for the effect they have on people. Conservation means not just conserving topsoil and trees and ducks, but conserving the values which make human beings human.

I think of what is presently called the farm problem in the same way. It is basically another problem of conservation—of conserving not only the very roots of our national economy but also a way of life. Some say the best way of life.

Three years ago I spent a week vacationing here in Wisconsin. I remember seeing, as we drove along, one proud, bustling dairy farm after another, with TV antennas on windmills the REA had made obsolete, new silos glistening in the sun—everything saying that the mortgage had been paid off, that this life was good.

Two months ago I drove the length of Wisconsin again and I heard it said that one of every ten of those dairy farms has now either gone broke or is a losing proposition. And the reason is clear. Butterfat brought the Wisconsin farmer 81 cents a pound in September, 1952; now he gets 62 cents. Milk was worth $4.39 per hundredweight then; now it is $3.35. The bottom suddenly dropped out of the price the farmer's wife got for eggs. And, even more important, the prices of the things the farmer buys in town have not gone down; on the contrary, they have gone up. The farmer is caught in a price-cost squeeze, and the consumer hasn't benefited either.

The farmer is 13 per cent of the population and receives 6 per cent of the income. He is getting fewer and he is getting poorer. Too often now his machinery is wearing out. There is a mortgage again. A lifetime's investment is dwindling.

It is small wonder that a lot of farmers, and not just Democrats, were bewildered by the news last year that cheese processors and distributors reaped a profit of $2½ million—of taxpayer money—on deals with the government for cheese that never left their warehouses!

It is unfair and dangerous that farmers, alone among the great economic groups in our country, are not sharing in the current prosperity. The farmer's lot gets worse while for everybody else things get better. This is not only unfair to the farmer, it is unhealthy for all of us. For when things go bad for the farmer it hurts a lot of other people.

The present Republican policy of sliding or flexible price supports is not working. Instead of eliminating surpluses, as advertised, it is eliminating farmers, as not advertised. After two or three years of heroics, ballyhoo, and unprecedented applause from the Republican press, our past problems are all still with us. Export subsidies, import quotas still sharply conflict with our declarations about freer world trade. There is still indefensible discrimination between different commodities, and between storables and perishables. And the burdensome surpluses are still burdening us. As a result the problem of controls, effective controls, also still remains.

Yet the difficulties that now beset the farmer pose grave problems and also dangerous temptations. It will be tempting to us Democrats to say: "Return the Democrats and the farm problem will be solved overnight." (And let me say, parenthetically, thank heaven it is a problem of too much instead of too little as it is in so much of the world where I've been.)

Well, it won't be solved overnight, and let's leave that kind of talk to the Republicans. For such promises, or even more moderate ones, will do us no credit in the eyes of an awakened American farmer. The farm problem is a desperately difficult one. It has been made more difficult by the neglect, the indifference, the postponement and the huckstering and slogan-making of these past three years. Let us not promise what we cannot perform. Farmers will trust the Democratic party next time but they will not trust it to perform miracles.

High price supports have served the farmer well, and by increasing production when needed they have served the nation well, too. They are the counterpart of the protection which the worker has for his wages from his union and which the manufacturing corporation derives from its flexibility and tariffs. As between price supports on the one hand and no price supports and no farm aid, on the other hand, I am for high price supports.

But I do not think the old program by itself, good as it may have been in its day, is good enough for now. The problem is to see that the farmer gets his proper share of the national income. The technique—the method—by which prices have been supported in the past, and which the Republicans adopted, is faulty. These loan and purchase programs work well for only a few commodities. They do not work well for any perishables; for some they cannot be used at all. That means that livestock and dairy farmers get a lower or less reliable protection than producers of storable crops, or they may be ignored entirely. And storable crop loans and purchase operations force the government to acquire stocks that are now vast and burdensome.

We cannot be satisfied so long as such shortcomings persist. We must be prepared to experiment with new techniques of insuring the farmer a fair income when the times turn against him. I think we should explore such devices as production payments and see if for some products, at least, they don't work better. The Republicans have already paved the way by adopting for wool the Brannan plan which they called "immoral" not so long ago.

We must also seek a more fundamental attack on the surpluses. No sensible steps should be ruled out. We should aid cotton producers in converting to better balanced farming systems, and surely the possibilities of conserving our basic asset, the land, by temporary or permanent withdrawal from grain production have not been exhausted.

Shouldn't we seek, too, an expansion of our livestock economy based on an expanded consumption of livestock products? Acres now growing unneeded bread grains would thus be turned to production of feed. Many more acres are required to provide a diet rich in animal proteins than one based on cereals. And, moreover, the products of grassland agriculture better serve the ends of soil and water conservation.

Plainly, with so many commodities to deal with and problems so complex, the farmers' plight is not going to be solved by any single remedy, be it sliding or fixed price supports. And certainly the farm problem won't be solved by Republican oratory and by pious admonitions to the farmer to grin and bear it, for Ezra Benson and the dear old G.O.P.

There looms, too, on the immediate political horizon, another temptation—the tax issue. Here again we face sobering distinctions between the politics of expediency and the politics of responsibility.

Let me say at the outset that if anyone doesn't hate high taxes, well, he just hasn't paid his taxes. And I think I know all the arguments for a tax cut. Business is good; tax revenues are rising. The budget, Mr. Humphrey says, is approaching a balance. International tensions are easing. And 1956 is an election year!

Yet we are entitled to consider a tax cut only in terms of a clear understanding of what it means.

I think of our needs. I see the number of public services which must be improved and strengthened. Our schools are crowded and inadequate as they try to serve the largest number of youngsters in our history. We are saving money and wasting children. Our highways are inadequate too—even the Republicans agree to that. There is wasting soil to be saved. There are still noisome slums to be cleared. Our public housing—for reasons of economy—is still grossly inadequate. Our rivers still get out of hand. There are watersheds to be protected. Our national parks have been starved. There are dams to build and the people's health to safeguard. There is the insistent problem of defense in a still troubled world, and tax reduction at the price of safety is not good economics.

All these needs, it seems to me, ought to be weighed against our natural desire to cut taxes further. And I say let our opponents cry out for tax reduction at any price. But we are the party of compassion and the party of responsibility. We at least must inquire whether at this juncture there are things we want more than tax reduction.

Haven't we always said that when times are good we should balance the budget, arrest inflation, and reduce public debt? Business is booming right now. If it slacks off we will want and *need* to reduce taxes in order to stimulate private spending. But we cannot be for tax reductions in *bad* times in order to stimulate spending, and also for tax reductions in good times just because there is the prospect of a balanced budget surplus.

We Democrats must not ourselves forget the lessons we learned and taught America during the great days of the New Freedom and the New Deal. It was our party, working against bitter opposition, which shaped this unique partnership between government and business and labor and agriculture— this fusion of private with public enterprise—this marvelously flexible mixed economy—out of which has flowered our present prosperity. Our guiding concept in this development was the realization that mass production must be matched in a free economy by mass purchasing power. The total national income must be so distributed, year after year, as to be effective in the market place. And it is this purpose—preventing the disastrous cycle of "boom" and "bust"—which should determine our taxation policy.

We don't oppose tax cuts. But we want to know what we are doing and where we are going. A responsible political party has greater responsibilities than winning votes at any price.

I have not recommended here, nor will I, a bipartisan approach to these issues of policy involving the farm program, taxation, or conservation. There is room, indeed there is need, for the pressing in such areas of basically different points of view.

These have been sobering days in the political life of the nation. We have been reminded as a people of the nearness of the will of God to the affairs of man and of nations. It is appropriate that we renew our pledge that we will be guided as a political party only by the politics of responsibility.

Yet it remains true, as always, that to be a Democrat is to feel strongly, to be impatient, to want mightily to see that things are done better. And we shall go forward—our obligations larger—our responsibilities greater—our purposes firmer and more clear. For we believe with all our hearts that the principles of the Democratic party rise from the roots of people's needs, that they are nourished by people's deepest convictions, that they will flower in the realization of people's dreams of a greater destiny.

The Crisis in Agriculture

BEHIND THE POLITICS of big talk and little action lies the simple fact that most of the big men who run this show want little government.

Let me say the aim of democratic government is to safeguard the interests, rights, and opportunities of all its members, which means to keep the balance between industry, labor, and farmers—to name the three biggest. The outlook for democratic balance is in danger when any one group gets control of the government. And that is exactly what has happened to us. The industry, money, management group has control of our political apparatus. What's more, the bulk of the press of the country nowadays is also numbered among that group, a group that already enjoys—in education, prestige, and wealth—most of the incidental means of power. Whatever the individual good will and virtue of the business leaders, such a concentration of power is dangerous. For the government must be the trustee for the little man, because no one else will be. The powerful can usually help themselves—and frequently do! And in that connection I noticed that the net income of one corporation, General Motors, after taxes, will be twice as much as the total income of all farm workers and operators in the whole state of Minnesota, before taxes.

That brings me to perhaps the greatest gap between Republican words and Republican deeds—the crisis in agriculture. Certainly we have no more stubborn, elusive problem. I don't think it can ever be solved unless you really want to solve it. I sometimes wonder how much these gentlemen who run the show in Washington believe in farm programs. For a generation they have denounced minimum wages, social se-

From an address at a Democratic rally, Duluth, Minnesota, October 29, 1955.

curity, aid to education, public power, etc., as "creeping Socialism." Of course they believe in fast tax write-offs and protective tariffs for business, but they seem to believe in a hands-off, free-market policy for everyone else. I have thought lately that I heard an echo of Calvin Coolidge, who said: "Farmers have never made money. I don't believe we can do much about it."

Mr. Coolidge's philosophy seems to have outlived him, in spite of President Eisenhower's reassuring words hereabouts three years ago, which you all remember so well: "The Republican party is pledged to the sustaining of the 90 per cent parity price support, and it is pledged even more than that to helping the farmer obtain his full parity, 100 per cent of parity." Farm income then stood at 102 per cent of parity; today it is at 85 per cent of parity. And if an innocent and gullible Miss Minnesota feels aggrieved by these gay deceivers I will gladly be a witness in a breach-of-promise suit against the Republicans, because I was at Kasson that famous day. And I am happy to recall that I did not outbid or even try to match the Republican promises to the farmers.

But the hollow words keep coming. "Our agriculture economy," said the Republican Vice President, "is basically sound." "Agriculture," the Republican Secretary of Agriculture echoed, "is fundamentally sound."

Across the years comes another echo—"Fundamentally sound." That's exactly the phrase a Republican President once used to describe American business. The year was 1927.

Fundamentally sound? Sixteen thousand more farm mortgages were recorded in the first six months of this year than last year.

Fundamentally sound? Why, sure, American agriculture is fundamentally sound. And I can't worry as much about having too much food and fiber as too little in a country which is growing at the rate of two and a half million a year, and in a world where more than half the inhabitants are undernourished. Our farmers are in trouble just now not because they have failed, but because they have succeeded; because they are producing more than we need and their prices are going down while their costs are going up.

What to do about it? Well, I'll tell you what one part-time

39

farmer thinks about it, and that's a bold thing to do in the presence of so many experts.

In the first place you have to want to do something about it. You have to feel with sincerity, with conviction, with passion, that farming is not only an essential industry entitled to its fair share of the national income, but it is something more; that farming, family farming, is also a way of life that must be preserved, that it is indispensable to the stability and the continuity of any civilized society.

And in the next place, it seems to me that we have to face the fact that there isn't just a farm problem, there are many, because there are many agricultural commodities and they all differ. It seems to me that in addition to the various proposals to stimulate consumption we need more than one string to our bow; that we need an arsenal of weapons which can be used or not as changing conditions require in a constant effort to keep supply and demand in some balance.

In the case of some commodities we may well find production payments or compensatory payments more effective, even more economical in the long run, than price supports. And surely we should explore without delay the great possibilities in the long-discussed land rental, soil bank, and conservation programs to take land out of uneconomic production and to store fertility in the soil instead of the bulging elevator. And I'm sure you also dread the devastating dust storms that we know so well and that can come again, for soil blowing away is worse than money blowing away. Money can be replaced, soil can't.

But until we can broaden the base of our attack on the farm problem we must rely largely on the loan and purchase price-support programs. It seems to me unfortunate that in the public mind, at least the Republican mind, the whole farm problem seems to be embraced within the controversy between flexible and 90 per cent price supports.

More than a year ago, at Sioux Falls, I said that flexible price supports would only hurt the farmer some more and would not eliminate the surpluses as advertised. Well, as we know too well, the farmer has been hurt plenty and production is not down but up. How much longer we must wait and the farmer must suffer until the Republicans admit the error of their ways I don't know, but the longer it is the more I will suspect that they don't much care about falling farm income.

So we must return to the 90 per cent supports which the Republicans thought so well of in 1952, until they decided it was time for a change—after the election. As I said then, and last year, and again this month, we know the imperfections in this program, but we also know that it will keep farm income up, at least for some commodities, and that's the crying need for now.

While firm price supports keep income up they don't keep surpluses down, and I say again that, lest the dam burst and engulf us, we Democrats must press on, with Republican help I hope, to develop the much broader national farm program which is required to restore the full parity of total farm income.

At the risk of misunderstanding and misrepresentation, I will say again and again that restoring 90 per cent price supports to meet the present emergency is not to say they are a solution, but only that it is a better program than sliding supports that slide only one way. And I have been waiting patiently to hear some Republican leader confess that the stable general price level to which they have been pointing with such pride these past few years has been largely due to the fact that the continuous rise in industrial prices has been offset by falling farm prices.

But what concerns me even more is the way the administration blames the farmers' difficulties on American labor. Neither the farm misery nor the Republicans' political misery is going to be cured by trying to drive a wedge between city and farm people. You in the Democratic Farmer-Labor party of Minnesota have shown perhaps best of all that the way to meet America's problems is not by playing groups of Americans off against each other but by joining people's common purposes.

Well, you'll have to give the Republicans credit for one thing: the highest living costs and the lowest farm prices—at the same time. They complain that it isn't their fault, that they inherited the farm problem from the Democrats. But let's not argue the point; let's just say to our Republican friends that whatever they inherited from us we're ready to take back.

And the farm problem isn't the only one we're ready to take

back. The conservation problem, the education problem, the minorities problem, the great and overriding problem of our national survival in this Atomic Age—none of these is just an economic or a budgetary question or an abstraction that may be safely left to those who compute statistics and feed tape into a Univac—that thinking machine which I sometimes suspect is making much of the policy these days in Washington.

Each of these problems breaks down into the reflection of the life and times of human beings—of wheat farmers in Minnesota, and factory workers in New Jersey, and fishermen in Maine, and orange pickers in California, and cotton choppers in Georgia. Here is our eternal concern as Democrats—with the way men live, and the way men dream, and with the opportunity each must have to take his rightful place in the long march of history.

The Legacy of Philip Murray

IT IS HARD on occasions such as this to distinguish between the lasting darkness of loss and the passing darkness of its shadow.

Our lives take their meaning from their interlacing with other lives, and when one life is ended those into which it was woven are also carried into darkness. Neither you nor I, but only the hand of time, slow-moving, yet sure and steady, can lift that blanket of blackness.

I am, of course, deeply conscious of the honor that I share in taking part in this tribute to the memory of Philip Murray. But even more keenly, I feel that it is appropriate for someone outside the labor movement, like myself, to participate in this memorial. I say that because Mr. Murray was more than the President of the C.I.O., more than a leader and spokesman for organized labor.

Those of you who worked with him knew him first and foremost as a trade-unionist, a man of sagacity at the bargaining table, a militant leader in your times of stress, and a shrewd negotiator. Those of you, among the thousands who called him "friend," knew him as a beloved companion, a thoughtful advisor, a generous man with a boundless sense of humor and kindness. As time softens the first sadness of his death, I think we can better see Phil Murray in perspective, and describe him properly in terms that would have embarrassed this unassuming man in his lifetime.

In the truest sense of the words that we often abuse, his life was a success story. The world is better off because he lived in it. Without that fact as a basic ingredient, you cannot give validity to a success story. Too often, in judging what man is a success, we think in terms of the market place, and measure him a success because he moved into the big house on top

From an address at the Philip Murray Memorial Dinner, Atlantic City, December 3, 1952.

of the hill. But the test is rather "how and why." And **Phil Murray's** success in life cannot be measured in a probate court.

The inspiration in Mr. Murray's life, the lesson for the world, lies in the fact that a boy humbly born in another country could come to America, his knuckles blackened with the coal dust of the Scottish pits, hew out an illustrious career for himself in service to his fellow man, and die a man of simple tastes and modest means, but leave a legacy of material goods in the homes of millions of workers in these United States—not only material goods measured in wages, in pension benefits, and other gains for the workers he led, but the goods of the spirit. Millions of workers have a personal dignity their fathers never knew because Phil Murray and others like him helped these workers to stand on their own feet.

My acquaintance with him was not intimate and my contacts were few. Perhaps that qualifies me all the better to comment on what to me was his most conspicuous quality. Humbly born, after a stormy life of democratic leadership and great achievement he humbly died. Yet it has been too often true that the very humbleness, even the disadvantages, of a man's beginnings have led him to abuse authority subsequently attained. Rank and power expose humility to the rust of pride. We know those who, in the very telling of how they "came up the hard way," acknowledge in the telling that they have lost the lesson of their experience.

Phil Murray's humility was deeper rooted. It did not change with the seasons of experience or the years of growth. He knew that in our system of things the conferring of authority on particular individuals is largely accidental, that its compliment is slight, and that the man who exercises it is no different from his fellow men or from what he was himself before he assumed the role of leadership.

It was often remarked, and to some it seemed strange, that the President of the C.I.O. was moved easily to laughter and not infrequently to tears. Perhaps his greatness found its sustenance there, or at least its reflection—for it is emotions that link us closest with each other. So much of democratic leadership is just the understanding of the people's needs and hopes, the looking to them rather than to one's own ideas for guidance and for strength, the maintaining of a oneness between leadership and following.

No democratic organization can afford the risk of leadership which lacks humility. It is that element which gives men —which gave Philip Murray—the ability to lead a people who distrust the power to command.

His was not an easy career. The path of the man who chose a career in organized labor in Murray's youth was not strewn with N.L.R.B. orders directing an employer to bargain. Too often the life of the labor organizer was more akin to the career of an underground leader, in terms of frustration, even terror.

What motivated and sustained him in the long struggle? What was the guiding purpose that drove him on with a disregard for self that resulted finally in death? I suspect the mature, the compelling purpose, was to bring dignity and meaning into lives which had lost these qualities. It was plainer to those in the coal mines of Pennsylvania in 1902 in his boyhood than it was to a good many other people in America what a price we had paid, in human values, for the fruits of the industrial revolution. The coal dust and the sweat and smoke of factories had settled not only on men's faces and in women's kitchens but on their lives. Work had become, for millions, something much less—much meaner—than it had been when men were carving homes and farms out of forests and wilderness and working as craftsmen in small shops. In too many minds the men and women beside the assembly lines became indistinguishable from the machines.

This, then, is our heritage from Philip Murray. It is no lesser for not being written in the words of great books or in the masonry of proud structures—for it is written rather in the lives of men and women and built into the meaning of democracy. It is the example of what leadership means in a system that finds its strength in its insistence that leaders be only servants. To realize this heritage is to deny all but the personal elements of loss, of ending, in what has happened. There are those who are ready to accept, to carry on—and even to build upon—the example which has been left, the tradition which has been established.

Behind the grief of great loss there is the stimulus to assume the increased responsibility to go on. The whole lesson of history is its essential continuity. It is the fullest recognition and memorializing of those who have departed that those who remain feel no despair—for otherwise the task was not fully done. I cannot presume to say that I know what Mr. Murray's view of the future was. But I do know that his life and work spanned a dramatic evolution in the status of labor and in our thinking about labor in this country. From the unspeakable conditions of fifty or sixty years ago he lived to see organized labor grow to its present vast power and influence in our economy and our society. And I suppose that this transition is as important a single fact as any in the past half-century.

While there are inequities and injustices in our laws that still demand remedy, labor's long battle for status and recognition has been largely won. Violence and ruthlessness by employers and unions alike are now obsolete. The doctrine that the end justifies the means should be a thing of the past in labor relations.

Labor has been afflicted with Communist infiltration. It has been afflicted with hoodlums and racketeers. These battles for clean unions have been fought and will be fought as long as necessary. But the bigger job of the future is the proper exercise of organized labor's vast responsibility, not just to the workingman but to the country. Some of the attitudes, habits of thought, and methods of the past are no longer relevant. How soon will the modern idea that Big Labor is here to stay, that its constituency is no longer just the union member but the nation, pervade the ranks of labor leadership? The largest task now, as I see it, is the conduct of relations with industry, always in the larger framework of the national interest on which labor and business and all the rest of us are dependent.

I'll say nothing poetic about the twilight of the era of your great gains. Rather it is for us to make this interval of labor's transition from "far-off things, and battles long ago," the dawn of a better era for all of us—for America.

I like to think that Phil Murray was familiar with these words: "A fool who stands fast is a catastrophe; a wise man who stands fast is a statesman."

It is, then, in a spirit of gratitude for what he did with his life and of gratitude for the opportunity that is the handmaiden of the power he helped bestow upon you, that we say to Philip Murray: "Hail and Farewell," and that we say to Death, "Be not proud."

The American Vision

I AM A GREAT believer in national humility, modesty, self-examination, and self-criticism, and I have preached these virtues vigorously, although, of course, I haven't practiced them very diligently. Of late I have been disturbed, as I am sure many of you have, by what seems to me to be the course at home and abroad of irrational criticism, abuse, and mistrust of America, its conduct, its motives, and its people. I don't mean just the voices that have been raised, we thank God, in protest against our current deficiencies, against the attacks on academic freedom, the pressure for conformity, our failures abroad, or the present wretched manifestations in Washington of our national neurosis. Nor do I mean the wholesome and continuous debate and self-examination that should and must go on among us and among allies; the candid controversy that makes for good neighbors and for good friends. Rather I am talking of the malice, distemper, and the new fashion of being cynical, sarcastic, skeptical, deprecating about America or fellow Americans.

There are rising voices here and abroad that forget that although America occasionally gags on a gnat, it also has some talent for swallowing tigers whole; voices that tell us that our national energy is spent, that our old values have decayed, that it is futile to try to restore them; voices that say that at best we are as Rome: that once our bridges, our skyscrapers, our factories, and our weapons fall before the iron law of decay, no trace will be left—no great issues, no great cause to mark our past in universal history.

And there are voices that seem to say that we are as Carthage, that our vital principle is commerce, just commerce;

From an address at the Columbia Bicentennial Conference, New York, June 5, 1954.

47

our ethics, our politics, our imaginative faculties, they say, are all bent and twisted to serve our sovereign—commerce. Other voices cry havoc, fear that America is not equal to the task; that Communism is the way to the future—is irresistible, just as Fascism was for them not so long ago. Even novelists and poets seem to have been infected. The very excitement in a time of change and testing is cynically suspect.

Some of this talk, of course, may reflect a wholesome attitude abroad and a wholesome attitude here of self-criticism, if in a slightly fevered form. Some of it may even mark the reaction to the easy and the groundless optimism of the nineteenth century. I don't know, but I do know that if we doubt ourselves we will persuade no one. If we doubt our mission in the world, we will do nothing to advance it. And if we are craven before the slanders that fill our ears we will secede from each other.

But to view our present and our future with such sickly anxiety is to ignore the lessons and the achievements of our past. For the plain truth is that we here in America have written the greatest success story in human history. The plain truth is that on the record of performance, we here in America have in a few years made Socialism obsolete, shown that Communism is nothing but a noisome stagnant pool of reaction.

And it wasn't merely in 1776 that America left its footprints on eternity. For in our lifetime, we, the seventh generation of free and independent Americans, have given a tidal force to the forward roll of what was set in motion by the first generation. If we but lift our heads for a moment above this storm of criticism, of abuse, doubt, and "un-American activities," and survey the past fifty years, I think you will say with me: "Hooray for America!"

The first and most obvious thing we have to cheer about is our material progress. The miracle of American mass production is commonplace. And under our capitalist system we have increased our wealth to an extent almost unimaginable fifty years ago, at the turn of the century.

Now this increase in our wealth has, of course, greatly changed our country. The change for the sake of change—as I've tried with a notable lack of success to point out to my

48

countrymen—isn't worthy of applause. What matters is not that we have changed but how we have changed.

Our national income is distributed far more equitably than it was at the turn of the century. As late as 1935–36 there were only about a million American families and unattached individuals, as they commonly say, with incomes of $5,000 or more, and 17,000,000 with incomes of less than $1,000. Fifteen years later, in 1950, these proportions were just about reversed, and even after allowing for inflation, the change is still dramatic.

It is not in terms of money and products that we can see most clearly the change that America has undergone. Rather it is in the attitude of the people and in the role of the government. For we have succeeded not only in making our society prosperous but in keeping it fluid.

And, while this was easy enough in the days of the frontier, it seemed all but an idle dream by 1900. The frontier was closed; the homestead land was gone; women and children labored in dingy sweatshops, and robber barons plundered at will. Miners in company towns and immigrants compressed into filthy tenements were fast becoming a miserable proletariat.

How could the roads of opportunity be kept open? How, short of revolution, could we adjust modern capitalism to democratic ends? To many it seemed hopeless. Yet see what happened: the gap between rich and poor has been greatly narrowed without revolution, without Socialism, and without robbing A to give to B—although there may be some dissent to that down in Wall Street!

Our wealth has been mightily increased and better distributed. The rising tide has lifted all the boats.

How has this transformation been accomplished? By increasing productivity and by putting government to the service of the people. Woodrow Wilson, Theodore Roosevelt, Robert La Follette, and so on, led a revolt of the American conscience, followed by the reforms under Franklin Roosevelt. They've altered the face of America.

The child labor laws, wage and hour laws, the antitrust acts, banking legislation, rural electrification, soil conservation,

49

social security, unemployment compensation, the graduated income tax, inheritance taxes—it may be too much to say that all this and more amounts to a bloodless revolution, but it certainly amounts to a transformation of our economic and social life.

Now why was all this done? Why did America adopt the concept of man's responsibility for his fellow man? Our decision that the well-being of the least of us is the responsibility of all of us was, of course, not merely an economic and a political decision; it was, at bottom, a moral decision. And it was not, as some are now saying in the nation's capital, all a sinister conspiracy of the great philanthropic foundations.

It rested upon the conviction that it is the duty of the government to keep open to all the people the avenues of opportunity that stretched so broad and so far before us in the days of our frontier. It rested upon the conviction that the government must safeguard the people against catastrophe not of their making.

But this great decision has brought us face to face with vexing problems which have engaged your attention, as I understand it, during this past week—the problems of the conflict between freedom and security, between the individual and his social safeguards.

It seems to me there is something gallant about man's fight to become the master rather than the slave of nature; but there is something rather tragic about his struggle to keep himself free from the impositions of his own social creations.

Now it would be fatuous to claim that we are anywhere near solving this conflict, in my judgment, as it would be fatuous to say that because our material well-being increases year by year all must be well with America. It isn't.

Too many of our people still dwell in wretched slums or on worn-out land. Once again our topsoil, our national skin, is blowing away out on the plains. Our schools and hospitals are overcrowded; so are our mental institutions and our prisons. Too many of our cities are wasting away from neglect. And how can we boast of our high estate when more than one of every ten citizens still do not enjoy fully equal opportunities?

Nonetheless our progress has been astonishing—more Americans are living better than ever before. The middle class,

50

whose disappearance Marx so confidently predicted, has expanded as never before in the history of any other nation. And while the Communist conspirators fulminate about the cruel capitalists, the lackeys of Wall Street, and the downtrodden masses, we have created a free society that promotes the general welfare of all far better, far more successfully than it has ever been promoted by any other system or social organization.

Briefly, I think America's record is "terrific"—if I may borrow a word from my sons. And it is my view that its performance abroad is even more spectacular.

Since the turn of the century we have successively and emphatically renounced, first imperialism, then isolation, and finally our historical neutrality. We have transformed our foreign policy as completely as our domestic policy. Twice America has decisively tipped the scales for freedom in a mighty global exertion.

Instead of isolation, our policy is total involvement; instead of non-co-operation we have been the prime mover in the United Nations; instead of neutrality we have organized the greatest defensive coalition in history. And in Korea we fought and bled almost alone for the United Nations and for collective security.

But this isn't all. In the process America has fathered three unprecedented ideas: Lend-lease for Hitler's intended victims in war, the Marshall Plan for Stalin's intended victims in peace, and Point 4 to help undeveloped areas. And to pay for it all Americans have borne a tax load, I mean a *collected* tax load, that is without counterpart save in Britain, and that few beyond our borders appreciate.

And what have we asked in return? Why have we done all of this? Some will say self-interest, and there is truth in that because Communism follows the geography of human misery. Some will say magnanimity, and there is truth in that, too. For it would have been easy to go home as we did after the first war, or go it alone as some of our people have proposed.

Call it what you will; the point is to help others help themselves, to help make independence and democracy work, to share the burdens of the less fortunate, to raise the tide a little all around the world, lifting all of the boats with it, just as we have done here at home. It was bold and imaginative. It was wise and responsible; it was good for them and it was good for us. As Edmund Burke said: "Magnanimity is not seldom the truest wisdom."

Now, while I emphatically approve and loudly cheer America's purposes abroad, past and present, I don't mean to imply for a moment that I approve of all our foreign policies and conduct, past or present—especially present!

My purpose has been just to suggest the main outlines of a success story in which we can all take pride. As we look back to 1900 and look around us today the infinite evidence of our creative impulses and of our vast achievements ought to be heralded, not mocked.

We have heard the "least of these." We have enlarged our vision, opened our heart, and we have disciplined our strength. We have turned it into a servant of justice—justice not alone for ourselves, but justice for the world-wide commonwealth of free men and of free institutions.

Here, indeed, is a case where mankind has a right to knowledge and to the use thereof—the knowledge of what America has done, how America has spread out the decision-making process, within its many parts.

It is the knowledge of how we have committed 160,000,000 people to vast social projects, not by coercion, but by persuasion and consent, and by a balancing of the rights of the one with the needs of the many.

I say it is a grand and glorious story. On the basis of the record we have outperformed any rival proposals of Communism or of Fascism; and America has nobly accepted her responsibility and proudly met her time for greatness in a troubled age.

Why then all this abuse and criticism? Why then have we of late grown afraid of ourselves? Why have we of late acted as though the whole of this nation is a security risk? Why do you suppose we have given in to the bleatings of those who insist that it is dangerous for a man to have an idea? Why do we talk of saving ourselves by committing suicide—in the land of Jefferson?

So, having said: "Three cheers for America—you've done a great job of work," we have to add: "But look out, America, your work has just begun; though you've nobly grasped the present you could meanly lose the future."

What's the matter with us anyhow? The usual diagnosis is ignorance and fear. Ignorance leads many to confuse ends with means, to act as though material progress were an end in itself rather than a means to great and noble ends. This, I suggest, is the peril of our hardheaded, pragmatic attitude that has helped us so much to achieve our vast social and economic transformation, for if we ever succumb to materialism the meaning will go out of America.

And ignorance begets fear—the most subversive force of all. If America ever loses confidence in herself, she will retain the confidence of no one, and she will lose her chance to be free, because the fearful are never free.

But I wonder if all of these alarming concerns are not America's surface symptoms of something even deeper; of a moral and human crisis in the Western world which might even be compared to the fourth-, fifth-, and sixth-century crisis when the Roman Empire was transformed into feudalism and primitive Christianity, early Christianity, into the structure of the Catholic Church, or the crisis a thousand years later when the feudal world exploded and the individual emerged with new relationships to God, nature, to society.

And now in our time in spite of our devotion to the ideas of religious and secular humanism, I wonder if we are in danger of falling into a spirit of materialism in which the aim of life is a never-ending increase of material comfort, and the result a moral and religious vacuum. Is this leading, as lack of faith always must, to a deep sense of insecurity and a deterioration of reason? And I wonder, too, if today mass manipulation is not a greater danger than economic exploitation; if we are not in greater danger of becoming robots than slaves.

Since man cannot live by bread alone, is not the underlying crisis whether he is going to be inspired and motivated again by the ideas of the humanistic tradition of Western culture, or whether he falls for the new pagan religions, the worship of the state and a leader, as millions of believers in the Fascist and Soviet systems have already done?

That we are not invulnerable, that there is a moral and a

human vacuum within us, is, I think, demonstrated by many symptoms, of which McCarthyism—which has succeeded in frightening so many—is only one.

But it is even more certain that there are millions who see or at least who dimly sense the danger, and who want to make life in its truly human meaning the main business of living; who want to express the humanistic tradition of reason and of human solidarity—who want to understand the truth and not be drawn into the mass manipulative influence of sentimentality and rationalization.

I venture to say that there are in the world many with a deep, intense longing for a vision of a better life not in a material, but in a spiritual sense; for love for human solidarity. There is a hunger to hear a word of truth, a longing for an ideal, a readiness for sacrifice. Churchill's famous speech at the beginning of the war is an illustration and so is the totalitarians' appeal to emotional forces rather than to material interests.

But the conventional appeal seems to be so often to the better life in *material* terms, I wonder if people are not eager to hear about the better life in *human* terms.

And I think that deep down the ideas of independence, of individuality, of free initiative, represent the strongest appeals to Americans who want to think for themselves, who don't want to be creatures of mass suggestion, who don't want to be automatons.

The question is, I suppose, whether the human and rational emotions can be aroused instead of the animal and irrational to which the totalitarians appeal. But fill the moral vacuum, the rational vacuum, we must; reconvert a population soaked in the spirit of materialism to the spirit of humanism we must, or bit by bit we too will take on the visage of our enemy, the neo-heathens.

As I have said, in my judgment America has accomplished miracles at home and abroad. But, despite all of this wisdom, this exertion, this goodness, the horror of our time in history is that things are worse than ever before. There is no real peace; we are besieged, we are rattled. Perhaps we are even passing through one of the great crises of history when man must make another mighty choice.

Beset by all of these doubts and difficulties, in which direction then do we look?

We look to ourselves—and we are not ashamed. We are proud of what freedom has wrought—the freedom to experiment, to inquire, to change, to invent. And we shall have to look exactly in the same directions to solve our problems now —to individual Americans, to their institutions, to their churches, to their governments, to their multifarious associations—and to all the free participants in the free life of a free people.

And we look, finally, to the free university whose function is the search for truth and its communication to succeeding generations. Men may be born free; they cannot be born wise; and it is the duty of the university to make the free wise. Only as that function is performed steadfastly, conscientiously, and without interference does a university keep faith with the great humanist tradition of which it is a part.

More than a hundred years ago William Ellery Channing defined the free mind this way:

I call that mind free which jealously guards its intellectual rights and powers, which calls no man master, which does not content itself with a passive or hereditary faith, which opens itself to light whencesoever it may come, and which receives new truth as an angel from heaven.

I wonder how many of us fulfill Channing's definition. And I wonder if our failure to do so could be part of our trouble today.

TWO

Democrats and Republicans

Campaign Mythology and the Public Weal

WHILE we may be a defeated party, we are not a beaten party. We are not a beaten party for many reasons, and the most important is that we have been honest with the people. We made no effort to sugar-coat bitter problems so that they would be easier to swallow. We told the truth; we spoke our minds. And we emerged from the campaign with more good will in the bank than any other defeated party in recent history. I am confident that if we continue to be forthright with the American people, our bank account of respect will continue to grow.

We must, therefore, be honest with the people by supporting the new administration when we believe it to be serving the national interest.

We have all been heartened by the occasions on which our new President, under the sobering responsibility of authority, has shown that he respects the public weal more than ebullient campaign oratory. He has quite properly rebuked Republicans in Congress for unseemly haste in cutting taxes before making the hard decisions on where, when, and if expenses can be cut. Democratic Congressmen, I am proud to say, supported the President with responsible realism.

And in the resolution he has just proposed, the President has repudiated the Republican campaign mythology about dark and sinister agreements at Yalta, Teheran, and Potsdam. The proposed resolution relates to the breach of those agreements by the Soviet government, shameless violations which have long been denounced by everybody, Democrats and Republicans alike. Let us, I say, no longer make cynical political capital by pretending that our country ever conspired in

From an address at the Western States Dinner, Los Angeles, February 26, 1953.

the tragedy that has befallen once great and independent peoples.

Tempting as it is, I shall not dwell on the unworthy and misleading words that have been uttered of late about the Seventh Fleet, words implying that President Truman's purpose was to protect Red China rather than Formosa.

But while supporting the Republicans when they act in the national interest, we have an equal responsibility to oppose them when they do violence to the public interest.

In the coming months many questions await resolution by the Congress and the people. One of the first is tidelands oil. On this issue I have long since expressed my views. But, however the Congress may decide the question, let us make sure that it does not set in motion the piecemeal dismemberment of our great public domain which is held for the benefit of all the people of the United States.

There are powerful interests who have interpreted the election as heralding an open season for the retail and wholesale transfer to the states of our great national assets—the forests, the grazing lands, the water, and the minerals.

In this connection, if you will indulge me for a moment, you may be amused, as I was, by a telegram to Senator Earl Clements from a man in Kentucky which I saw the other day:

Chattanooga Daily Times . . . quotes Senator Walker in Lincoln Day speech as favoring sale of Post Office Department to private interests. Please advise when bids are to be opened. I represent eight plumbers and one Republican who wish to acquire this property. Also interested in United States Mint and Fort Knox if they are for sale.

I hope we don't forget that the public domain belongs to Democrats and Republicans alike, and, as Theodore Roosevelt warned us long ago, the descendants of both will pay the price if we do not preserve their heritage. And I confidently expect that the Democrats in Congress will be the public's guardians of our forests and our parks; our grazing lands and our minerals; guardians, too, of our great reclamation programs and our family-sized farms; and of low-cost power for all the people.

Likewise, we must vigilantly protect the great programs of

social progress which we have initiated in the past twenty years and which may be in for something less than sympathetic treatment.

Incidentally, I had been under the very distinct impression, a few months back, that the Republicans had made off with the Democratic farm plank. I guess I was wrong. They just borrowed it temporarily, and returned it immediately after the election.

But it was not so much of these things that I wanted to talk tonight. One of the most exhilarating aspects of the 1952 campaign for me was the activity of so many independent-minded citizens, many of whom had never before participated in a political campaign. They found it exciting and satisfying to join in making the nation's greatest decisions; what our government is to do about war and peace; about depression and prosperity; about human rights and human liberties. But politics, good politics, is not merely a quadrennial or biennial burst of enthusiasm; nor is it a function reserved to the so-called professionals. In its highest and truest sense, politics is leadership; and leadership is a time-consuming, brain-consuming, and energy-consuming job—a job that is open to all citizens.

This means that we must organize in our communities; we must get and give the truth. In the places where our organization has been deficient we must set ourselves to the tough task of putting our house in order.

Forty years ago the Democratic party was just assuming power, after a long period out of office. In that moment of triumph Woodrow Wilson said this in his First Inaugural Address: "The success of a party means little except when the nation is using that party for a large and definite purpose." Now that is a chastening statement of principle which our Republican friends would do well to bear in mind. And each of us as citizens, owing as we do our first allegiance to the purposes of our country rather than to those of our party, should be careful never to obstruct the one in order to advance the other.

Wilson's sober appraisal of the significance of party victory can be validly applied to our own present situation. A political party which cannot in defeat make itself an effective instrument of larger national purposes is without significance in the future political life of the country; and sooner rather than later, it will be so marked by the people to whom it must look for the return of trust and confidence and victory.

One of the most challenging aspects of this job is that it seems never to have been done well in the past. Latterly, in twenty years of opposition, the Republican party never distinguished itself except by the shrill vehemence of its criticism of the imperative adjustments to the facts of life, both at home and abroad, which were made under the imaginative and determined leadership of Franklin Roosevelt and Harry Truman. Our Republican friends evidently thought the definition of minority was the converse of maturity; that responsible conduct was not required until they attained majority status. Growing up is always a painful process. The necessity for doing so swiftly makes it worse.

There is, then, a unique opportunity for our party to achieve a new distinction. If we make the most of it, we not only best assure our own eventual triumph, but we may create a pattern of political conduct for others to see and follow, to the lasting benefit of the nation. For the party out of power, principle— and not patronage—must inevitably be the only solvent. Let us not fail to make a virtue of our necessity.

Yes, we Democrats have a special duty—we who chafed under the yoke of responsibility during the postwar years while Europe was saved and Communism stopped—we who suffered all the while the taunts of irresponsible opposition. We must continue, I say, to tell the people the truth; that there are no magic, cheap, short solutions to global conflicts long in the making.

We must not yield to the temptation to goad the Republicans to produce quick miracles and dazzling successes. Let us never sow division when it is so important to harvest unity.

The tensions and difficulties may get worse before they get better in Europe, in the Middle East, in Asia—all around this world, divided and in revolution. Millions of people are as sorely puzzled as many of us here at home. The nature of the struggle is by no means clear to them and, unlike this heaven-favored land, there is lacking to many the same incentives to make the struggle. We must labor to increase these incentives, to prove to misery-laden millions that democracy can provide the right to think, to believe, and to eat, as well as vote.

That others have reservations about our unerring wisdom, that some cannot or will not fall in step at our pace must not exasperate and defeat us. And, in the dark majesty of the issue of life or death, none of us will advance our overriding interest in peace by outbursts of temper against each other or by ill-considered muscle-flexing against the common foe. We shall have to take care not to amuse our foes and frighten our friends.

Patience—firm, intelligent, understanding—seems to be in short supply. Yet it is the indispensable quality of leadership of the diverse elements of the free world and of the uncommitted millions groping their way into the sunlight of a better world. It is also the essential quality of a political party which, after the exhilaration of executive responsibility, finds itself in the less dramatic role of proving again its qualifications for public confidence.

What we as a party must cultivate is what the nation must have. In defeat we can make ourselves servants of the national purpose for peace. There is no greater or better political destiny.

Crusades, Communism, and Corruption

This speech closely followed two important pro-nouncements by Republicans—Senator McCarthy's at-tacks on the Democratic administrations as "Twenty Years of Treason," and Secretary John Foster Dulles' statement of his doctrine of "massive retaliation."

I DO NOT propose to respond in kind to the calculated campaign of deceit to which we have been exposed, nor to the insensate attacks on all Democrats as traitors, Communists, and murderers of our sons.

Those of us—and they are most of us—who are more Americans than Democrats or Republicans count some things more important than the winning or losing of elections.

There is a peace still to be won, an economy which needs some attention, some freedoms to be secured, an atom to be controlled—all through the delicate, sensitive, and indispensable processes of democracy—processes which demand, at the least, that people's vision be clear, that they be told the truth, and that they respect one another.

It is wicked and it is subversive for public officials to try deliberately to replace reason with passion; to substitute hatred for honest difference; to fulfill campaign promises by practicing deception; and to hide discord among Republicans by sowing the dragon's teeth of dissension among Americans.

The loyalty and patriotism of a whole political party, of one-half of the nation, has been indicted. Twenty years of bipartisan effort, highly intelligent and highly successful, have been called "Twenty Years of Treason"—under the auspices of the Republican National Committee.

From an address at the Democratic National Committee Southern Conference and Dinner, Miami Beach, March 7, 1954.

When one party says that the other is the party of traitors who have deliberately conspired to betray America, to fill our government services with Communists and spies, to send our young men to unnecessary death in Korea, they violate not only the limits of partisanship, they offend not only the credulity of the people, but they stain the vision of America and of democracy for us and for the world we seek to lead.

That such things are said under the official sponsorship of the Republican party in celebration of the birthday of Abraham Lincoln adds desecration to defamation. This is the first time that politicians, Republicans at that, have sought to split the Union—in Lincoln's honor.

This system of ours is wholly dependent upon a mutual confidence in the loyalty, the patriotism, the integrity of purpose of both parties. Extremism produces extremism, lies beget lies. The infection of bitterness and hatred spreads all too quickly in these anxious days from one area of our life to another. And those who live by the sword of slander also may perish by it, for now it is also being used against distinguished Republicans. We have just seen a sorry example of this in the baseless charges hurled against our honored Chief Justice. And the highest officials of the Pentagon have been charged with "coddling Communists" and "shielding treason." General Zwicker, one of our great Army's finest officers, is denounced by Senator McCarthy as "stupid, arrogant, witless," as "unfit to be an officer," and a "disgrace to the uniform." For what? For obeying orders. This to a man who has been decorated thirteen times for gallantry and brilliance; a hero of the Battle of the Bulge.

When demagoguery and deceit become a national political movement, we Americans are in trouble; not just Democrats, but all of us.

Our State Department has been abused and demoralized. The American voice abroad has been enfeebled. Our educational system has been attacked; our press threatened; our servants of God impugned; a former President maligned; the executive departments invaded; our foreign policy confused; the President himself patronized; and the integrity, loyalty, and morale of the United States Army assailed.

The logic of all this is—not only the intimidation and silencing of all independent institutions and opinion in our society, but the capture of one of our great instruments of political action—the Republican party. The end result, in short, is a malign and fatal totalitarianism.

And why, you ask, do the demagogues triumph so often? The answer is inescapable: because a group of political plungers has persuaded the President that McCarthyism is the best Republican formula for political success.

Had the Eisenhower administration chosen to act in defense of itself and of the nation which it must govern, it would have had the grateful and dedicated support of all but a tiny and deluded minority of our people.

Yet, clear as the issue is, and unmistakable as the support, the administration appears to be helpless. Why? The Stevens incident illustrates what preceding events have made memorably plain: A political party divided against itself, half McCarthy and half Eisenhower, cannot produce national unity—cannot govern with confidence and purpose. And it demonstrates that, so long as it attempts to share power *with* its enemies, it will inexorably lose power *to* its enemies.

Perhaps you will say that I am making not a Democratic but a Republican speech; that I am counseling unity and courage in the Republican party and administration. You bet I am!—for as Democrats we don't believe in political extermination of Republicans, nor do we believe in political fratricide; in the extermination of one another. We believe in the republic we exist to serve, and we believe in the two-party system that serves it—that can only serve it, at home and abroad, by the best and the noblest of democracy's processes.

And there is nothing, by the way, except abuse of democracy's processes in this deception about the employees allegedly removed from government jobs as "security risks."

We were told in October, 1954, by the White House that 1,456 government employees had been removed as security risks. The President later raised the figure to 2,200. And we were told—by Governor Dewey of New York, the Postmaster General, the Counsel to the President, and countless other Republican leaders—that most of these were "subversives," "spies and traitors" who had been "kicked out of government." Some of these orators even suggested they had been planted in the government.

You remember all the campaign talk about Communism and corruption, and what the Republicans were going to do if they won to clean up "the mess in Washington," as they called it. Well, as you may have heard, they won, and when they didn't find the government "crawling with spies and traitors" they started this numbers game to show how well they were doing.

The figure has now been raised to 2,427; but the only thing we know for sure is the government's reluctant admission that out of more than two million federal employees only one alleged active Communist has been found.

It looks as though the Great Crusade had practiced a Great Deception. They may consider this good politics. But it is vicious government. We will await the final results with interest, and also the administration's apologies to the many innocent, loyal people who have been injured by this unscrupulous, un-American numbers racket.

Everyone hopes the administration will find and remove all the real subversives and keep them out of our government. For a single disloyal or dangerous employee is one too many, and I do not hold that the past should be closed. On the contrary, experience will remain a powerful, ever-present reminder of the price of anything less than eternal vigilance. But I do hold that past errors do not excuse new ones; that democracy's ideals and vitality must not be despoiled by those who purport to defend them.

The President has said he disapproves all these goings-on— this slander and deceit, this bitterness and ugliness, these attempts to subordinate a nation's common purposes to a divided party's political ambitions. He has said so repeatedly in statements to the press—but the nation's ideals continue to be soiled by the mud of political expediency.

This internal crisis makes it all the more urgent that the Democratic party remain strong, responsible, and attentive to the nation's business. I note that no Democrat has charged that the whole Republican party is corrupt merely because three Republican Congressmen in a row have been convicted of defrauding the government. We know that Republicans and Democrats alike want better government—government that measures up to the ideals of proud people, to the dignity which befits the leader among nations, to the standard we think of as the reward citizens receive from a democracy for which they pay and work and pray and fight, and see their sons die to preserve.

Now, more than ever, America must be a citadel of sanity and reason. We live in a troubled, dangerous world where the great issues are peace or war and the stakes are life and death.

Perhaps these melancholy diversions explain, for example, why there has been so little public curiosity about such a genuine concern as the "new look" in national defense and foreign policy. I had hoped that there might be a resumption of the bipartisanship of President Truman's administration when Secretary Dulles and many prominent Republicans, including the President himself, served in important roles.

At all events, without the benefit of bipartisanship, the administration has unveiled this "new look." It has been presented to us as a program of more for our money, national security in the large economy-size package, "a bigger bang for a buck."

While I don't presume to understand its full implications, they are sobering enough to require searching, responsible discussion. The background of any evaluation of this new program must be stern realization that the peril of the free world is not diminishing.

We are told, and I am quoting the words of Secretary Dulles, that we have rejected the "traditional" policy of "meeting aggression by direct and local opposition." We have taken the decision, he says, "to depend primarily upon a great capacity to retaliate instantly, by means and at places of our choosing." But some "setbacks to the cause of freedom," some "Communist successes," Mr. Dulles says, should be regarded as "normal."

All this means, if it means anything, is that if the Communists try another Korea we will retaliate by dropping atom bombs on Moscow or Peiping or wherever we choose—or else we will concede the loss of another Korea—and presumably

68

other countries after that—as "normal" in the course of events.

Is this a "new look" or is it a return to the pre-1950 atomic deterrent strategy which made some sense as long as we had a monopoly of atomic weapons together with a strategic air force. Yet even then it didn't deter attack, and brought us to the brink of disaster in Korea where atom bombs were useless, and we were only saved by heroic exertion to re-create conventional ground forces.

But, you say, we did not use the bomb against Russian and Chinese targets for fear of enlarging the war. Exactly; and if we should now use them in retaliation that way it would certainly mean World War III and atomic counter-retaliation. For the Russians have massive power of retaliation with atomic weapons just as we do, and our cities are also susceptible to destruction.

Another question: what if we are confronted with something less than a clear case of overt aggression? What if we had relied exclusively on a policy of "massive retaliation" since the close of World War II? Would we have resorted to global atomic war in order to meet the Communist threat in Greece and Turkey? To counter the Berlin blockade? To resist aggression in Korea?

If the answer is no, then the so-called "new look" in foreign policy is no "new look" at all, but merely a continuation of the policy of adapting our methods of resistance to the method of attack—a policy that has brought the free world through many crises without precipitating a Martian catastrophe.

Instead of greater freedom of choice, does this decision to rely primarily on atomic weapons really narrow our choice as to the means and the places of retaliation? Are we leaving ourselves the grim choice of inaction or a thermonuclear holocaust? Are we, indeed, inviting Moscow and Peiping to nibble us to death?

This is the real danger. This is the real problem. Will we turn brush fires and local hostilities into major conflicts? Will our allies go along?

Using weapons short of war, and relying upon our reluctance to embark on global war, the Communist imperialism will attempt to absorb country after country, to close the ring around us, and to decide the issue between tyranny and freedom long before a final outburst of atomic fury.

It seems to me that the new weapons—even if we had a complete monopoly—are no answer to all the complicated aspects of this world-wide struggle, for armed aggression is only one of the many shapes of the Communist menace. And the only thing new about the "new look" appears to be the weakening of our Navy and ground forces and reducing the non-atomic programs and policies that we need to win the cold war.

Was the administration caught between two conflicting sets of promises—to reduce the budget and simultaneously strengthen our defenses? Did it choose the former because the one thing that could not be cut, the *sine qua non* of our security, was the new weapons and air power?

I don't know, but if true bipartisanship in the formulation of policy in matters of such grave import is impossible, at least we are entitled to the facts and the truth unadorned. If our military policy is beyond the further financial endurance of the country; if this reliance on retaliation is the only reasonable policy for the long haul, then frankly tell us so and why. But don't confuse us and frighten our allies by misbranding disengagement as advance and retrenchment as initiative. Don't tell us we have something new and better for less, when we haven't.

It may be that they don't mean what they say or that I have misinterpreted what they say. But issues of life and death should be clarified and not clouded, for security in our age cannot be brought by slogans and gimmicks.

It is only in the strength of freedom, in the fortitude and sacrifice of free peoples; it is only in the humility of all men under God that we can create a future not scratched from the wreck and rubble of war or from the chaos of domestic disorder but rising from the love and faith and devotion of unconquerable humanity.

I hope that we can begin to talk with one another about our affairs more seriously, moderately, and honestly, whether it be our foreign policies or the patriotism of our people and public servants. There has been enough—too much—of slander, dissension, and deception. We cannot afford such wastage of our resources of mind and spirit, for there is important work to do which will be done together or not at all. It is for us, all of us, to recapture the great unifying spirit which still surges so strongly through the hearts and minds of America. Let us, as Democrats, resist the ugly provocations of this hour and try to cut the pattern of America's future, not from the scraps of dissension and bitterness but rather from the full, rich fabric of America's ideals and aspirations.

"Let us," in Thomas Jefferson's words, "restore to social intercourse that harmony and affection without which liberty and even life itself are dreary things," and without which, I could add, tomorrow's misfortune will mock today's expectations.

The Congressional Campaign Begins

WE ARE on the eve of another momentous election. The time is approaching when we must pass judgment on the parties and their candidates again—which is not just our privilege as citizens; it is also our obligation, and on the quality of our decisions largely depends the quality of our government.

The Republicans have been in office for twenty months—or long enough to elect Maine's first Democratic governor in twenty years. About the only danger our Republican friends don't face this fall is the danger of overconfidence.

But of course there is nothing new about this loss of public confidence in the G.O.P., and the political doctors have been proposing larger and larger doses of expediency to salvage what they once called the "Great Crusade." A couple of months ago in Milwaukee, the Vice-President of the United States set the tone of Republican political education and statesmanship by blaming the defeat of the French in Indo-China on the Democrats in Washington. A couple of weeks ago in Cincinnati at the Republican strategy conference Mr. Nixon's ennobling advice for his teammates was mostly to avoid discussing the issues at all and to stay out of debates. And a couple of days ago, over in Ohio, Mr. Nixon defined the Republican task: it is to figure out what to do to win and then do it. Anything goes, apparently—and the farm program went quickly. Mr. Benson, the Secretary of Agriculture, promptly took this advice and totally repealed his "total acreage allotment" plan to control farm surpluses. The farm belt, it seems, was chafing tender Republican skins. It will be interesting to observe how the nation's press, which recently applauded so vigorously the President's farm program and Mr. Benson's

From an address at the Democratic Dinner, Indianapolis, September 18, 1954.

72

courage, will react to this hasty retreat and this application of the Nixonian doctrine of political expediency.

As in every election, state and local issues, the merits of the individual candidates, catchwords, and the weather will affect the results. Of the weather I have little to say and nothing to promise. As to the Republican slogans I've said quite a bit from time to time about government by merchandising. Nor can I say much about individual candidates, except, of course, that we are proud of ours. But I do want to say a word about the spirit of a Congressional campaign in this age of perpetual, troubled motion in human affairs. I want to say a word about the similarities of our great parties, which may seem a strange way to talk on the eve of a fateful political contest. And I hope this audience won't think it heresy for me to suggest that we Democrats could have anything in common with the Republicans.

An election tends, of course, to emphasize our political divisions. This is as it must be, for to vote is to divide and in selecting one candidate or party we necessarily reject the other. An election is both a selection and rejection; it is a choosing up of sides. It matters greatly whether reason or passion guides our choice. Reason will enlighten and elevate our understanding and it will discover in controversy the springs of a new unity. But passion will poison the political atmosphere in which the nation must meet the tests of the future.

The fact is that we are Americans, first, last, and always, and may the day never come when the things that divide us seem more important than the things that unite us. We have many differences with the Republicans on specific issues of national policy, and we want to discuss and debate them because we think they are important. But I hope we may never forget that we hold far more in common with our friends, the Republicans, especially Republicans like Wendell Willkie, than we hold in dispute. Were it not so, neither party could govern, for government rests less on majorities at the polls than on the abiding unity, good sense, and obedience of the people.

Even in these sobering times it would be too much to hope, I suppose, that there might be an end to extravagant claims that one party represents all that is good and the other all that is evil. And we know that shrill voices filled with bitterness and hate have already been raised in our land. A strange and, it seems to me, truly un-American violence has stained too many utterances in recent months. It was the Republican Governor of New York, twice his party's candidate for President, who damned all Democrats for all time with words too ugly to repeat and too grotesque to believe. It was the Republican Attorney General of the United States who impugned the very loyalty of a former President of the United States—a man who has done more to combat Communism at home and abroad than all the Republican politicians put together—Harry S. Truman. It was a Republican Senator from this great state of Indiana who described Democrats as betrayers. And it was the Republican National Committee itself which sponsored, in memory of Abraham Lincoln, the slogan "Twenty Years of Treason" to describe the two great Democratic decades.

Now this, of course, is not the language of reasoned political debate. This is the language of clan warfare, of civil war, of flaming passions and unreason. And it is more dangerous than just the debasement of our political dialogue and our political morals, because as it exploits it also aggravates the unhealthy national mood of fear and suspicion of one another that has so hampered the unemotional discussion on which wise public policy must be based; a mood that has so dangerously diverted us from the main jobs of establishing sane foreign policies and evolving sound domestic programs.

We shall hear more and more of these unscrupulous, shrill voices before the people must judge in November. What will the response be? Will the people reject or applaud those who do not even hesitate to recklessly divide America into ugly, bitter factions?

I think the good sense of the American people will prevail and that America has already made its decision on those demagogues who rely on defamation, deceit, and double-talk. At any rate, whatever the provocation, we must not be guilty of contributing to irreconcilable divisions in our country and to political delinquency. And, whatever the provocation, I hope and pray that we Democrats will both recognize and respect the difference between cynical politics and principles, between ruthless partisanship and patriotism.

Now I have spoken seriously, indeed piously, about this because the preservation and strengthening of America requires above all the preservation and strengthening of our mutual trust and confidence. No election victory is worth the damage of these central elements of our strength. Weakness begins at home, in doubts, suspicions, and whispers, and if the spirit of America is enfeebled, it will be the result of self-inflicted wounds.

So I say let us dispute our honest differences honestly and let the people decide them on the merits, but let us Democrats at least not be guilty of sowing discord, mistrust, and hate in this lovely land. As bearers of an honorable and ancient political tradition let us so conduct this momentous campaign as not to weaken but to strengthen the nation in this troubled hour.

Kansas—A Kind of Prophecy

THERE IS A deeply historical reason for the attention which will be focused nationally on political events in Kansas this year. It is the feeling which many have that Kansas, by reason of history and location at the very heart of our continental power, is a kind of social, political, and cultural barometer for all America. Kansas seems to anticipate the national mood; Kansas, we feel, right or wrongly, is often a long-range forecast of the political and cultural weather of the United States. William Allen White, whom I knew and worked with just before the last war, said that Kansas "is hardly a state" but "a kind of prophecy," for, as he put it, "when anything is going to happen in this country, it happens first in Kansas."

In this year of Territorial Centennial celebrations, I need hardly remind you that Kansas was a fighting Idea, a symptom as well as a focus of impending national crisis, even before she was a fact of political geography.

One hundred years ago last spring Kansas was an empty land; aside from a couple of military posts and a few Indian trading posts, there were no white settlements in all the vast area between the Missouri and the Rocky Mountains. Of every hundred white men in all these immense solitudes, probably ninety-nine, in the spring of 1854, were on their way to somewhere else by the Oregon, the Santa Fe, and other trails. The skies arched a brooding silence among the hills, the valleys, and the mighty sweep of the Western High Plains.

But this peace which lay virtually unbroken upon the Kansas landscape was in marked contrast to the noise, the violence even, which focused on Kansas as an Idea in the Senate of the United States, and throughout the nation, in May of 1854.

The Kansas-Nebraska bill which repealed the Missouri Compromise and substituted the disastrous "squatter sovereignty"

From an address at Wichita, October 7, 1954.

principle whereby the issue of slavery was to be decided by vote of settlers on the Kansas land passed the House in March. In May it passed the Senate. On May 30 it was signed into law by the amiable Franklin Pierce, whose lack of deep conviction made him a pliant tool of single-minded men.

What followed was predictable. What followed is what *always* follows, sooner or later, when basic moral principles are compromised. We have seen many examples of it in our own time. We've seen it in the attempts of the Kerensky regime to appease the Bolsheviks in the Russia of 1917. We've seen it in the attempts of social democratic parties of Italy and Germany to appease the Fascists and Nazis during the 1920's. We've seen it in the attempts of misguided conservatives in Britain and France to appease Hitler in the 1930's. And, in a different dimension, we saw in that sordid public exhibition last spring the culmination of the Republicans' effort to appease Senator McCarthy, to have it both ways, to use and to abuse him at the same time. (I have been tempted a few times to remind our Republican friends of a Chinese proverb—who rides a tiger may not dismount.)

"Bleeding Kansas" was born of the Kansas-Nebraska Act, an act of appeasement designed by Northern "middle-of-the-road" politicians—and out of "Bleeding Kansas" came national Civil War. These rich plains became for a decade another "dark and bloody ground," a landscape of guerrilla war, of murder and pillage, suffering and violence.

The ways of Providence, however, are inscrutable. Sometimes it appears in history that good arises out of evil—just as evil sometimes, though less often, arises out of good.

And one of the good things that arose out of the Kansas-Nebraska Act was the Republican party (which I hope isn't heresy in this audience!)—a regrouping of the discontented—Whigs mostly—to resist the further extension of slavery. I have always been proud and thankful that my own great-grandfather was one of the founders of the Republican party in Illinois in that troubled spring of 1854. And I'm thankful too that he can't see it now.

I have heard it argued that the evils of Kansas' first years also had good consequences. The perilous times placed a premium on alertness and flexibility of intelligence, as well as on courage, iron will, and endurance. Strong characters, original minds, and vivid personalities came to the fore. The Kansas community which emerged from the struggle was a various one; with all manner of tensions and ideas between its components, it had a dynamic quality all its own. In the years that followed the Civil War, these tensions and this variety were maintained; they were even increased. The Puritan idealism transplanted from New England was sustained by an influx of religious colonists in the 1870's and after. The frontier pragmatism of the Old Northwest was encouraged by the harsh living conditions as your settlements moved westward. And the gambling, fighting qualities of the Old South were echoed by the wild cowboys of Abilene, Wichita, Hays, Dodge City, and by the daring ranchers and farmers who moved out onto the High Plains—a land where one's very existence was a gamble. Those were the years of railroad building through hostile country, of Indian massacres and sod-busting, of economic exploitation by Eastern capital, of devastating droughts and grasshopper plagues—a "sea of troubles," in Hamlet's phrase, against which Kansans bravely took arms—and conquered.

During its first fifty years Kansas became what I think every state in the Union *ought* to be, and *must* be, if the doctrine of "states' rights" and "local control" we hear so much about these days is to have real meaning for the future. Kansas became a laboratory of social experiment for the nation. The frictions between opposing views and interests struck sparks which fell upon the rich tinder of a daring spirit and lit creative fires.

One new social device after another was tried out, here on the Kansas prairies, between the close of the Civil War and the end of Teddy Roosevelt's Bull Moose in 1912. Some of these experiments failed ludicrously. Others had only indifferent success. But a surprising number of them succeeded so well that other states, and then the nation as a whole, imitated them. Kansas did indeed become, in those creative years, a "kind of prophecy," in White's phrase.

Prohibition, rightly or wrongly, railroad regulation, "bluesky" laws, women's suffrage—all were pioneered here in Kansas. In the 1890's this was the center of that creative political ferment known to history as the Populist Revolt; out of which came many of the progressive measures adopted by the administrations of Teddy Roosevelt and Woodrow Wilson. In the early 1900's, Kansas showed the way in the field of sanitation, public health, compulsory medical insurance, workmen's compensation, etc.

Kansans created during those years a great tradition. And, of course, also created legends of painful righteousness and piety through their more fervent efforts to legislate the private morality of citizens. But for the most part, puritanism and progressivism were joined in happy wedlock upon these plains, producing at decent intervals offspring, characterized by a practical idealism—and Kansas households exhibited great pride and self-respect.

But then, alas, something happened. While Kansas has somehow resisted all the pressures which tend to destroy regional differences and has maintained herself as a distinctive state of mind to a rare degree, many historians share the opinion that in the second decade of this century the remarkably creative forces of Kansas began to be dissipated.

I have an excuse for commenting on Kansas' recent history. For what happened in Kansas forty years ago had national implications, just as what happens here this year has national implications.

In 1912 what happened was Teddy Roosevelt's Bull Moose. It came raging across Kansas as it raged across America, splitting off from the Republicans that wing which believed that no great political party can properly devote itself, with single-minded exclusiveness, to the special interests of businessmen. "The worst government of all," Teddy Roosevelt said, "is the government of the very rich . . . the government of a plutocracy." Yet the faith in plutocracy and service of a single interest has been—save for the strange interludes of Lincoln and T.R. himself—the dominating influence in Republicanism. And when the Bull Moose collapsed, progressivism in Kansas was left leaderless, disillusioned, and cynical—for the principal Progressives returned, chastened and discredited, to a Republican party now completely dominated by the Old Guard.

If Kansas continued thereafter as a kind of prophecy for all America—as I think she did—what she prophesied was no longer a various, a dynamic, a progressive America, permeated by that rational controversy which is the very essence of the democratic process. William Allen White himself recognized and recorded the unhappy change. Whither, he asked plaintively in a 1934 magazine article, have the old Kansas giants departed? What has dampened the fires of Kansas' old flaming idealism? Why has a timid mediocrity triumphed in a state once notable for the courage of her experiments, the colorful vigor of her politicians, and the vivid intelligence of her country journalism? White never found the answer to these questions—or at least never admitted that he had—but since he did ask them I think he might agree that what Kansas had begun to prophesy by that time was a conformist America committed almost exclusively to economic values.

Of course this prophecy was far from perfect, for which we may all be thankful: it did not come wholly true, either within Kansas' borders or in that larger world whose cultural weather Kansas seems sometimes to forecast. But it definitely *tended* in certain respects to come true, to the dismay of all who really care about human freedom.

For we Americans do well to recognize that unthinking conformity is fatal to genuine liberty. By developing a standardized mental environment, conformity breeds the most insidious and permanent tyranny of all, in that its subjects are unconscious of their slavery—and in so far as it prevails it weakens our mental and moral fiber, limits our flexibility of thought and action, and reduces our most potent defenses against totalitarianism.

Thus it might be said that as the range of interests represented by the Republican party narrowed and contracted, Kansas suffered a loss of human freedom—a loss confirmed by the failure of efforts to develop an opposition party or an opposition press to perpetuate the great traditions of Populism and Progressivism.

I have indicated that when the Bull Moose collapsed after 1912, its leaders here in Kansas returned, hat in hand, to a Republican party more reactionary than it had formerly been. They were not forced to do so; they *chose* to do so. And what were the consequences, the very sad consequences, of that choice?

Consider, for example, the case of the beloved William Allen White. He used to explain, defensively, as many of you may recall, that he remained in Republican ranks, comporting himself as a party regular at election times despite his disapproval of party policies and candidates, because he wished to reform the party from within. He wished, he said, to liberalize it. But, of course, he didn't succeed.

Instead he suffered what seems to be the common fate of so many progressives who seek to achieve their aims under the banner of modern Republicanism. For the progressive in Republican ranks is likely to find himself isolated and ineffective, or else a front man behind whom the same old special interests continue their aggressions upon the general welfare—and we, the people, are largely robbed of his services.

Senator George Norris of Nebraska, for example, was lonely and ineffective in the Republican ranks in the 1920's. Not until Franklin Roosevelt's time did his creative bills become law. And if he were alive today he'd find his greatest monument, TVA, branded as "creeping Socialism" by a Republican President, and a Republican administration actively aiding unprecedented raids on the public domain—the land, mineral, and water resources—which George Norris fought so hard to preserve for the benefit of all the people.

The story of the younger Senator Bob La Follette of Wisconsin is a misfortune not only for him but for the nation. In 1946 when he decided that the Wisconsin Progressive party should go into the Republican camp, young Bob, a great defender of civil liberties, was defeated in the Republican primary—by Joseph McCarthy.

Senator Wayne Morse, of Oregon, who stayed and struggled from within the Republican camp as long as he could bear it, is another case in point.

Obviously a great majority of Kansans were sickened by the discovery that their state has long had a secret government of special interests who have been able to promote or prevent legislation at their pleasure. They want a change. They *demand* a change. Their vote in the Republican primary proves it.

A Truth Beyond Politics

I WISH the world could better know this country for what it really is—not just a greedy economic giant crouching fearfully behind its walls—not just a panoplied warrior nervously fingering his weapons—and not a sordid civil war between the officers of our government—but as *this*—as a people who gather together in thousands to give a people's government its essential vitality.

Some day the world *will* see again—as it does not now I regret to say—the vision of the real America. And when it does it will be a brighter day for international understanding, for confidence, for good will, and for peace on earth.

For beyond and beneath the turmoil of a political campaign are principles and great objectives—and it is because I believe them to be more fully embodied in the Democratic party than in any other that I am myself a Democrat. Our aim as Democrats is not the concentration of authority in the hands of feudal overlords or of a totalitarian state, but the diffusion of power as well as of well-being among all the people. We strive to enable free competitive enterprise to withstand the machinations of monopolistic or cartelized power. We strive to enable honest saving and investment to protect itself from fraud, chicanery, and overreaching. We seek to enable the farmers and the workers to maintain a fair and equal bargaining position on the markets for their products and for their labor.

This is the New Freedom which seeks the prudent use and husbandry of the nation's resources and their protection from ruthless exploitation and despoliation at the expense of future generations.

It strives to conserve not only our material resources but our human resources—the self-respect and dignity of all

From an address at the Hollywood Bowl, October 9, 1954.

members of our free and independent society. It demands protection of every individual and his dependents from the unavoidable hazards of old age, sickness, and unemployment. Our new freedom would give every individual without regard to color or religion or age or wealth or physical handicap a stake in freedom worth defending.

There is no doubt that we are living in a changing world. Progress in science and technology has awakened the hope for a better life and increased well-being everywhere.

The Kremlin tells all those throughout the world yearning for change that our free system has nothing to offer them and would leave things as they are; that only imperial Communism offers them a hope for a change and a better life.

But we believe that we have a better way—the way of consent instead of force. And we must give proof that our way of life is now with a new freedom bringing a greater degree of continuing well-being to all our people than has ever been enjoyed in all history by any people. The struggle with evil, error, and tyranny is everlasting, but never vain. And even the most fanatical ideology must adjust itself to revealed truth or perish. The job is to cling everlastingly to the truth; to try everlastingly to find it in the clatter and confusion of these times—and to find it even in the storm of words of a political campaign.

Rapier versus Ax:
A Constructive Opposition

WHEN, in 1952, the American people decided that it was time for a change, they assigned to the Democratic party a new but challenging task—that of playing the role of a responsible minority in the halls of Congress.

That, at any rate, was the conclusion shared by party leaders, including Senator Lyndon Johnson and Representative Sam Rayburn, who joined in pledging themselves to the constructive purposes of a loyal opposition. All were agreed that the interests of the Democratic party must and would be subordinated to the interests of the nation.

Now that we are on the eve of another national election, it seems only fair and proper that, in addition to casting a critical eye upon the record of the majority party, independent voters should likewise examine carefully the performance of the minority. How, in short, has the Democratic party lived up to its pledges to the American people?

To my way of thinking, the record of the Congress shows that Democrats have not only talked sense to the American people—they have made sense to the American people. Rarely, if ever before, has a minority in Congress so successfully spurned opposition for opposition's sake, or so strongly supported the Executive without in any way forgoing its own interpretation of the nation's best interests.

The record is especially impressive when it is contrasted with that of the Republican minority during the previous twenty years of Democratic rule. Nor, I should add, is the contrast made any the less striking by the record of the Republican majority during the last twenty months.

Indeed, the single most important issue debated during the

Originally published in the New York Herald Tribune, *October 13, 1954.*

Eighty-third Congress found Democrats defending the President against irresponsible members of his own party. The Bricker Amendment threatened the very foundations of the President's authority in the conduct of foreign relations, and, had it been passed, the American people would have lived to rue the day. To their everlasting credit, Democrats joined with a few responsible Republicans to turn back this unwarranted and infinitely dangerous attempt to amend the doctrine of the separation of powers.

In other matters, too, Democrats fought with the President to repel Republican snipers, as in the attack against the nomination of Charles Bohlen as our Ambassador to Russia. And the nation will not soon forget the spectacle of the McCarthy hearings or the plight of a Republican Secretary of the Army forced to seek help from Democrats to protect the Army from a Republican Senator.

The election of 1952 did not mean an end to the Democratic party's traditional support of freer foreign trade, or, for that matter, the Republican party's equally traditional protectionism. So it is not surprising to find that, when the President proposed a three-year extension of the reciprocal trade agreements act, together with other trade reforms, Democrats worked enthusiastically to give the President what he said he wanted (and what they knew the country needed), only to fail in the face of unanimous opposition from the Republicans.

As significant as are these instances of minority support for the President, the Democratic party can be just as proud of its record of constructive opposition. For in this record is to be found proof not only of our determination to "fight them to the end when we think they are wrong" but of our desire always to propose something better.

Take, for example, the administration's tax bill, a measure which provided a much-needed overhauling of federal tax law, but which also gave to corporations and high-income families the lion's share of tax relief. Democrats argued that this was neither equitable nor economically sound, and proposed a much broader division of tax relief by increasing the individual exemption from $600 to $700. The Republican majority voted solidly against this proposal.

Democrats took the lead in exposing the pretensions implicit in the administration's "new look" defense policy, and in decrying the cutback in Air Force appropriations last year and in Army ground forces this year. And when Democrats moved to maintain Army strength at nineteen divisions, the Republican majority voted solidly for seventeen divisions.

No less indicative of the Democratic party's concept of its responsibility as the minority party was its stand on one of the most complex, yet most important measures considered by the Eighty-third Congress—the revision of the atomic energy act. Provisions of the administration's bill threatened to leave the future development of atomic energy for industrial purposes in the hands of a few utilities and chemical companies, despite a paramount public interest in maintaining free access to the potential fruits of this immensely promising source of power. Democrats fought staunchly, and to a large extent successfully, to take out the monopoly features of this bill.

Democrats did not succeed, however, in blocking legislative authorization for the Dixon-Yates contract,* which ensuing disclosures have shown to be a major item in the Democratic indictment of Republican philosophy and performance.

All of these issues, I believe, are pertinent to our current political debate, and if, in the nature of things, it is the Republican majority that is standing trial, Democrats are no less anxious that their record as the minority be weighed in the balance.

In the past, many of us who sincerely believe in our two-party system of government have been saddened by the spectacle of a minority demonstrating its unfitness to govern by acting on the premise that the role of the opposition is to oppose everything proposed by the President of the majority party.

In the past two years we have witnessed a refreshing novelty. We have seen a minority party carry out a program of selective, perceptive opposition—sometimes defending the President against the majority of his own party, sometimes opposing steps it considered wrong and proposing a constructive alterna-

* After considerable Congressional criticism, and after the city of Memphis decided to build an equivalent power plant, the administration finally dropped its Dixon-Yates project.

tive, sometimes amending and altering administration proposals to improve them, or, in the case of bad ones, to lessen their potential danger.

We have seen the rapier replace the meat ax. We have seen the stop-and-go sign replace the permanent block. We have seen a minority party demonstrate its fitness to govern again.

The Congressional Campaign Ends

As THIS campaign approaches its end, I want to discuss as soberly as I can what is at stake on Tuesday for us all—what is at stake so far as government measures and policies are concerned; and then what is at stake so far as the election affects the health and responsibility of our democratic system.

Let me first discuss with you why I think a Democratic Congress would be good for the country—indeed, why it might even be good for the Republican party!

Now it is both customary and fitting that the President should desire and ask for a Congress of his own political persuasion, for the President is also the leader of his party. But it is an entirely different matter to say that the President is somehow and in some way *entitled* to a Congress of his own choosing. It is not the President but the people who choose the Congress; and our biennial Congressional elections were specifically designed by the Founding Fathers to provide the people an opportunity to periodically record their judgment of an administration.

I might add that I do not recall the Republicans ever advancing the argument that a President was entitled to a Congress of his own party when there was a Democratic administration in Washington. Nor do I think it very likely that they will be making this argument in, say, 1958!

But President Eisenhower has been offering another argument as to why the people should give him a Republican Congress. He has said a Democratic Congress would usher in a cold war with the White House, but if we are to judge by the record of the last Republican Congress, there can be no war colder, or hotter, than the internal conflict in the Republican party. I need only remind you of the proposed Bricker Amend-

From an address at the Democratic Rally, Cooper Union, New York, October 30, 1954.

ment which was perhaps the most serious Congressional attempt in recent times to strike at the authority and integrity of the presidential office. It was conceived and executed by Republican Senators. And the coldest political warfare waged within living memories between the executive branch of government and members of Congress was the attack on the Eisenhower administration by Senator McCarthy and his Republican followers—an attack which heartened our enemies and dismayed our friends. The contradictions of the President by his majority leader, Senator Knowland, of the cabinet by one another, of the Vice-President by the Secretary of State and so on, have become a subject of sorry mirth not only here but abroad where it is no longer clear who speaks for America.

But on Thursday night General Eisenhower once again summarized his case for a Republican Congress by suggesting that "confusion can be avoided and steady progress assured only by electing a Republican majority." After two years of confusion and retreat under a Republican Congress, I could hardly believe my eyes when I read this. Indeed I would like to use these words of the President's as my own text. For I deeply believe that the only way to avoid the lamentable confusion which has characterized our policies at home and abroad in the last two years—the only way to achieve a resumption of social and economic progress—is to elect a Democratic Congress next Tuesday.

A Democratic Congress would not only be more likely to enact legislation for the benefit of all the people. The irony is that in addition a Democratic Congress would be more likely to enact more important parts of President Eisenhower's own program than a Republican Congress would.

I could even add that it is the only way to rehabilitate as an effective instrument of government the Republican party, now so hopelessly divided on policy, program, and philosophy.

Let us consider foreign affairs. Our foreign policy, the level of our military strength, and our system of alliances have been systematically imperiled by compromises, contradictions, and appeasement of the Republican Old Guard; except, that is, when the Democrats have rescued the President from his own party and his own leadership. Democrats, for example, tried to resist the policy of reducing our national strength. Democrats tried to save President Eisenhower's own foreign trade program from the Republican protectionists. Democrats effected the confirmation of his Ambassador to Moscow against Republican opposition.

On twelve key administration bills on foreign policy the Democrats not only provided the margin of victory, but on each one the Democrats actually gave the President more votes in both Senate and House than he received from his own party.

But the Democratic minority could not always save us from the Republican Old Guard.

When the President insists, as he did on Thursday, that his administration has been more faithful to bipartisanship in foreign policy "than any previous administration," one must charitably assume that he has been misinformed again. Under the Roosevelt and Truman administrations, dozens of Republicans shared in the responsibility for the formulation and execution of foreign policy in exalted positions—including General Eisenhower and Mr. Dulles, themselves. Where, I respectfully ask, are the Democrats who play similar roles in this administration? Where, even, are the Republicans who served under Democratic administrations and have been dismissed to please the Old Guard?

Either to please the Old Guard, or to get votes, the administration embarked on a perilous course of foreign-policy-by-slogan and foreign-policy-by-bluff. The reckless words about "liberation," "atomic retaliation," "seizing the initiative," "unleashing Chiang Kai-shek," and the like may have warmed the hearts of the Old Guard. But abroad they frightened our friends if not our enemies—whose aggressions have steadily increased in the past two years.

Thanks to the Republican primitives, the administration put a muffler on the Voice of America and our overseas psychological warfare at just the time that Soviet propaganda was scoring new triumphs.

To please the Old Guard, in short, our Army has been cut back, our foreign trade program scuttled, our foreign service harried and demoralized, our allies intimidated and alarmed, our unity of purpose exploded into a sorry mess of conflicting statements, conflicting policies, and conflicting hopes. And, on every one of these issues, it is the Democrats in Congress who have consistently stood for steadiness and strength.

The President asks us to believe that all will be different in the next two years—that he can do with a Republican Congress what he couldn't do—with a Republican Congress! He asks us to believe that a Republican victory will somehow cause the Old Guard to change its spots and reappear in the next Congress purified and repentant. But I say that experience is the best teacher and that a Republican victory will only give them new confidence and deepen the divisions in the Republican party, and the peril to all of us. It will encourage their attacks on the great coalition of free peoples and on our own political and military strength. Indeed, is there any way to liberate our foreign policy from these baleful influences and destructive divisions—is there any way to end the compromise, babble, and confusion which this appeasement has produced—except to elect a Democratic Congress on Tuesday?

And all this holds equally true for domestic policy. At first the Republicans laid claim to a record of legislative achievement. Latterly we've heard less about this record and more about Communists in government, subversion, and sin. Probably this is because most of the positive accomplishments of the administration were made possible only by Democratic votes. But I shall only mention the other parts which were put through without Democratic votes—for only that represents the distinctive contributions of this administration and only that would be threatened by a Democratic Congress.

What has President Eisenhower sought in the domestic field against Democratic opposition?

Against Democratic opposition, he put through a tax program in which the main benefits went overwhelmingly to the corporations and to stockholders. Against Democratic opposition, he has sponsored a wide and various give-away program. Ranging from public power development to grazing lands, from Dixon-Yates to oil, from atomic patents to water-power sites, the administration has not only reversed a bipartisan conservation policy of fifty years but has disclosed an alarming disposition to transfer our national possessions and resources from the many to the few.

Against Democratic opposition, the administration has en-

91

acted a new farm program. As a matter of good faith in politics, it seems to me reprehensible that this program was erected on a foundation of false pledges and broken promises. But, what is more important is that it means lower farm prices, with no corresponding decrease in sight in the cost of what the farmer has to buy.

More disturbing still is that not just the Vice-President and the Republican campaigners, but now the President himself, has affirmed the proposition that prosperity under the Democrats was achieved only at the price of war and bloodshed. This, of course, has been standard Communist propaganda for years and is believed by many to prove that the United States is ready to precipitate war in order to save capitalism. I am sure that the President must have spoken thoughtlessly and carelessly; and let me say to our friends and our enemies beyond the seas that no one who sincerely believes in free capitalism can believe that war or preparation for war is the price of prosperity.

Moreover the facts contradict it. The President evidently forgets the successful transition from war to peace in 1945 and 1946, when in a single year eight million men were released from the armed services and defense spending fell ten times as much as in the past year. Yet, in 1946, we had far less unemployment than we have today. One must assume, too, that the President has not been informed about the prosperous peacetime years of 1947 and 1948 when defense spending was less than one-third as large as it is today, and yet unemployment was at least a million less.

Of course, a Democratic Congress will not solve all our problems. But the election of a Democratic Congress on Tuesday will check the tendency of the last two years to separate the United States from our allies in world affairs. It will stem the drive to cut back further on our own armed strength. It will diminish the passion to give away our natural resources. It will stop further Dixon-Yates deals. It will restore the dignity of the Congressional investigation and will strengthen the atmosphere of individual freedom. It will chasten the administration's complacent attitude toward the millions of Americans who cannot find jobs. It can do much to bring back intelligence, sobriety, and purpose, to the American government. And a Republican victory this fall can only confirm and intensify the tendencies which have brought us into such disrepute abroad and into such disunion at home.

And a Democratic victory will mean a gain for responsibility in another way—in a way perhaps more important than the substantive issues at stake in the campaign. For the success of our democracy depends on the extent to which politics can serve the end of education, of justice, and of truth. Those who would degrade our political processes threaten to destroy the very essence of a free system. If these methods succeed today, then they will be used again and again, until freedom, dignity, decency themselves sink from sight into quicksands of confusion, mistrust, and fear.

All thoughtful citizens have been concerned about the progressive degeneration of this present political campaign. We have observed with sorrow the effect that the pressures of partisanship and political ambition have had on the top leaders of the Republican party. When the campaign began, the President said that the only issue was the record of his administration. But the end is a reckless campaign of smear, misrepresentation, and mistrust. No reputation, no record, no name—no Democrat in short—has been immune from savage or sly attack on his integrity, his good sense, his very loyalty. A few days ago, when the President was asked what he thought of this kind of campaign, he said that he had not heard about it. But within twenty-four hours—and despite his earlier protestation that Communism was not an issue in the campaign—he wrote the Vice-President expressing gratitude and admiration for his contribution to political enlightenment. And yesterday on his airport tour the President himself found it in his heart—or in his script—to take up these themes himself.

This is the end of the "Great Crusade." This Republican campaign has become a program of slander that began a year ago when Mr. Brownell, President Eisenhower's Attorney General, impugned the very loyalty of President Truman, when Governor Dewey identified all Democrats with death and tragedy in Korea, and when the Republican National Committee sent Senator McCarthy around the country to characterize the Democratic administration as "Twenty Years of Treason." Evidently the President couldn't control the campaign of slander, then, and evidently he has embraced it now.

I am sure that President Eisenhower could have accepted this strategy only because he has forgotten what I believe he really knows, and will once again remember—that *how* one wins in politics is as important as *what* one wins.

If ever our system should rise to the highest dignity of its tradition and its responsibilities, it is today. If ever we needed politics which would leave our people informed and united, not confused and divided, it is now. If ever smears, slander, innuendo, misrepresentation were out of place in our national life, it is in this time, at this place, in this world.

Our nation faces grim years ahead—years which will test to the utmost our resolution, our will, and our faith. The realities of our existence—the severe and menacing problems which hang over us—will be as harsh on the day after the election as they were the day the campaign began. After a responsible campaign our country and our people would have been better equipped to cope with these realities than we were three months ago. Instead, the nation has been recklessly torn apart in the search for votes with careless disregard for our self-respect and our unity of national purpose.

The challenge is not just to win elections. The greater challenge is to live in pride and freedom in a future so precarious and so threatening that we can risk no missteps or miscalculations. We need to unite our country, not to divide it; to heal wounds, not to enlarge them. The times demand, not mistrust and suspicion and fear, but more mutual respect and confidence and understanding than ever before.

This does not mean a suspension of hard and healthy debate, for that is the essence of democracy. But hard and healthy debate has to do with real problems. It has to do with legitimate differences in policy and program. There is plenty in the realm of valid difference between our two parties to provide material for a dozen hard-fought political campaigns. No one needs to invent issues or to misrepresent them or to falsify them. No one needs to make confusion a policy and corruption a faith.

I say corruption, because this kind of campaign threatens to corrupt the very processes on which the functioning of democratic government depends. To say that one or another American or party lacks patriotism or favors Communism or wants to subvert our society—when his only crime is disagreement—is to shake our system to the foundations. If we lose our faith in each other, we have lost everything; and no party victory is worth this. Those who seek victory at this price can be rebuked in only one way—that is, at the polls. And this, I think, is the deepest meaning and the greatest opportunity for the American voters on Tuesday.

I would plead with all Americans to cleanse their minds of suspicion and hate; to recognize that men may differ about issues without differing about their faith in America or their belief in freedom; that politics must be a means, not of compounding our weakness, but of consolidating our strength.

If we do justice at the polls to our own conscience and sense of responsibility, then alone can we do justice to the nation we love; then alone can we make our beloved land a symbol and shrine of hope and faith for all free men.

The Challenge to Political Maturity

Now THAT the dust of the campaign has begun to settle, following the recent elections, we are in a better position to discern the permanent realities in our national life—above all, to recover that sense of unity as Americans which underlies the discord and conflict between us as Republicans and Democrats.

I have always insisted that far more unites us than divides us. And I have always regarded this, not just as a fortunate fact, but as a grim necessity for our survival. If we cannot achieve essential harmony, especially in the conduct of our foreign policy, then our divisions will expose us to ghastly possibilities of catastrophe in this troubled world.

The last campaign, it must be frankly said, seriously imperiled our sense of unity. Cruel, unjust, and foolish things were said, patriots were slandered, evil motives imputed, parties traduced and defamed. And by the most exalted of our adversaries too.

Frank and responsible debate is the essence of the democratic way; but recklessness and irresponsibility in our political discourse—frauds, hoaxes, and falsehoods—can strain our democratic fabrics to the breaking point. And the technique of "the big lie" must never become a standard weapon of democratic dialogue.

Let us never forget that self-government was designed for men who had first of all learned to govern themselves.

Perhaps it was too much to hope for an end in this campaign of the sort of guerrilla warfare that has been waged against us Democrats in the past few years; perhaps it was too much to hope that ambitious men would forswear low roads to high places; perhaps it was too much to hope that the awesome

From an address at the Democratic National Committee Conference and Dinner, New Orleans, December 4, 1954.

circumstances of these times would elevate our discourse, or at least halt the downward drift of our political controversy.

Indeed, there is probably much political realism for Democrats in Carl Sandburg's little poem about the soldier of fortune who entreated the Sphinx to reveal the wisdom of the ages in one sentence, and the Sphinx replied: "Don't expect too much."

But not expecting too much does not mean that we should reconcile ourselves to accepting this sort of campaign with resignation. It means something very different. It means that we should recognize these methods as a degradation of the democratic process that strikes at the very foundations of the republic. To remember this, to resist the provocation of retaliation in kind, to match evil with good, falsehood with honesty, is never easy and the results are not always reassuring. But this remains the greatest challenge to our political maturity, a challenge that our party met, I think, with honor in this last unlamented campaign.

In the end the people reaffirmed their confidence in the Democratic party in Congress and in many state governments. But, as Democrats, we must not merely rejoice in what victory has done for our party; rather we must look forward and ask what our victorious party now can do for the country.

There is a relation between legitimacy of power and responsibility. The insecurity of knowing that power must be gained by tricks and deception breeds dynamic words coupled with irresponsible action. But power which comes legitimately, as ours has, can be responsibly exercised with reason, patience, prudence, and wisdom. It is only from that sense of security that wisdom can be joined with innovation and that new paths can be explored with security.

From the past we all have a heritage of error. But we cannot dwell on the past, for the future is too challenging and too peremptory. I am sure that the great majority of Democrats and of independent voters agree in wanting this administration to succeed as it never has before in its task of defending the security and property of our own people and of expanding the hope for freedom and justice for all peoples. It is in this spirit that I speak tonight. It is in this spirit that the Democrats will act in the Eighty-fourth Congress.

We Democrats do not propose to usurp the powers and responsibilities of the Republican executive. As the loyal opposition we should not propose either to find the answers for executive problems or to impede the executive in the proper carrying out of its responsibilities. We wish to see the government do its job better; not to impede its operations.

I foresee as a consequence of the campaign the beginning of a restoration of responsibility to our discussion of public affairs. Nowhere is this responsibility more greatly needed than in the discussion of foreign policy. And nowhere is unity, manifested in intelligence and harmony of purpose, more important. I should add that unity—bipartisanship—can never be an end in itself. No man or party would be justified in surrendering principles deemed essential to national honor and safety simply for the sake of harmony. But where the independence and survival of the nation may hang in balance, we must all work together, lest we all perish together.

Bipartisanship, or whatever we choose to call it, in foreign policy cannot mean an artificial or coerced unity. It cannot mean a device for restricting legitimate discussion or suppressing honest criticism of the conduct of foreign affairs. Nor can it mean the development of new mechanical arrangements which might impair the constitutional and traditional authority of the Executive in the foreign field.

But what it must mean, first of all, is the elimination of domestic politics from the conduct of foreign affairs.

We all know that domestic politics have had too often a powerful influence in determining the tone and even, on occasion, the measures our government has adopted in the foreign field. We all know that decisions have been made in foreign affairs in the late years less to produce results abroad than to produce applause at home. We all know that great damage has been done to our national interest abroad for the sake of showing the domestic audience what big, tough boys we were. We all know that appeasing Republican leaders at home has sometimes had priority over recognizing realities abroad. If our foreign policy is to be manipulated in order to score political points in the domestic debate, then obviously unity in foreign affairs is not very likely.

Actually, the problem of co-operation between the two

major parties in foreign policy has not arisen from the Democratic party in modern times. Since the first World War and Woodrow Wilson's heroic exertions, the Democratic party has been willing to co-operate at home and abroad in effective action. The problem has always been a Republican problem—the problem of how to get unity where one of the parties continues bitterly divided within itself, the problem of trying to ascertain the mind and will of the restless and contradictory combination of forces within the Republican party.

Currently, indeed, the matter can be put in more specific terms. How the government functions in domestic affairs as well as foreign affairs during the next two years will depend more upon the President's success in leading his own party than upon Democratic willingness to co-operate with him. If President Eisenhower can conclude a non-aggression pact with Senator Knowland, and if he can find some means of peaceful coexistence with a large segment of his party, I think he will find us Democrats easy to get along with.

There will continue, of course, to be sharp divisions between the parties in the new Congress. I am sure that the Democrats will fight as manfully as they can for the public welfare, as they see it—against the giveaway of the people's property; for a better deal for the farmer, the wage earner, and the small businessman; for an expanding economy; for our traditional Democratic belief in equal rights for all—special privileges for none. I am sure that the Republicans will fight us back just as hard in terms of their beliefs.

But this conflict on domestic issues need not mean inaction in the foreign field. What should our main objectives in foreign affairs now be? To answer "peace" is to express an aspiration rather than to define a policy. All Americans—all human beings—want nothing more than to live at peace with their brothers. But wishing will not make it so.

To attain it we must have within ourselves an affirmative vision of hope which we can share with the rest of mankind. We cannot be any stronger in our foreign policy—for all the bombs and guns we may heap up in our arsenals—than we are in the spirit which rules inside the country. Foreign policy, like a river, cannot rise above its source. The image we project

99

to the world will, in the end, reflect what we ourselves are and what we feel in our minds and hearts.

If we do not stand unequivocally at home for civil freedom, we cannot hope to stand as the champion of liberty before the world.

If we do not stand at home for equal rights for all our citizens, regardless of race or color, we cannot hope to stand as the champion of opportunity before the world.

If we do not stand at home for steady economic growth and widening social welfare, we cannot hope to stand as the champion of progress before the world.

We should stand for all these things because they are the least to which our people are entitled. We must stand for them because they are our great sources of strength in the world conflict. Unless we stand for them, our moral pretensions are hollow. Unless we stand for them, we have no hope of achieving the peace we long for.

This is the vision which must underlie our foreign policy. The main obstacle to realizing this vision, of course, is Communism, but it is not the only obstacle. If the Soviet problem could be solved tomorrow, our present-day world would remain ravaged, hungry, and explosive. Many of the people of Asia, Africa, South America would be in about the same state of aspiration, unrest, and upheaval as they are today.

Yet while the social revolution of these times must lie always in the background of our mind, the implacable power of the Soviet Union, the new turbulence and attraction of Communist China, and the intricate and sinister operations of the world-wide conspiracy clearly represent the immediate threat to peace.

Personally I am weary of the long semantic argument about coexistence. If we exclude the solution of atomic war, and if we exclude the solution of surrender, all we have left is some form of armed truce which we can call coexistence or anything else you like. Armed coexistence is certainly a bleak prospect. But it is better than no-existence.

The problem we face is how to restrain this new Communist imperialism, and at the same time maintain peace in the world and hold out hope to peoples presently striving for a new life. It is my belief that we are seeing today an important shift in

Soviet tactics. The massive Western rearmament after 1950 has checkmated the armed power on which the Soviet relied for intimidation and aggression. Hence, they have begun to switch to the social and economic battlefield and to try, through diplomatic means, to split the Western coalition. Employing these new tactics, Communism has made significant gains in those parts of the world striving for a new power and a new dignity. And it may gravely disturb the unity of the alliance of the free peoples of the West.

Yet, while the Soviet policy has become more flexible, we have become more rigid. While Soviet leaders astutely utilize the weapons of social agitation and political subversion, we continue to act as if Communism is primarily a military threat. While we cannot for a moment relax our vigilance on either the military or the conspiratorial fronts, Communism is also a powerful social movement, making a profound appeal wherever people are aspiring or insecure or frustrated. The probability is that, so long as we maintain our own military strength at sufficiently high levels, the chief threat in the next period will be Communist exploitation of social and political unrest. This analysis implies two main obligations for the United States.

If it has been the growing strength and unity of the free world which has deterred new adventures on the Korea model, then obviously our first obligation is to maintain our own strength and the unity of our coalition.

And if the conspirators are concentrating today on social and political aggression, then our second obligation is to show peoples struggling for economic and national deliverance that they can fulfill their aspirations better in association with free peoples and by the methods of consent than they can by submitting to the iron yoke of Communism.

Let us look first at our strength—our strength in unity, in purpose, in dedication, in productivity; our strength in military equipment, trained manpower, and readiness; our strength in the skill and morale of our foreign representatives, in the clarity of our policies, and in the nobility of our ideas. Everything which contributes to our strength heartens and encourages our allies, our friends around the world, and particularly those who would like to be our friends. Everything which contributes to our strength increases the respect and the caution of those who are hostile to us.

But we have permitted our armed strength to decline, and we have abused that other bulwark of our national safety, our system of alliances. Some Americans, indeed, have made a career in recent years of attacking our allies.

I hope these tendencies will be sharply reduced in the new Congress; I hope it will ask the most searching questions concerning the adequacy of our air-atomic power, the adequacy of our Army, and of our system of defenses. I believe a Democratic majority in Congress can be relied upon to restore a serious and realistic concern for national defense and for the proper development of our military strength.

And along with this goes the necessity of assuring our allies that our determination to play our part with them in the common defense is fixed and permanent. This is essential to our joint strength, and it is essential to the restoration of confidence in the United States as a trustworthy, steady, and respected power in world affairs.

The act of the Senate this week (adoption of the McCarthy censure resolution) in reaffirming its dignity and the simplest principles of conduct will go a long way in restoring not alone our self-confidence and self-esteem, but also the respect of our friends. And I am glad that among the Democratic members at least there was no confusion about the standards of behavior of the Senate of the United States.

So, in brief, I feel that we have much to do in developing our own strength and alliances and helping the less fortunate in their struggles for life and freedom. If we employ serious and sensible analysis in place of slick phrases and the techniques of advertising, we will be able better to recognize our problems and make headway with their solution. I wish, for instance, we could in an atmosphere of open and reasoned discussion examine the dilemmas facing us from across the Pacific instead of pretending that they do not exist.

Although the two great parties have fought bitterly, sometimes recklessly, on almost every other issue, our policies in Europe have largely remained on neutral ground. There have been differences and criticisms, of course. I have voiced my own concern on many counts. But on the whole we have worked out common policies. And with a Democratic Congress the prospect for now moving forward toward more liberal foreign trade is brighter.

But in Asia our performance is in sharp and melancholy contrast. The fall of China, the war in Korea, the disaster in Indo-China, all have been accompanied by discord and disunity and some of the worst demagoguery in the history of the republic. While Communist influence has steadily increased in Asia, sentiment in many areas has steadily turned against us. And this situation presents both political parties with a challenge of profound importance. While the initiative is clearly in the hands of the Republican administration, the responsibility of the Democratic Congress-is also clear.

The first step in the development of a sensible Asian policy, while there is still time, is to take Asia out of American party politics.

Next I believe we must recognize the limitations of American military power in any situation short of a world war. It is, for example, folly to assume that we can somehow painlessly bring about the collapse of world Communism through the good offices of our good friends Chiang Kai-shek and Syngman Rhee.

And then we must face the fact that security and freedom in much of the world depends today more on economic progress than military defense. The number one problem in Asia today is not Communism but that millions of people want a better life and have discovered that poverty, hunger, and pestilence are not the immutable destiny of man. If they can't make progress by the voluntary democratic methods of consent, they will turn to the involuntary methods of coercion, as China already has. There is some evidence, and it is welcome to me, that our government is beginning to perceive this and to change its major emphasis from military to economic considerations.

So our obligations are many and complex. Military strength, allied unity, economic growth—these I think are the solid foundations of the collective power of the free peoples.

Peace is not the work of a single day, nor will it be the consequence of a single act. Yet every constructive act contributes to its growth; every omission impedes it. Peace will come, in the end, if it comes at all, as a child grows to maturity—slowly, imperceptibly, until we realize one day in incredulous surprise that the child is almost grown.

So patience may reward itself. Let us cleanse our minds of the recriminations of the past. Let us abandon the illusion of quick and final solutions. And as we face—all of us together—a journey into an unknown future, let us recognize that there is no substitute for restraint, honesty, and work—yes, and most of all, for the loyalty of Americans to one another.

I am confident that I speak not only for you, the leaders of our great and triumphant Democratic party, but also for all my fellow Americans when I say to President Eisenhower, to his associates in the executive branch of our government, and to the new Congress—may God grant you the fortitude, the forbearance, and the wisdom to lead a united nation toward our goal of peace and security for all people.

On Giving Government
Back to the People

OUR BUSINESS is politics, and I propose to get right down to business.

We mean by "politics" the people's business—the most important business there is.

We mean the conduct of the people's business by all the people, in open meetings where we can say what we think, and what we think should be done—about what we think!

Leaders of the Democratic party have met in Chicago to discuss plans for the coming year. The discussion has been of policies and principles—not of men. The happy truth is that the Democratic party maintains an essential unity of purpose which does not depend upon the individuals who may carry its standard. And no other political party, I might add, can make that statement!

We have heard Democratic leaders report from all parts of the country. The reports add up to this: We are going to win in 1956!

We are going to win next year just as we won the special Congressional elections in 1953, both houses of Congress in 1954, and last week's municipal elections.

These victories demonstrate again that what the Democratic party stands for is what most Americans stand for—the principles individual men and women in this country believe in and are proud of.

This is what I want to talk about tonight—what we Democrats are for, and, yes, what we are against. I shall be speaking not so much to you as for you—trying to say some of the

From an address at the Democratic National Committee dinner, Chicago, November 19, 1955.

things I know are in all our hearts and minds, the things that give us the right to call ourselves Democrats—and Americans.

We propose not to make issues where there are none, nor to be critical without being constructive. Our disagreement with the central principles of Republican policy runs deep, but it does not diminish our respect for those who sincerely hold that political faith. We respect the leader of the Republican party, President Eisenhower, who is President for Democrats as well as Republicans, and we rejoice alike in the progress of his recovery.

Our first, our greatest, our most relentless purpose is peace. For without peace there is nothing.

Now that the mists of illusion have risen from last summer's meeting at the summit we must again face the fact that the cold war is still in the deep freeze, that our security system is deteriorating, and that a safe and orderly world is still a distant goal. Certainly we must have learned by now that peace and security cannot be had for the asking, or by slogans and tough talk, or by blowing alternately hot and cold, rash and prudent. Certainly we must have learned that sound foreign policies cannot be devised with one eye fixed only on the budget, and the other on the divisions in the Republican party. Certainly we must have learned that in the fluctuating market of world affairs there is no bargain basement where peace is for sale cheap.

But let us be very clear that Republicans want a safe and sane world every bit as much as Democrats. And in this day, when our position is more perilous than it has been since Korea, let us also profit from our past mistakes, while we deplore them, and let us think of foreign policy not as partisans but as Americans. Let us, indeed, remember that who plays politics with peace will lose at both.

Our world is dominated by two facts—expansive Communist imperialism with the hydrogen bomb in its arsenal, and the great revolutionary upsurge of the less privileged peoples who long for peace and a share in the better things of life.

These facts present a complex challenge. We and our allies must be strong to check Communist ambition. Yet we cannot allow fear or envy or frustration to alienate the vast mass of the uncommitted peoples.

Unhappily, this balance, so painstakingly created following the war, has not been preserved. America's military strength has been reduced—while at the same time we talked louder and tougher. But if our threats were sincere then our pretensions of peace were insincere. And if we did not mean what we said, then we were bluffing.

Small wonder that distrust and fear of us became so widespread that the world received with profound relief President Eisenhower's assurances at Geneva that America was really and truly a peaceful nation. But let us not forget how people had been led to think otherwise.

We must restore the balance in America's relations with the world—the balance between our strength and our concern. To guard the ramparts of freedom we must uphold the stability of our alliances and maintain our military strength. But martial strength is not an end in itself. It can be only the firm base from which we are prepared to negotiate, whenever negotiation seems fruitful, and from which we will seek to create with tireless patience a workable system of controlled disarmament.

To this restored vision of a firm, consistent, peace-loving America, we must add a refreshed concern for our less fortunate neighbors. We must play our generous part in the bettering of the human lot; and we must do so not just to compete with Communism, not to preserve colonialism, and not to impose Americanism. We must make the world understand again what it once knew—that at the roots of our faith we recognize that we belong, all of us, to the family of Man.

Here at home, no less than in our foreign affairs, primary importance attaches to the genuineness of our concern for human welfare. It is the fundamental faith of our party that in a democracy the individual citizen is all-important—that ordinary men and women have the sense, the integrity, and the decency to make choices and to decide for themselves how best to improve their lot and use their human span. Our aim is simply to secure the widest distribution of well-being. And we know this can only happen when responsibility for policy making and participation in government are also widely shared.

The sense of democracy as a partnership in which all of our people share and participate has been blurred in these past three years. Instead, in whatever direction we look—tax policy, regulatory policy, resources policy, credit policy, or what not —we see the sharp outlines of what can only be described as special-interest government in Washington, something we haven't seen since the Republicans were there last! Instead we are coming to realize that we are being treated more as customers than as partners—gullible customers, susceptible to the huckstering advertiser arts of salesmen for a special interest.

Well, you know the people own this business, and they don't want anybody forgetting it. We climbed, together, from the trough of depression which we Democrats had inherited from the Republicans. And today most Americans dwell upon the plateau of prosperity which the Republicans inherited from us.

But even though they had never had it so good, the Republicans promised a lot of changes back in 1952. I don't know why we complain so much about their broken campaign promises. It's those they keep that hurt. Every change they've made has caused us trouble, but the things they haven't changed are working fine.

Among other things they have adopted a new farm policy—to get rid, they say, of the farm surpluses. Well, it hasn't reduced the farmer's production, but it has sure reduced his income. And today the only reason we have a stable general price level is that rising industrial prices are offset by falling farm prices. The balance in our interdependent economy is threatened, and the well-being of twenty million Americans is sinking, while the Republican cheer leaders shout: "Everything is booming but the guns."

Our society needs the farmer more than anyone else. And the farmer needs a fair share of the national income. He hasn't got it just now. And there is precious little evidence that the "team" in Washington wants to do anything about it. But to help the farmer in this passing crisis you have to want to help the farmer, even as sympathetic Democrats have for a generation.

But I hear there may be a change. Prices are not the only thing that's flexible about Republican politicians, and it is no secret that they are dusting off some of the old Democratic production control proposals with a view to bringing them out—under Republican labels, of course. It is strange what an election year does to those crusaders who believe so devoutly in good old-fashioned, rugged individualism—especially for the farmer, and especially between elections.

In our natural-resources policy there has also been a change—a determined attempt to undermine conservation and power programs which are serving the interests of millions of people—particularly small consumers.

Today's fast dollar is being put above tomorrow's needs—Hell's Canyon goes to a private company for only partial development of its power; an effort is made to sabotage the preference clause in our public power contracts, and to cripple the great rural electrification program; the dubious Dixon-Yates deal is contrived in secrecy and the TVA attacked publicly.

This Republican inability to make a proper distinction between public and private business shows up elsewhere. We hear now about waste and privilege in the housekeeping department. And the Secretary of the Air Force is decorated for his services after getting his public and private business affairs embarrassingly mixed up—while at the same time thousands of honest and conscientious government workers, littler people, have been coldly pushed around so that the crusaders could boast about cleaning up something.

And surely one of the most remarkable alibis in years was offered last week by another high-level administrator who found it convenient to resign; admittedly he pressed his company's claims against the government—but only, he insists, on his lunch hour!

As Democrats we deny the soundness of helping only the large corporations with the pious hope that something will trickle down to the rest of us. We oppose special tax advantages to anyone, let alone a favored few. We oppose the policy of giving the lion's share of defense contracts to the large companies.

Twenty years of Democratic leadership went into making America economically strong by increasing and broadening and stabilizing consumer buying power. And we still claim that the best thing for any business is people coming in the door with money in their pockets.

I suggest that this whole pattern is a reflection of the basic philosophy our new managers brought to Washington in 1953. "We are here in the saddle," the Secretary of the Interior said, "as an administration representing business and industry." Well, after two or three years I'm convinced he knew what he was talking about!

Let us be quite clear about this. There is no conflict between the Democratic party and business. What we criticize is not business, but the virtual exclusion of everyone else. Eight of the ten members of the cabinet and almost three-quarters of the men appointed to high executive office in the past three years come from the same segment of the community, big business. Is this a good thing? I doubt it, and I suspect businessmen by and large doubt it too.

We do not question the honesty of these men, or their good intentions, or their right to hold office. But we do question the breadth and variety of their collective vision; we say that this republic is imperiled when government, which belongs to all the people, falls into the hands of any single group.

What do we Democrats mean to do about this when we take up the reins of government once again? I think you could sum up our aim very simply—we mean to return the public interest to the center of public policy, and to restore the sense that government is the concern not of a single dominant economic interest but of all the American people.

But there are those who say, let well enough alone, all is well, don't rock the boat. And I agree that this is an age of abundance, as well as an age of anxiety. I agree that it is a time for catching our breath; I agree that moderation is the spirit of the times. But we best take care lest we confuse moderation with mediocrity, or settle for half answers to hard problems. A democratic society can't stand still, and the world won't stand still. Both are living things and the meaning of life is in growth, in working always toward something better, something higher. Moderation, yes. Stagnation, no! As the history of nations reminds us, nothing fails like success.

We must tackle the problem of agriculture. We are committed, as I say, to restoring farm income to fair levels, by a many-pronged attack, I hope.

Democrats do not contend that price supports, firm or collapsible, are the whole answer to a healthy farm economy.

110

On the contrary, we have always contended, as we do now, that price supports must be employed in conjunction with a whole series of both supplementary and complementary measures. The real key to the farmer's welfare is an intelligent, sensitive, and responsive administration of agriculture on a day-to-day basis—and that is something that can only be accomplished by the party which is in office.

We will seek to protect the place of small business in our free enterprise system. Enterprise depends upon opportunity—opportunity for a man with talent and energy to branch out on his own—to build his own business, own his own plant, take his own risks, make his own decisions. And at the rate smaller businesses are going bankrupt or being swallowed up by bigger business these days, you can't help but be anxious about the future of enterprise as we have understood it.

We will give urgent consideration to the plight of substandard families, and of the blighted or depressed areas—the stagnant pools into which the tide of prosperity has failed to flow.

We will continue to fight to preserve the nation's heritage of natural resources—our sources of power, our public lands, our national forests, our soil, our parks. We propose, very simply, to reinstate the principles which for forty years underpinned a bipartisan conservation policy initiated by Theodore Roosevelt, and interrupted for the first time in 1953.

We will attempt to bring our great public services back into balance with our expanding wealth. For are we really prosperous when our national income is going up but our schools are becoming more crowded, our teachers more outnumbered, our hospitals more inadequate, our roads more dangerous, our conservation more timid, our slums more contagious? Sure the figures on the pay check are important, but is a family really prosperous if it lives in an urban jungle where juvenile delinquency takes growing children for its prey?

We Democrats are for a country in which the schools are worthy of the children—and adequately staffed by teachers supported as their honored profession merits.

We are for a country where no man's home is blighted by smoke, dirt, and noise, and cut off from sunlight, trees, and air.

111

We are for a country where no family lives in dread of crippling disease that adds to the pain of the stricken the fear of intolerable expense.

We are for a country where older people are not doomed to live out their last, empty years with only the solace of a small pension.

We are for a country where all of our people can work under fair labor standards, and where responsible unionism is encouraged by laws that guarantee free collective bargaining.

We are for a country where we defend the liberties of all by defending the liberties of each, where the Bill of Rights and the Golden Rule are part of our being, where there is freedom to think, to speak, to doubt and dissent, and to be yourself.

And we are for a country where no family's aspirations are bounded by unyielding barriers of race or religious prejudice.

These are some of the things we have not yet fully achieved—and because we have not there is among us a spiritual uneasiness, an empty feeling, a feeling that we have settled for too little, that we have accepted today's creature comforts at the price of the old ennobling dreams.

To see all these things is not to see failure, but only the job that still needs doing. America is well and strong above all nations in all time. We are the luckiest people in the world and we know it. To see these things, and to roll up our sleeves and start doing something about them, is only to suggest, if you will, what we Democrats are for.

I talked of these and other matters recently with a beloved elder statesman of our party. How, I asked him, can all these complexities be reduced to simple terms? He pointed out the window to a man and woman and child walking down the street—a family any of us might count among our neighbors.

"Just ask yourself," he said, "who's looking out for those people down in Washington these days."

Well, there it is. Those people are not customers of our government; they are owners too.

The problem, and the Democratic answer to it, are as old as our party. Woodrow Wilson put it in these words: "I understand it to be the fundamental proposition of American liberty that we do not desire special privilege because we know special privilege will never comprehend the general welfare. This is the spiritual difference between adherents of the party now about to take charge of the government and those who have been in charge of it in recent years."

We reassert tonight this simple yet essential faith—that democracy serves no one except as it serves us all.

THREE

The Common Welfare

Farewell Report to the Citizens
of Illinois

I WISH I could review here everything that has been done or attempted since 1949 to improve our state government. I should like to review these crowded years department by department—from hunting and fishing and wildlife conservation to insurance regulation—our successes and our failures, our triumphs and defeats, what I've learned that's so and what I've learned that isn't so. I would like to talk to you about politics and patronage, about law enforcement, gambling, corruption, about human beings, the good and the evil, and all the things that have made these four relentless years here in Springfield the best in my life.

You would understand better then why I am so grateful for the opportunity you, the people, gave me and why I wanted so desperately to continue here in Springfield. But my party asked me to run for President, and, after preaching the gospel of public service so long, I didn't see how I could consistently decline. The consequences are familiar to you, and acutely familiar to me now, on the eve of my return to private life!

But all that is past, and it is with the future that I shall deal. I have listed some ten major future goals for the state. They contain no sensations. In the past four years we have instituted extensive legislative and administrative changes. I am happy to say that most of the ambitious original objectives I had four years ago have now been accomplished in whole or in part. What follows are the principal things that remain to be done as I see it:

1. *Foremost is the highway program.* It must be completed as soon as possible. The tempo of that program has been set.

From the farewell report as Governor of Illinois, Springfield, January 8, 1953.

Last year $86 million in new contracts were awarded, not counting $23 million of work carried over from 1951 and $11 million contributed by the state to the Cook County superhighway development. This was more than twice as large a program as in any prior year in Illinois history.

Moreover, a sound pattern for completing this program in the next ten years has been established. Under laws enacted in 1951 the contribution to the cost of that program will be shared on a more equal basis by highway users—the private vehicle owners and the truckers. I strongly urge the legislature to resist efforts that may be made to radically disturb this fair apportionment. To jeopardize the highway program itself, or to grant special advantages or concessions to particular classes of vehicle operators, at the expense of other classes, would be a grave injustice and disservice.

2. *The urgent needs of the public schools must continue to be recognized.* The schools represent our greatest asset. Important forward strides have been taken in recent years to strengthen the schools of Illinois. To do this the legislature in 1951 appropriated in round figures $150 million to the common schools for the current biennium. State aid has been almost doubled in my four years.

What have been the results? They cannot be measured alone in higher appropriations, but they can be measured in better facilities, better curricula, better trained teachers. The Illinois School Problems Commission surveyed 1,396 schools for the year of 1948–49 and reported that nearly one-half of the elementary schools and almost one-fourth of the high schools had to be rated "inferior." The same schools, surveyed for the year 1951–52, showed that the number of elementary schools now falling short of the foundation program is barely one-fourth instead of one-half. The "inferior" high schools are now fewer than one-fifth. This means that thousands more Illinois children are now receiving a satisfactory instead of an inferior education.

I think the legislature might well consider the creation of a School Building Authority which could finance construction of desperately needed school buildings on a long-term revenue bond basis when local resources are insufficient.

3. *We must extend the gains in welfare services and admin-*

istration. As in the case of schools, accomplishment here cannot be measured alone in terms of dollars spent. Real progress has been made in reducing overcrowding and understaffing in the mental hospitals and correctional institutions, but they have by no means been overcome. Our threefold approach has been: Increased efforts to reduce mental disease and public dependency through research and community efforts; extension of the career service idea in the recruitment of more and better hospital personnel; and continuing enlargement of our physical facilities.

On the whole, I think nothing has pleased me more than the improved care and treatment of our unfortunate wards in these past few years and the nationwide recognition of our progress in Illinois.

4. *The state penal system must be re-examined.* Some of our prison facilities are outstandingly good, but others are not. The Menard Penitentiary presents special problems of administration due to obsolete physical plant and the illogical location there of the psychiatric division where mentally deranged criminals are kept. These problems were brought forcefully to public attention by the recent riots that endangered the lives of a number of guards.

It seems to me obvious that the psychiatric division should be moved to another location where psychiatrists and adequate facilities for the treatment of mentally ill prisoners would be more accessible. If the old prison is to be retained some of the buildings will have to be modernized and more shops and facilities provided to keep the prisoners occupied with useful work while they learn trades and skills that will help in their rehabilitation.

In that connection, consideration might well be given in Illinois to the use of the safest prisoners to do necessary work in the state parks and forests. Uncle Sam and one or two other states do it. Some such plan might eventually be extended to solve the old problem of reclaiming, through reforestation or otherwise, the thousands of acres of strip-mined land that now are unsightly and largely useless.

More important to me, however, is that our penitentiary system from the wardens on down should be taken out of politics and put on a professional career basis to make it attractive to the most competent people. I have already taken steps in that direction and I hope more will follow.

5. *Law enforcement must be tightened.* Through increased emphasis and activity on the part of the Attorney General and the State Police, we have made conspicuous progress in law enforcement. The overweight truck laws are now being well enforced, but our gambling laws are inadequate and I again urged the General Assembly to give increased powers to the Liquor Control Commission to suspend or revoke tavern licenses where commercial gambling is permitted. Also, since we outlaw gambling, I think it would be consistent to prohibit the manufacture of slot machines and other gambling devices within the state.

Removing the State Police from politics and placing them under a merit system, which I recommended in 1949 and the legislature approved, has already paid important dividends in terms of performance and morale, and I pray that this great reform will be encouraged in letter and spirit in the future.

6. *Efforts to modernize the state Constitution and the state government should continue.* We must have a better judiciary and quicker justice in our courts. Our procedures for the administration of justice are over a century old and clearly outmoded. The Chicago and Illinois Bar Associations have made careful studies of this problem and their plan for modernization of the judicial structure will be presented to the General Assembly at this session.

The proposal to amend the revenue article of the Constitution, which narrowly failed of adoption in the last election, should be restudied and again submitted to the people at the earliest opportunity. The inequities and abuses of our present tax system can never be corrected until the revenue article is brought up to date.

A constitutional amendment giving a greater degree of legislative representation to Cook County's preponderance of population is long overdue. Gross inequalities in population as between the districts within the metropolitan area also must be corrected.

Many recommendations of the Commission I sponsored for reorganization of our state government have already been put into effect, but the General Assembly can accomplish more

120

toward further efficiency and economy by favorable consideration of the remaining recommendations of this Commission.

7. *Better mine safety and labor laws are needed.* The new
federal legislation will not, it now appears, relieve the states
of their obligation to enact and enforce adequate safety regula-
tions in the mines. Consequently the need continues for a new,
up-to-date, effective code of mine safety laws. Illinois also
needs a workable state minimum wage law, and a system of
temporary disability insurance protecting wage earners from
the loss of wages through illness.

8. *The civil rights of all citizens must be steadfastly protected.* Discrimination in any form on account of race, religion,
or national origin is repugnant to our ideals of liberty and
justice. The proper and most effective initiative in attacking
discrimination, wherever it exists, rests with the states. I again
express the hope that Illinois will join the other progressive
states which have adopted fair employment practices laws.

9. *A single board for higher education should be created.*
Little has been done, except in the teachers' colleges, toward
the integration of our system of higher education. There is no
orderly, co-ordinated state-wide program; there is much expensive and unnecessary competition and duplication. Two years
ago I was convinced that the creation of a single board for
higher education, that would take the place of the three
virtually autonomous boards we now have, would facilitate
that process. I still think so.

10. *The merit idea in personnel policies and recruitment
should be extended.*

The efficient functioning and integrity of government depend upon attracting to public life honest, competent, loyal
men and women. Of all the things I have tried to do nothing is
more important than the progress we have made in bringing to
and retaining in the state service capable men and women
without regard to politics.

The State Civil Service has been expanded and revitalized;
the State Police merit system has been established; training
programs have been started in the welfare, revenue, public
safety, and other departments which need trained career personnel. These are examples of what is needed to improve
personnel practices and performance.

121

When I took office, only 53 per cent of the eligible state employees had civil service status. Today 70.3 per cent are certified. This is a major accomplishment, and it came about not through any magic formula or last-minute manipulation. It has been a slow, steady gain.

If better personnel practices are to have lasting value, this work must go on. I hope very much it will go on here in Illinois because I believe the ultimate results in terms of better service, less cost and waste, and restored public confidence will be tremendous.

Indeed, if I had my way, I would wish history to judge the total worth of my administration by what has been done in this and three other major areas of responsibility.

One of these is the highway program, which I consider the most urgent and vital of the immediate tasks confronting the state. Another has been the dawn of a new day of recognition and state support for our public schools. The third is the positive progress which has been made in meeting the state's welfare responsibilities vigorously and intelligently.

There are many, many accomplishments of other departments and agencies. I have in mind the divorcing of the Commerce Commission, which regulates utility rates, etc., from partisan control and restoring public respect for it; closer screening of public assistance rolls to eliminate many ineligibles; better salaries for state employees; reorganization of the Purchasing Division to place state buying on a strictly business basis; tightening up on abuses in the use of state cars and expense accounts.

And I could go on and on—how the revenue collection services have been improved with reduced personnel, how the Highway Division has been able to carry out its heavier work load without increase in technical staffs, how the Department of Public Health has helped build 17 community non-profit hospitals in areas where the need was greatest, with 21 more under construction.

I'm particularly proud of economies along the way—the weeding out of non-working political payrollers, the reduction in personnel in many departments, the saving of a million dollars a year through new highway resurfacing techniques, the saving of another half-million a year on the State Fair, and the like. Had it not been for many savings, plus various cuts in operating appropriations, we would not now enjoy our substantial treasury balance. The finance department has computed total savings and reductions in appropriations during the last four years at $60 million, almost the exact equivalent of the general revenue fund balance.

This then is my report on the condition of the state:

Our financial position is strong, significant changes have been initiated in state government organization, the people are getting the kind of public service at the state level which they are entitled to expect. Our regulatory agencies have acquired a reputation for objectivity, competence, and freedom from influence. Public employees expect to do, and do, a full day's work for a day's pay.

There has, in short, been a brightening of the tradition of state government in Illinois. With the type of public responsibility we have sought to achieve, with a fearless facing of the people's needs and demands, we can make effective state government a reality, and thus avoid those failures of performance which so often cause public functions to move up the ladder to Washington.

Government—local, state, and federal—is not something separate and apart; if it is to be good it must share the attitudes and the competence of the best in our society as a whole. Both business and government are gainers when the best among us from private life will make the sacrifice, if need be, to fill vital public positions.

Illinois, where my family have lived and prospered for a century and a quarter, means a great deal to me, and I am humbly thankful for the opportunity that has been mine to serve it. I leave my high office content in one respect—that I have given to it the best that was in me. It has been a richly rewarding experience, and the satisfactions have far outweighed the disappointments.

To the people of Illinois who have honored me so generously, and to the associates in this great undertaking whose friendship and loyalty have meant so much to me, I shall be eternally grateful.

And now, with a full heart, I bid you all good-by.

Medicine and Public Policy

DEMOCRACY'S ways are such that even in areas of the public welfare where we depend so much on professional competence and leadership, great importance still attaches to the thinking, the help, the backing up of the community generally. Just as people's superstitions once held back the growth of medical science, so their understanding and appreciation of its promise can contribute greatly to speeding medicine's full maturity.

There is substantial basis, I think, for the proposition that a veritable revolution is going on today in our thinking about our health, and that this revolution is of vital importance to the future of medical science and service.

Not many years ago the prevailing attitude, as it had been for centuries, was to accept illness and disease and premature death fatalistically. There seemed no choice but sad resignation. The struggle was that of two or three people sitting in a quiet room trying with love and prayer and little more than trained intuition to battle the unknown and to even the struggle a little. Often, too, there was unconscious association of sickness with shame, and certain ravages of the body were discussed only in whispers and camouflaged with euphemisms in the obituaries. We faced the problem of our health, perhaps more than any other, virtually alone, as individuals, and hardly at all as a community.

Yet today there have come, almost suddenly, unmistakable signs that we are ready to mobilize in this area our capacities to do by united effort—not necessarily through government, but just together—what we have wanted but have been unable to do alone.

This change comes in part, I think, as a consequence of the

From an address at the New York University-Bellevue Medical Center Dedicatory Exercises, New York, June 2, 1955.

recent wide circulation of medical statistics. Figures tell so little of any story of human suffering, but these have been a shock treatment:

One of every seven of us, as things are, will die of cancer;

Ten million of us are today suffering from arthritis, a million permanently disabled;

Sickness in the nation's work force idles more employees than lack of work;

And one of every twelve children born this year will at some time need institutional care because of mental disorder—unless new ways are found to combat diseases of the mind.

These are only partial statistics, and they say nothing of the grief and suffering and loneliness which are their true dimension, nothing of the appalling public as well as private expense of disease. Yet they have served, I think, to waken us to what stands today as the test and challenge of the true wealth and genius and brotherhood of Americans—for there is agreement that ways can be found to meet all or most of these afflictions.

Yet if we have been shocked by these figures of tragedy and waste into an almost frantic desire to do *something*, it is another equally startling report that gives us the courage to know that there *is* something that can be done. Indeed the other factor contributing most to this current revolution in our thinking about this problem of health is the grateful realization of the astonishing recent advances in medical science.

We hear, hardly daring to believe yet knowing it is true, the story of the results, during an eight-year period, of new medical research and education:

Deaths from influenza were reduced between 1944 and 1952 by three-quarters;

Those from appendicitis and acute rheumatic fever dropped two-thirds;

Fatalities from syphilis, kidney disease, pneumonia, and tuberculosis were cut in half;

In the last decade alone, the nation's death rate has been reduced by over 9 per cent, the average life expectancy increased five full years.

And now there comes, almost as from Heaven, this great new strength against that dread disease which seemed to hurt us most because it struck with greatest viciousness at our children. I had not thought to enter the Salk vaccine controversy but if anything were predictable in our uncertain world, it was the immense and imperative demand for anything which promised to check the dread scourge of polio. I don't think it required any special clairvoyance to anticipate the demand for the vaccine, the supply and the hazards of production and distribution, or to foresee, with the happiness and lives of all our children involved, that here was a situation above all others that called for foresight and meticulous planning and preparation.

But to return to the spectacular achievements. Although I am neither physician nor statistician I suspect that part of the reason the death rate for heart disease and cancer is going up is that the rate for diseases that strike earlier in life is being pressed down. You doctors will have to accept the inevitability that we are never again going to be satisfied. It is grim irony that your profession can never do more than postpone ultimate defeat.

Yet the central fact remains: that people are now awakened —partly by the shock of learning the facts of our weakness, and partly by learning what can be accomplished—to a willingness and a great enthusiastic desire to contribute fully toward this accomplishment.

How? What form is this help to take? What is there for us, the people, to contribute to this essentially technical job? Money? Yes, of course. But more than that too. It is vitally important that there be a people's program for their own health —so that they may marshal the support which is needed, may indicate the broad outlines of the non-scientific aspects of a democratic health policy, and may be at least able to make fullest use of scientific advance in this field.

This is not the occasion for even an attempt at formulation of such a policy. Yet there are several points on which agreement seems to be emerging.

One is that methods must be worked out for making medical service better available to all who need it, and this without crippling cost to anyone. We are spending more than $10 billion a year for medical expenses. We are willing, if we have to, to pay more. But we want to make this expenditure as effective as possible, to realize the economy of *preventive* medicine, to assure the distribution of medical service on a basis of need for it, and to remove the haunting fear in so many American homes that if serious sickness strikes it will wipe out every cent of savings, perhaps cut off all earning power, and destroy life's dignity even if life itself is spared.

We are appalled by the report that over a quarter of a million people die each year "whom we have the knowledge and the skills to save."

We think it not right that a million American families will have to spend over half their income this year for medical care, that there will be 500,000 cases of catastrophic accident or illness which will consume the entire family income, that eight million American families are today in debt for medical care, and that two million of these had to borrow at high interest rates from personal finance companies to cover the cost of medical treatment. In too many American homes a parent at some time or other looks down at a sick child, knows that something should be done and that there isn't the money to do it.

There is emerging impressive evidence of agreement that the most promising approach to this problem of distribution of medical service lies in the development of voluntary, private, prepayment health insurance programs. Indeed, three out of every five people in this country are now enrolled in some program of this type, although in very few cases is the coverage comprehensive and so far only a small percentage of total medical costs are taken care of this way.

This principle of private health insurance seems ideally fitted to the necessities of the problem of distributing medical service. Prepayment encourages resort to preventive medicine, with resultant reduction in the amount of costly hospitalization. In their most effective form these plans bring the ministrations of specialists to families who could not otherwise afford them— a purpose so admirably recognized and served, incidentally, by the work New York University faculty members are doing at the Hunterdon Medical Center in Flemington, New Jersey. These prepayment plans level out the peaks of unpredictable cost of major illness. They bring more service to more people on more reasonable terms.

It is an important element in this prepayment insurance development that it represents a private, non-governmental answer to a problem requiring group action. And these private prepayment plans are America's better answer, we think, to the similar needs that have resulted, elsewhere, in the state taking over this function. They represent a resourceful application of the American principle of mutual self-help to meet a big problem without substituting state for individual responsibility.

But the application of this new principle is still at an experimental stage. Certain barriers to its development must be broken down, particularly objections and even discrimination against forward-looking doctors. In half the states there are restrictive laws, passed in haste, which prevent responsible private groups of doctors and patients from working out effectively the prepayment plans they consider best.

And it is recognized, fortunately by the leaders of both political parties, that some degree of government assistance in developing this new program is necessary. The proposal to meet this situation by offering federal reinsurance to voluntary health plans has already been rejected on all sides as only a gesture. Reducing the uncertainties of insurers' risks may help a little, but it doesn't really approach the central problems of raising the money to get these programs started and then covering in them the low income and older people who are most in need of more medical service.

Much nearer the mark, I think, are the proposals to make long-term, low-interest-rate loans to new prepayment groups and to subsidize part of the cost of comprehensive service to groups including some whose financial means are limited but whose medical needs are no less great.

The situation is then that a sound new principle for improved distribution of medical service has been approved by a substantial majority of Americans, and that the ways and means to implement it are at hand. This represents actually a great experiment in private, neighborly meeting of the ever-enlarging problems which are so characteristic of our expanding society. It is very important that there be understanding and co-operation here between the medical profession and the community

128

generally, for our health is everybody's business. And it is imperative that discussion not be frustrated by the familiar shouts of Socialism that seem to bedevil all forward steps in our country.

Another point of now very general public agreement is that we need a good many more doctors and dentists and nurses, and a substantially larger medical plant—more hospitals and more or larger medical schools.

There were, we are told, fewer medical school graduates in 1950 than in 1905, and there are fewer doctors today in proportion to the population than there were a hundred years ago. Small wonder we are also told that we need at least 25,000 more doctors.

On this occasion it seems appropriate to press only one aspect of this problem. This new Medical Science Building and the developments to follow add appreciably to the nation's facilities for medical education. But still this remains the obstacle to enlargement of the medical profession. New medical school construction which will cost a quarter of a billion dollars is needed, and there is the further formidable problem that it costs four times as much to educate a medical student as he can be expected to pay in tuition.

We gratefully applaud the fact that private funds made possible this building we dedicate today. But it gets progressively and painfully clear that private philanthropy cannot, alone, meet the doctor shortage which is already upon us. Where the stakes are literally life itself, it would seem proper to use democracy's emergency methods.

The U.S. Senate expressed unmistakably the national will when, in 1949, it passed unanimously a bill to assist medical schools. The American Medical Association opposed that bill and it died in a House of Representatives committee. The expressed concern was about federal domination. But research in these schools has been subsidized by many millions of dollars of federal grants without a hint or whisper of domination. And for my part I don't believe government has any desire or intention to dominate medical education, and I think most all of us have complete confidence in the profession's development of an educational program. We are ready to do almost anything we are asked in order to get the doctors we need. The stakes, I repeat, are people's lives, and I hope it isn't heresy for a people's government to take an interest in that!

Of the need for more hospitals it may be said that more is being done on this front than on any other. But the need remains great, and the cost of hospital care so high that it is a constant anxiety in many American homes. But there is at least awareness of the proportions of this need, and we have had for some years an active and expanding program of public and private participation for trying to meet it.

Finally, there is a powerful emergent demand today for an acceleration of the medical research program. The incredible achievements of barely a generation, the sulfa drugs, penicillin, streptomycin, and now the polio serum whose author, Dr. Salk, you honor today, are eloquent evidence of what's to come in research.

And here again, in spite of all that has been accomplished, we are shocked by the uncompromising figures:

That with ten million American men and women suffering from heart disease we are spending $16 million a year on research in this field—or $1.60 for each person presently afflicted;

That with cancer having marked one of every seven of us as its victim, we are spending this year to solve that cruel mystery, only $25 million—15¢ apiece;

That with mental illness costing incalculable suffering, and almost $1½ billion a year, we are spending $11 million, less than one per cent of that cost, to combat it;

That we are investing this year about a penny a person for research on arthritis and rheumatic diseases—cripplers of ten million Americans.

It seems a little strange, I think this audience will agree, that the Department of Agriculture will spend this year for research on plant and animal diseases ten million dollars more than the Public Health Service is spending for research on cancer, arthritis, mental illness, neurological and heart disease combined.

This just doesn't make sense!

Yet the National Advisory Council's recommendations last

130

year for a federal medical research budget for five key programs were cut in half before it went to Congress.

And I would speak out, too, against the administration's policy of cutting off grants for private research where there is no conceivable security consideration, just because a question is raised—by rumor or other unproven, untried report—about the health researcher's loyalty. What sickness, what awful timidity, is this that is now permitted to stop even inquiry into the secrets of biology and of man's physical survival?

Nor does the argument that we can't afford to spend more on medical research seem very persuasive when 576,000 men and women who are unable to work because of arthritis and rheumatism mean a loss to the federal government of almost $300 million a year in income taxes alone. Likewise, $2 million a year on research into the causes of blindness does not seem very large when tax losses from exemptions to the blind amount to 180 times that amount every year. One could go on and on to demonstrate that good health is good business, and that few public investments pay off like medical research.

But it is not to increase the national income that we seek to stop needless sickness and death. It is in terms not of dollars but of humanity that the case for medical research is to be made. And we want to be led toward health even as toward prosperity and peace. We have answered willingly, and often, leadership's call for crash programs to build better instruments of death. And now we ask humbly for leadership—from the profession and the government—for programs to build better instruments of life. We seek, together as a people, freedom—including the freedom to live.

I have tried then to suggest what seems to me the tremendously important fact that there is emerging today substantial accord about important points in the nation's health program. We want to work together here, as we have in other areas of the common welfare, with the least possible reliance on "government." We want to experiment with new ways to make medical science available to all who need it, encouraging its preventive use, spreading the impact of its cost so that in no home will the tragedy of serious illness be compounded by economic disaster. And we want to press fast now toward the beckoning horizons of hope already revealed by medical research. We seek also to enlarge our medical staff and facilities.

It is from these common aspirations that this new Medical Center will draw its basic strength, and in their furtherance find fulfillment of its broadest promise. Thus will it become not only a house of healing, a center of scientific progress, but more than that a place of democratic achievement, where professional skill is blended with a people's hopes—to make a better life.

Here, too, there will be served the still broader cause of the brotherhood of man. For healing, like music, is a bridge between races and nations. The secrets of life-giving, unlike those of death-dealing, can be made humanity's possession, binding the giver and the receiver ever closer together.

Public Lands, Public Interest,
and Republican Promises

THEODORE ROOSEVELT said that: "Of all the questions which can come before this nation, short of the actual preservation of its existence in a great war, there is none which compares in importance with the great central task of leaving this land even a better land for our descendants than it is for us." I believe that. I think we all believe it. And for fifty years we, both parties, have been working out a policy based on the belief that the rivers are the property of all the people, that they should be developed and the water and power resources used to promote democracy, equality of opportunity, genuinely competitive free enterprise; and that the electric power generated at the dams should be sold first, if wanted and needed, to non-profit electric systems, to cities, to public power districts, and to R.E.A. co-operatives. The balance has always been sold to industry or to private power corporations, and this too was part of the policy.

The federal power policy and water resource development which the administration inherited was simple and forthright. The Republican platform had promised to continue this program. But what counts, as we have learned again and again of late, is not a Republican promise, but a Republican performance. The record of performance suggests, to say the least, that the administration's aim is to destroy the water and power policy that has been fifty years in the making.

There has not been one new start on a multiple-purpose water and power project in two years. Construction of projects already under way has been slowed to a walk or stopped. Bills were introduced to give away Niagara Falls power to five private power companies. The greatest remaining power site in

From an address at Albuquerque, October 15, 1954.

the United States, Hell's Canyon, has been abandoned to a utility whose plans for development contemplate using little more than half the potential. Other abandonments are sure to follow.

Now listening to Republican oratory one might think that public power was a misbegotten offspring of the New Deal; a product of the black art of a conspiratorial cabal of what Secretary Wilson and Vice-President Nixon are fond of calling "left-wingers." But our friends are not only minting new meaning for old words, but also rewriting history, including some of their own better pages. For it was in the first decade of this century, a safely Republican decade, that public power was recognized in legislation.

As for coining new words, the new Republican power policy is called "partnership," a joint enterprise of Uncle Sam and a private utility company or local group. Now I should think such arrangements, which are not wholly new, would work out in many cases to the advantage of both partners. But it would appear that in the Republican lexicon a "local partnership" means that both parties build the project and one partner gets the profitable part, the power, and the government—you and I—get the flood control, storage, reclamation, and unprofitable parts.

Increasingly the nation's taxpayers have come, I think, to recognize power projects as a sound investment—we get our tax money back with interest, the nation still has an income-producing asset, and much local wealth is produced which benefits us all. But it is hard for us to see why all of us, as taxpayers, should support the non-paying part of these developments while private utility companies take a guaranteed return out of the profitable part. I can't understand why an investment of tax funds is called "creeping Socialism" if there is an arrangement for repayment of the investment, but is a wholesome "partnership" if both partners pay and only one collects.

Speaking at the dedication of the McNary Dam on the Columbia River not long ago, President Eisenhower seemed to be praising that project named in honor of a great Republican public power advocate, and at the same time paraphrasing his "creeping Socialism" argument with which he has already denounced TVA. He set up a straw man and then indignantly knocked it down in the sacred name of private enterprise. According to the President, this straw man spoke for people, presumably Democrats, who were out to establish a federal power monopoly to "supply all the power needs of our people." But no one has ever proposed such a monopoly, no one in twenty years of Democratic loyalty to the power policy of Theodore Roosevelt has ever even glanced in its direction.

All over the country the pattern is the same. The Republican-dominated Federal Power Commission tries to get a bill which would force existing federal projects to subsidize construction of private facilities. In spite of federal court decisions, Secretary McKay refuses to abide by contracts between the government and farmers' co-operatives in Oklahoma and Missouri. The President asks for a large reduction in R.E.A. loan funds, but after Democratic Congressmen had forced a much higher appropriation the President congratulated his R.E.A. administrator on lending so much money to co-operatives.

But, let me turn from this to a major aspect of the giveaway with which the people of New Mexico are familiar. For in New Mexico are some of the greatest installations of the atomic energy program. It has been a prodigious effort by all the people and we have spent $12 billion of the people's money on it. It created what many think is the major deterrent to global war in these perilous days, and it has also created the brightest hope man has ever had for a golden age of plenty and release from poverty and toil. For the same energy that can obliterate us can also be harnessed to produce power so cheaply and in such quantities that, as one of the engineers has said, in the future it may not pay to meter it. It is estimated that the national reserve of atomic fuel is more than sixteen times the total energy tied up in all our assured reserves of coal, oil, and gas.

In 1946 the Democrats passed the McMahon Act, which provided that this great resource should be used to promote democracy and free competitive enterprise. Speaking in Albuquerque Vice-President Nixon made the extraordinary statement that the philosophy of government espoused by the present administration would bring to the people of New

Mexico and the nation the greatest benefits in the field of atomic energy development. Well, I'm not sure I understand that, but I do know that the administration introduced a program to give away our atomic energy resources that many thought made the surrender of the tidelands oil look like small potatoes.

The debate on the administration's atomic energy bill may well have been the most important debate in many a year. The Republican leadership pushed their atomic giveaway through the House of Representatives in a hurry, and would have done the same in the Senate if it had not been for Clinton Anderson of New Mexico. When the bill was rushed to the Senate he alone was prepared to discuss it with any knowledge of what it was. So, half sick from overwork, he rose and talked for five hours while his fellow Democrats studied the bill. He gained the time necessary to prepare a defense against what Senator Lehman of New York has called "a colossal giveaway, bigger than anything that has ever existed in this or any other country." Through the days that followed, he and his Democratic colleagues prevented a $12 billion investment and resources beyond comprehension from being turned over to a handful of big corporations. Not all was saved that the public was entitled to, but the savings were mighty important and the citizens of New Mexico are not the only Americans who don't believe in monopolies that are indebted to Clinton Anderson for another great service.

Step by step we have seen the pattern unfold and the Great Crusade become, as someone said, the Great Grab Bag. It is the familiar Republican pattern of friendly consideration for the few at the expense of the many—government of the many, by the few, for the few. But we cannot say that we were surprised, for at the very beginning of this new Gold Rush, the Secretary of the Interior, Mr. McKay, said: "We are in the saddle as an administration representing business and industry." And I guess he knew what he was talking about.

The federal power to regulate the price of natural gas has been relinquished. The Secretary of the Interior has announced plans to sell the government's helium plant. Experimental plants for converting coal into oil and recovering oil from oil shale have been shut down or gone on the block.

The Soil Conservation Service has been crippled, its top staff placed upon a political spoils basis, and its appropriations cut down. The national forests have been attacked. And in an interesting effort to stimulate local initiative by removing the incentive for it, the administration tried to abolish the appropriations for federal co-operation with state and private forestry. Fatal inroads on the public's power to regulate the public lands were stopped by the Democrats, joined by a handful of conservation-minded Republican Congressmen.

In short, the bipartisan conservation policy that has reserved our public lands in the public interest and preserved our public heritage for posterity, has been under repeated attack from the administration. And it looks as if the new philosophy regarding our public wealth, protected and developed for more than fifty years and now enormously valuable, is that if somebody can make a profit from it, then it should never have been a public asset in the first place.

The word "giveaway" may sound unkind and perhaps it is a little inaccurate, but it is certainly descriptive of these past two years, and I haven't even mentioned the Republican tax bill which gives 91 per cent of the savings to corporations and individuals with incomes in excess of $5,000 and 9 per cent to everyone else, which is 80 per cent of us. What would happen in the next two years if the administration had its way I don't know, but I'm suspicious. It takes time to halt and reverse a resources policy that has been developing for fifty years. But over the door of the National Archives are carved the words: "All the past is prologue," and I wonder if that means, in the vernacular, that "You ain't seen nothing yet."

In 1908 Theodore Roosevelt warned of "a threat of great corporation control of the water powers of the country."

"The country?" some critics ask. "Why, these great projects are local or regional, helping isolated slices of the country, at all the taxpayers' expense." But again the facts are that an integrated development enriches and enhances the entire national economy. For example, the use of electrical appliances has vastly increased, private businesses and industries have multiplied in the seven states directly served by TVA, which means more and more equipment, machinery, transportation in New York, Pennsylvania, Ohio, etc., where new opportunities for investment and employment have been created. It is the old story of wealth begets wealth. Yet there are those in high places who think and even speak of TVA and its power program as an illustration of "creeping Socialism" and constricted initiative, who would have us believe that the great developments in this country during the previous twenty years were merely the creations of uncontrolled zealots.

What we see, then, is not so much a sweeping single retreat from previous Democratic policy, but a slow bloodletting—strict limitation on construction of transmission lines which eases the pressure on private power rates, no new requests for power dams, new contract conditions, devious changes in criteria, back-door raids like Dixon-Yates. Individually these incidents are complicated by small print, verbal veils, and something less than candor. But taken in sum total they constitute a compelling repudiation of a public policy whose ingredients have a history going back almost to the time when electricity was first used. If clearly analyzed and illuminated, it is clear that the sentence is death by slow strangulation.

I feel very strongly that the preservation of our soil, the use of our land, which means the tending of our rivers, watersheds, and forests, is about our most important public responsibility. Perhaps I feel more acutely about it than others because I've seen the vast, arid, stony wastes of our earth that once richly nourished great civilizations. Yes, and I've seen the ugly tracks of the careless, improvident, and greedy across the plains and foothills and forests of our great West.

Erosion, desiccation, doom, move with such subtle, sinister imperceptibility. And no one stands at the mouths of our rivers and counts the value of the soil that daily washes out to sea. No one stands on our riverbanks measuring the unharnessed power and life-giving water flowing by.

"I will lift up mine eyes unto the hills, from whence cometh my help," is as lovely a sentence as there is in our language. The trouble is that in the physical world it just isn't true. The help doesn't come. What comes is disaster, and the broken stones of departed civilizations are the everlasting testimony. They have failed, not because of engineering which has performed miracles in all civilizations, but because of lack of

138

understanding of the land. And our civilization in the West could fail like the others.

But it need not, it must not. The correct management of our resources—how human society can be conducted in harmony with the conditions set by nature—is now a matter of scientific knowledge. We know enough; all we have to do is to act, act boldly, on what we know. If we do, the West, our great national storehouse of undeveloped natural resources, will play its mighty part in our expanding economy. If we don't, history's ugly lesson may be repeated in this beautiful land.

Education, a National Cause

No SINGLE issue of domestic policy is more in need of clarification, public understanding, and bold action than education. It is unfortunately true that educational inadequacy is less obvious to the naked eye than is the sight of a man out of work, of a factory shut down, or of a hungry family. Yet to look squarely at the issue of education is to face nothing less than the central question of whether civilization is to prove a fulfillment of divine and rational purpose—or a bitter mockery.

In a very real sense the central issue of education is the central issue of today: how a civilization which has reached, at least in America, unprecedented heights of material well-being and unlocked awesome secrets of the physical world is also to master the ways for preserving its spiritual and moral and intellectual values—for preserving, if you please, those very things that are the essence of civilization.

In a narrower, more political sense the issue of education is how democracy can be made an instrument by which a people work together to mobilize the strength of the community to fight ignorance as effectively as we have fought every other enemy which has threatened us.

Yet crucial as these issues are, I would nevertheless emphasize first that any discussion of education cannot be cast just in terms of national needs, or a national policy, or a national program. For education can serve the ends of democratic society only as it meets those of the individual human being. The essential condition of the system of free choice between conflicting ideas and leaders, which we call democracy, is that it be made up of all different kinds of people—which means that what we demand most of education is the development of informed people who are at the same time unique, different,

From an address before the National Education Association, Chicago Stadium, July 6, 1955.

unpatterned individuals. I think this means, in turn, that any national educational policy must encourage difference, experimentation, and flexibility in educational practice.

May I add a word about the things that have happened these past two or three years which undoubtedly make some teachers think that we want our children taught only certain things in a certain way. This just isn't so!

It was an unprecedented historical coincidence that brought together the flames of war across the world, the atom's unlocking, and the emergence of aggressive Communism that created dangers—at first not fully realized—of insidiously organized disloyalty. This coincidence of crises induced the fever of fear, and there were unfortunately those among us who insisted on treating this fever in medieval manner by applying leeches to the bloodstream of freedom itself. Public servants, particularly teachers, were regrettably the victims of these frightened attacks of scared people.

But the fever is now subsiding. We know about the precautions which are necessary against organized disloyalty, and we have also experienced the excesses of overcaution which are both unnecessary and dangerous. The Supreme Court has forthrightly rebuked the government's abuse of education's Dr. Peters. And the Senate has voted, despite administration opposition, to review the whole security program.

This battle for freedom, of course, is not over—as freedom's battles are never over. But it is very important, I think, that teachers realize that America's confidence in itself is coming back after our unpleasant nightmare—and that we insist no less strongly than before that the teacher's job is to teach the way of inquiry, to prepare each generation to meet its new problems, to improve its new opportunities, to explore civilization's always new horizons, to open minds and not to close them.

A second principle underlying our national educational policy is that whatever control of public education is required should be exercised by local authorities. Our public schools take much of their strength from the millions of private citizens who are involved directly in their affairs—the boards of trustees, the parent-teachers associations, the room mothers, and all the others. Local control keeps alive continuous debate and the freedom to experiment. It insures a wholesome diversity in educational plans and practices. It helps to keep public education from becoming an instrument of stifling conformity and uniformity. Not sentimental attachment to tradition, but hardheaded good sense demands that by keeping control of education in the local community we keep the spreading branches of an ever-enlarging democracy always close to its roots.

Yet we have reached the point where the financing of education, as distinguished from its control, can no longer everywhere be taken care of entirely from local or even from state and local revenues. This is not a matter of more, or more expensive, education. Nor is it a matter of opinion or of politics. It is a matter of plain arithmetic, and it is a matter of necessity.

The key fact is that by law most schools must rely very largely for their support on property taxes. But property tax revenues do not go up as the population and the community income and production go up. And the tax revenues which do rise in proportion—the income and excise taxes—have been largely taken over by the state and federal governments.

Our thinking about adequate financing of public education must still start from an insistence that it is first of all a responsibility of local and state governments; that they must make available the largest possible revenues to sustain our public education system. State and local governments have no higher duties and there are too many instances today of failure to do that duty courageously and imaginatively.

Yet it is obvious, over all, that some measure of assistance to public education from the federal purse has now become necessary, and that this necessity will become increasingly acute in the next few years.

Two centuries of American history and experience testify that this need for federal financial assistance can be met without the slightest degree of domination by the central government.

No such domination followed Congress's grant in 1785 of a section of every township in the federal domain for the maintenance of public schools.

Nor has President Lincoln's approval of the Land Grant College System resulted in federal control.

The GI Bill of Rights has done great good. So has the Fulbright Fellowship Program. And there has been no accompanying federal domination.

It seemed a fair conclusion some years ago when Senators and Representatives from both parties, notably Senators Lister Hill and Robert Taft, sponsored government aid-to-education proposals, that there was at least to be no political division on party lines about federal action in this field.

And in February, 1953, just after he assumed office, President Eisenhower said: "Our school system demands some prompt, effective help."

Yet when this need has become acutely critical, nothing has been done. Instead of "prompt, effective help," we await a conference on education to be held at the White House next fall. Now a conference is fine and it will dramatize the great significance of our educational system and its critical deficiencies. But it seems to me a pitifully inadequate excuse for years of doing absolutely nothing about America's number one domestic need—schools and teachers.

I do not mean to ignore the President's recommendation to Congress last February. We need, he said, seven billion dollars' worth of new schools. But to help get them, he recommended that Congress pass not a law but a miracle. For meeting this seven-billion-dollar need the President proposed grants of $66 million a year for three years. This is 33¢ a year to meet every $35 of admitted present, crying need.

The President's recommendations also included federal loans for school construction to be repaid with interest. But the proposed amount was sufficient to cover only one-seventh of the needs the President listed, and when the fine print was read it developed that even these loan provisions were so drawn that they could never be used.

It is, I think, interesting if disheartening to reflect that while proposing an effective grant of only $66 million a year for three years for school construction aid, the President at the same time proposed a federal grant for highway construction aid—mostly on a matching basis—of three billion dollars every year for the next ten years! This is $45 of federal funds for highways to every $1 for schools.

I will resist the temptation to draw inferences from the unequal competition between automobiles and education in our government these days, but I deny that this 45-to-1 ratio between highways and schools represents the standards or the priority of values of the people of America.

There is, however, no point in belaboring the inadequacy and deceptiveness of this administration's school program. The chief education officers of forty states have said that it would be of no help whatsoever in their states. And Congress has long since buried the President's bill.

What then should our federal school financing policy and program be?

It should be to face, honestly and forthrightly, our educational shortages, to hold the states and local communities responsible for meeting all of these shortages they can, and then to allocate from the taxes we collect from ourselves whatever is necessary to do the rest of the job.

The figures on the shortages are well known despite the efforts in Washington to conceal them by confused and conflicting pronouncements. Enrollment in primary and secondary schools increased as much in the school year just ended as it did in the entire twenty years between 1930 and 1950. Six million children went to school this year in firetraps. Seven hundred thousand children are on a split session basis and get only half-day schooling.

We are currently short at least 250,000 classrooms—which is rooms for 7½ million children. Extraordinary efforts by local communities throughout the country are improving the situation a little bit. But with a million and a half more school-age children every year now drastic measures obviously have to be taken—and there can be no excuse for further delay.

The shortage of teachers is in some ways even more ominous than the shortage of schoolrooms. It is generally agreed that we need 180,000 more teachers than are presently available. Yet only 70,000 qualified teachers enter the profession each year. Somehow we must double the number. We note the urging today in Washington for a strong military reserve. It seems to me high time that we also pay attention to the schools' crying need not just for a teacher reserve, but for filling the large gaps in education's front-line trenches.

To meet this appalling situation we must start, it seems to me, with immediate support of the proposals now before Congress for $400 million of federal funds each year for the next four years for school construction to be matched by state funds.

While this program, together with the provisions for extending credit to certain school districts, will by no means meet the whole construction need, it would be a long American step in the right direction. And I hope that what is good for all will not be lost to all by any linking together of the school aid and desegregation issues which would delay realization of our hopes and expectations on either or both of these vital fronts. In the long run segregation and discrimination, like other obsolete heritages, will yield quickly to the general advance of education.

The need for more teachers—145,000 new teachers a year to man the teaching ranks and meet the deficit—also means more money, higher salaries to make teaching a more attractive profession, and more funds for educating teachers. Careful calculations indicate that a federal grant to the states of approximately $50 million a year, if matched by an equal amount of new state funds, will at least break the back of the problem—instead of breaking the teachers' backs.

So much for the present. Over the longer run it may be best not to tie federal assistance to specific purposes, such as school construction, but rather to make unrestricted cash grants to the states on a per pupil basis. State governments would then have much greater flexibility to distribute these funds among local school districts for whatever purpose would most effectively advance education.

In view of the financial difficulties of the states, I also have misgivings about making federal grants to education permanently on a matching basis. But in any event, to insure that federal assistance is given only to those states which already make a proper effort to support public education, and to avoid the further risk that federal aid might result in relaxed state and local effort, some stated minimum local effort should be required as a condition of federal assistance.

Moreover, in the interest of narrowing somewhat the present

wide gap in educational opportunity among the children of the various states, it seems to me that there are cogent reasons of fairness and good sense for higher per pupil assistance to states with the least ability to finance education as proposed by that great champion of our schools, Senator Lister Hill.

Finally I would suggest a modest program of national scholarships to promising candidates who upon graduation would undertake to give some years to teaching. To encourage outstandingly competent teachers, scholarships might also be awarded for special teacher training to graduate students, or for advanced work for already experienced teachers.

Just as we recruit promising young people for West Point and Annapolis, and for such professional fields as the Merchant Marine, science and engineering, we should now consider the same methods of attraction to our great public school system. Moreover, the cost of such scholarships would be small; the return on our investment would be immeasurable.

Yet there should be no evading the fact that the composite program I am suggesting here will be expensive, and it is just a beginning. Beardsley Ruml has proposed federal expenditures to salvage our public school system of about $700 million next year, and possibly as much as $3 or $3½ billion a year ten years hence.

These are sobering figures and demand the closest scrutiny. Yet they are no excuse for either economic alarm or political timidity.

It is said that our national income should be rising at the rate of $15 billion a year during the next decade. This will mean increased federal tax revenues, at present rates, of $4 billion a year. So what I suggest, in effect, is that we agree with ourselves, to spend on education—until we have caught up with our children's needs—say 20 per cent of our federal tax collections from our new national wealth.

Bad education isn't cheap either. Its high costs are paid from other budgets—for poverty and sickness and unemployment and juvenile delinquency. The question is not only "What will an adequate education program cost?" The question is even more "What is the cost of not having such a program?" I cannot imagine the American people responding with anything but eagerness and enthusiasm to a proposal to give our children better education, which means a better chance, and fuller education, which means fuller lives.

I have suggested here what seem to me the outlines, the elemental necessities, of our public educational system. Yet we all recognize that there is infinitely more to the problem than simply providing a classroom and a person with a teaching certificate for every thirty children between the ages of five and seventeen.

The larger challenge that we must meet together—as teachers and parents and public and private citizens—is to prove that mass education can also be good education.

Good school buildings are an asset—but they are not the essence of good education. The real heart of good education remains, as always, good teaching. We must, if we want to improve the quality of education, attract into teaching and hold there a far larger number of our ablest young people. Compensation must be geared to ability and performance, and opportunity afforded for advancement to a high level based on merit, as in other professions.

And, above all, teachers must be freed of the shackles of bigotry and anti-intellectualism, and the indignities of loyalty oaths and unwritten blue laws which no longer apply to other citizens.

It is another accepted requirement for improving educational quality, I think, that we be clearer as to the tasks and priorities of our schools. Today they are being asked to perform not only their traditional jobs but, more and more, functions traditionally recognized as the obligation of the family, the church, the employer, and other social institutions. Under pressure of this group or that, courses of study are becoming laden with activities whose educational value is at least subject to serious question.

In a growing and changing society, the primary tasks of the school must also grow and change. But we must be clear that if we expect the schools to do too much, if we expect the teacher to play too many roles, we are bound to be disappointed with the results. If our educational purposes are unclear, if the curriculum is chaotic and cluttered with distractions, if the teaching staffs are overburdened with an indiscriminate array of responsibilities well beyond their reasonable capacity to carry, we must expect that our children will be educated for mediocrity instead of for something better.

I do not mean to trespass upon areas of what I know to be strong—and healthy—controversy among you who are so much more experienced in this field than I. But it is our common concern that we recognize and that we resist the pressures to let mass education become education for mediocrity. The dangers of mass education seem to me as much our problem as are its necessities.

We are well advised, I think, to take very seriously the admonition that education for all may come to mean real education for none. The struggle is very real today between massiveness, standardization, conformity on the one hand, and on the other the spirit of individualism which has given freedom and democracy and life itself their meaning.

We must, then, work together to forge better tools for the ever-enlarging job of educating fast growing numbers of our children for an always more complex life. Equally must we struggle everlastingly to keep education a process of enrichment—of the mind and spirit of the young American whose destiny is measured only by his wisdom.

FOUR

First Principles

This I Believe

WHAT DO I believe? As an American I believe in generosity, in liberty, in the rights of man. These are social and political faiths that are part of me, as they are, I suppose, part of all of us. Such beliefs are easy to express. But part of me too is my relation to all life, my religion. And this is *not* so easy to talk about. Religious experience is highly intimate and, for me, at least, ready words are not at hand.

I am profoundly aware of the magnitude of the universe, that all is ruled by law, including my finite person. I believe in the infinite wisdom that envelopes and embraces me and from which I take direction, purpose, strength. First to my mind there spring those words of the 27th Psalm, my favorite:

For in the time of trouble [the Lord] shall hide me in his pavilion. . . . He shall set me up upon a rock. . . .
I had fainted unless I had believed to see the goodness of the Lord in the land of the living.
Wait on the Lord; be of good courage, and he shall strengthen thine heart. . . .

Yes, I believe in and I have experienced His goodness in the land of the living. And I have found no rocks of certainty or safety but His.

And if *doing* is part of *believing*, I find a great design in the simple counsel of the old prophet Micah: "To do justly, to love mercy, and to walk humbly with thy God."

But having beliefs, or at least enunciating them, is only part of it. Living up to them for me is much harder; for, as someone said, it is easier to *fight* for one's beliefs than to live up to them. And I wonder if the chief cause of discord in human affairs is not so much the undesirable nature of beliefs as it is the fight-

Recording made at Libertyville, Illinois, by CBS, May 21, 1954.

ing for them, the competitive indoctrination among them. In effect this is what we have across the entire fabric of human affairs: rents and tears caused by the constant vendettas carried on by competing faiths: religious, social, political, and ideological.

I believe in liberalism, in individualism, in freedom of conscience; and if there is anything that the whole idea of liberalism contradicts it is the notion of competitive indoctrination. So I believe that if we really want human brotherhood to spread and increase until it makes life safe and sane, we must also be certain that there is no *one* true faith or path by which it may spread. But it is not easy to banish the notion that there can be universal brotherhood just as soon as everyone gives up *his* faith and accepts *ours*. That day will never come, for the richness of human diversity cannot be abolished any more than Mars or Jupiter. It can be resented and fought, but only at appalling cost. Difference is in the nature of life. It is part of our moral universe. Without difference life would become lifeless.

So I reject the ideal of total conformity, compulsory or complacent; the faith that is swallowed like pills, whole and at once, with no questions asked. I believe in helping ourselves and others to see the possibilities in viewpoints other than one's own; in encouraging the free interchange of ideas; in welcoming fresh approaches to the problems of life; in urging the fullest, most vigorous use of critical self-examination. Thus we can learn to grow together, to unite in our common search for truth within a better and a happier world.

The basic faith in liberty of conscience has an ancient ancestry. It is by no means exclusive with us. It is in fact our bond of unity with all free men. But I believe we are its ordained guardians in this age of assault and anxiety when so many seem to believe their doubts and doubt their beliefs.

Finally, I should like to *live* and not just believe those strong words of faith in St. Paul's letter to the Galatians: "Stand fast, therefore, in the liberty wherewith Christ has made us free, and not be entangled with the yoke of bondage."

Free Speech: A Duty

IN MAY of 1827, Elijah Lovejoy left his native village in the state of Maine for his first journey to his future home in the Mississippi Valley. As he came by schooner into Boston Harbor on the first leg of his long and arduous trip, he saw a frigate which had been taken from the British in the War of 1812 by the gallantry of American arms. This chance encounter moved him to write in his diary: ". . . as I gazed upon her and thought of the glorious achievements of my countrymen, my heart beat thick and proudly."

The youth of twenty-five who wrote those words had perhaps not yet learned what was to be borne in so hardly upon the man of thirty-five—that the glorious achievements of our countrymen are not all to be found in our military and naval annals; what he was yet to learn is that ordinary living affords many occasions for men to dare greatly, to live dangerously, and even to die nobly.

A decade from the time Elijah Lovejoy set out in such exuberant spirits to live and work in the great new Middle Country, such an occasion came to him. And, as he met it— bravely, directly, unyieldingly—so do our hearts, in his phrase, "beat thick and proudly" as we remember the first martyr to the freedom of the press, the freedom not just to denounce heretics, but to pronounce heresies, the freedom to say lawful but unpopular things.

To many of his contemporaries it must have seemed that Lovejoy's cause had ended in defeat. His own life was gone, his family stricken with grief and destitute, his hearse and his memory reviled by those who wanted no talk of human freedom to disturb their complacency and the existing order of things.

From an address at Lovejoy Historical Marker Dedication, Alton, Illinois, November 9, 1952.

Lovejoy embraced a great idea in an early and perilous stage of that idea's development. And that is usually dangerous, particularly when the idea is a new idea, disturbing to existing institutions, habits, and prejudices. His idea was that the enslavement of black by white was wrong and should be ended. That was a very radical idea and much more blood was to flow, the lives of millions more were to be wrecked, before that idea was to prevail.

But the measure of Lovejoy's triumph is to be found in the fact that only a quarter of a century was required to establish it as the law of the land. And across this scene of Lovejoy's death there fell, some twenty years later, the shadow of the tall, gaunt man who was to be the instrument to do this work. For not far from the plaque we dedicate today is the marker commemorating the last of the Lincoln-Douglas debates, held here in Alton in October, 1858.

Elijah Lovejoy, however, served a greater cause than that of the abolition of Negro slavery. And it was his devotion to this cause which we will remember long after the struggle over the abolition of slavery has been all but forgotten. This greater cause was the right—and the duty—of the individual to speak out for the truth. I make the reference to "duty" advisedly because that was the way Lovejoy thought of it. To his fellow citizens of Alton in meeting assembled to protest the turmoil provoked by his outspokenness, he said: "I am impelled to the course I have taken because I fear God. As I shall answer to my God in the great day, I dare not abandon my sentiments, or cease in all proper ways to propagate them. . . . If the civil authorities refuse to protect me I must look to God; and if I die, I have determined to make my grave in Alton."

There are many vigorous and powerful statements of the right to be permitted to speak freely, but I know of none more moving. And in these days of clamorous and jostling assertion of rights and privileges, it is sobering to be reminded by these words of duties as well as rights.

Lovejoy saw the problem in terms of what he felt obliged to say, not merely of what he might be entitled to say. The distinction is an important one; and only those who observe the one as well as claim the other serve fully the cause of truth.

154

Human character being what it is, heroes in the classic mold of Elijah Lovejoy are rare. Of such stuff were the martyrs made. Neither is it given to many to see the truth in human affairs with the clarity and depth of Lovejoy's crusading conviction. But we can have confidence in the ultimate triumph of truth, and in the certainty that our fellow men will seek it out and follow it if only they can hear and speak and sift the true and false in untrammeled peace.

Some of the residents of Alton did not have that confidence in 1837. Some of our fellow citizens of America do not have that confidence today.

One of the greatest and wisest of living Americans, speaking in the detachment and wisdom of his retirement from the bench, found words for his countrymen not long ago when he said: "I believe that that community is already in the process of dissolution where each man begins to eye his neighbor as a possible enemy, where non-conformity with the accepted creed, political as well as religious, is a mark of disaffection; where denunciation without specification or backing takes the place of evidence; where orthodoxy chokes freedom of dissent; where faith in the eventual supremacy of reason has become so timid that we dare not enter our convictions in the open lists to win or lose."

The American conviction could not find a more accurate statement than this by Judge Learned Hand. It has been the American conviction from the beginning that men are only free when they respect each other's freedom.

It is said that religious creeds are written to mark the graves where heresies lie buried. There is a common heresy and its graves are to be found all over the earth. It is the heresy that says you can kill an idea by killing a man, defeat a principle by defeating a person, bury truth by burying its vehicle. Man may burn his brother at the stake, but he cannot reduce truth to ashes; he may murder his fellow man with a shot in the back, but he does not murder justice; he may even slay armies of men, but as it is written, "truth beareth off the victory."

It is fitting that we dedicate this memorial to Elijah Lovejoy here in Alton, as a constant reminder of our eternal battle. For we fight not against flesh and blood, but we fight, in the long run, against the spiritual enemies of man himself.

155

It is the genius of American freedom that we admit our mistakes, even as we confess our sins. So we confess our sins even as we reaffirm our faith, that "Truth crushed to earth, will rise again," that a people, under God, can have a new birth of freedom, that every age needs men who will redeem the time by living with a vision of things that are to be.

Faith, Knowledge, and Peace

IF I WERE asked what the greatest danger is today in the conduct of democracy's affairs I suppose I would think first of war —but second, and immediately, of a very different kind of thing—of what seems to me the possibility that we in America are becoming so big, so organized, so institutionalized, so governmentalized—yes, and so standardized—that there is increasing danger that the individual and his precious diversity will get squeezed out completely.

Of freedom as an abstraction, as a concept, as a general principle, I know nothing new or different to say. Pericles stated freedom's character in his Funeral Oration in Athens in 430 B.C. And its contemporary hazards and applications have been made pointedly and persuasively plain in enduring volumes written within the year by Elmer Davis, Henry Steele Commager, Irwin Griswold, Walter Lippmann, that brilliant Englishwoman, Barbara Ward, and others.

Freedom—effective freedom—does not exist as a formula which can be written out by some and then used by others. The term itself is used as an argument for everything from absolutism to anarchy. Freedom is not what the government does. It is not something that is either won or lost in the world's capitals or on its battlefields, or that can be preserved by law —except for a moment or two in history's expanse.

The freedom that counts is simply what is in the minds and hearts of millions of free people. It is nothing more than the total of the feelings of people as they are expressed in the way we, the people, deal with our own families and our own neighbors and associates. This is freedom's hope today on the other side of the iron curtain. And, paradoxically, it is part of freedom's danger here at home.

From an address before the General Federation of Women's Clubs, Philadelphia, Tuesday, May 24, 1955.

Someone said: "The world is so big and I am so small, I do not like it, at all, at all." But if all of us could only realize that *we*, as individuals, are the guardians of this thing called freedom, this "Holy Light," that we as individuals are its makers, its destroyers, we might get rid of this debilitating illusion that we no longer count in a system of things that has gotten discouragingly big. If we could only realize that all freedom really amounts to is the way *we* think about and treat a non-conforming neighbor, a dissenting teacher, the minority view among us, people of different races and religions, people from the other side of town—then citizenship might become more meaningful, and freedom infinitely more secure.

My first point then may be very simply stated: It is that freedom begins at home. In the current phrase, this precious treasure has to be, by its very nature, a do-it-yourself business.

Yet to recognize freedom as essentially a personal thing is not to disregard the conditions of its endurance in society—of keeping the Holy Light burning. I think of three such primary conditions. Freedom, to change the figure, is a plant which grows only from *knowledge*. It must be watered by *faith*. It will come to leaf and fruit and flower only in the benevolent sunlight of *peace*.

We have long recognized in this country the essentiality of knowledge to freedom. We accept without dissent Jefferson's pronouncement that "if a people expects to be both ignorant and free, it expects what never was and never will be." We have accordingly made ourselves perhaps the most literate people in history. Our children go to school; not merely 10 per cent of them as in many places; not half of them as in others, but *all* of them. We do a job of opening up to them civilization's accumulated learning that is a far, far distant goal to most of mankind.

But that knowledge which is the seedbed of freedom is much more than the absence of ignorance, than the memorization of the accumulated truths, facts, and assumptions which we call learning. It is the capacity for *new* learning that counts, for learning the things which are still unknown, for learning what mistakes we are making, what better answers there are. If knowledge is essential to freedom it is equally true that freedom is essential to learning, to new knowledge—freedom to

158

criticize, to disagree, to dissent, to inquire, even to be wrong, to err in the attempt to be right or to discover truth.

We applaud in the fields of physical science this freedom to look for *new* truth. The whole urge there is to do things differently from the way they have been done before, to assume that old assumptions are wrong, to assert that there are four dimensions where only three have previously been recognized, to unlock particles of matter, and unleash immeasurable forces —to everlastingly probe and penetrate the unknown.

But in social and economic and political relationships our attitude is very different. The work of the heretic, the questioner, in science is applauded; but in society it is different. We grasped eagerly, desperate for the great new thoughts which came from Einstein and Oppenheimer about the relativity of matter, but their views on the relativity of men were suspect and unsafe. We seem to realize too little that the same kind of thinking which split the atom and is now controlling (I hope) the virus which caused polio may be needed to teach us how to control the use of the atom and to stop the virus which causes war.

We must come to the realization that *new* knowledge, some criticism and some dissent and some new ideas, will be required to level out cycles of our economy, to merge our markets with the world's, to get "farm surpluses" into empty stomachs, to replace men with machines and swords with plowshares without causing unemployment, and to create a more meaningful place in society for those whose life's work is done.

Our recent inclination to turn upon our thinkers, to sneer at intellectuals and to hold them up to ridicule, to suspect, denounce, and require oaths of them, is not just an attack on their dignity and freedom as individuals. It impairs, too, our hopes for the enlarged freedoms for all of us which could be the product of their unchallenged right to dissent and to explore. It seems so wrong to take a gun this way and blow out our brains.

May I add here just a footnote of further and not unrelated concern about the latter-day emphasis in our schools upon "the well-adjusted individual." I'm not coming out in favor of the maladjustment of individuals, but at the same time overemphasis on the "well-rounded," "well-adjusted," "well-balanced" personality seems deliberately designed to breed mental neuters. In actual practice mental neutrality means docile support of the *status quo*. And when students and teachers alike are discouraged from a critical evaluation of society, we are taking a longer step into the Age of Conformity than we may wish.

I have not meant to seem either despondent or critical about our current attitude toward the knowledge element in freedom. It is probably just a feeling that we come so close to our goals in this area that prompts a kind of agonizing about our falling short.

But, to move on, if knowledge is freedom's mind, its heart is faith. There must be a moral basis for asserting the worth of the individual, the essentiality of his freedom. This basis is for me, simply the belief that man is the child of God, that he holds within himself some portion of divinity, that he is the instrument for developing the meaningfulness of a divine order.

When we speak of individual freedom we hark back ultimately to the psalmist's words: "Thou hast made him a little lower than the angels; Thou hast crowned him with glory and honor and hast set him over the work of thy hands." Isn't this the sense of freedom?

There is cause for concern among freedom's friends, I think, that faith—the heart and meaning of freedom—has become less a part of our everyday life. We profess less, and perhaps share less, the religious faith of an earlier time which bade us love and trust one another—and accordingly respect each other's freedom. I recall that declining faith evoked Matthew Arnold's disheartened lines:

> The Sea of Faith
> Was once, too, at the full, and round earth's shore
> Lay like the folds of a bright girdle furl'd;
> But now I only hear
> Its melancholy long, withdrawing roar. . . .

Another poet speaks of "Freedom's Holy Light." And it must be a holy light or it will be no light at all. It will glow only in a cherished faith that all men are brothers, and that they are brothers because each contains within himself a spark of the divine. It falls on each of us but only as it is reflected from the countenance of others. It can prosper and wax bright only in a widening dawn of human conscience, an awakening into a time when we became each day a little better able to see ourselves in each other.

But, in the immediate view of it, the keystone, the indispensable ingredient, of liberty is peace.

The international scene is calmer; the music of the doves, albeit a little hoarse and hesitant, has suddenly replaced the harsh words and threatening gestures of a couple of months ago. The days are brighter in Europe, and a softer sun comes up each morning out of China, " 'cross the bay," or at least it appears to. For these new tunes here and abroad we are grateful.

Yet to speak of peace in terms of the demands of lasting freedom, to speak of it as members of the human race, is to think today far beyond a stalemate of arms, a cease-fire, a treaty. Peace means today facing squarely into the deadly, hypnotic eye of the hydrogen bomb—facing it and finding the answer. And there is only one sure answer.

With the unlocking of the atom, mankind crossed one of the great watersheds of history. We have entered uncharted lands. The maps of strategy and diplomacy by which we guided ourselves until yesterday no longer reveal the way. Fusion and fission revolutionized the entire foundation of human affairs. It has placed mankind, in the words of Sir Winston Churchill, "in a situation both measureless and laden with doom."

The words we use when we talk of this terrible force are so absolute as to be almost meaningless. We say that civilization cannot survive an atomic war, that there can be no victory and no victors, that nuclear weapons can annihilate all life on this planet. All these statements are true. But it is nearly impossible for us to understand them.

This scientific revolution in man's capacity for self-destruction calls for an equivalent revolution in man's capacity for self-preservation and the conduct of our foreign affairs. It will not do to rely only on the orthodox, time-tried methods of foreign policy which the great states have used in the past; for war was one of these methods; and today either war must become obsolete, or mankind will.

In the long run nothing will meet the needs of the people of our nation or of the world short of abolishing the very

161

institution of war as an arbiter of disputes or a tool of annihilation.

We must, of course, continue to preserve and to build our alliances, to help free nations gain strength to preserve their freedom, to develop our own armed strength—indeed, until the aggressors come to tolerable terms we must even continue building our own nuclear power.

But this is not enough. To stop here is to dwell still in the house of the past, with a bomb ticking in the basement. We can no longer rest contentedly on the framework of the old diplomacy and the old strategy of preponderant or balanced power. We must move beyond to that brighter day envisioned just ten years ago when the Nazi nightmare died and the United Nations came to birth in San Francisco amid great rejoicing. We must resume the attack on the institution of war itself.

Let no one deceive himself about the enormity of this task. The roots of war lie deep, not only in rivalries among peoples and conflicts among nations and ideas, but in the dark, tormented depths of the human heart. To abolish human rivalry and conflict would be a utopian dream. But to try and make sure that human rivalry and conflict will not abolish us is just not a possibility: it is an imperative necessity.

The differences between ourselves and the Communists are great and terrifying. They will not be easily resolved. I doubt if they will be resolved in our lifetime. Our effort must be to make sure that their resolution will take place, not in the old arena, where war was one of the weapons, but in a new arena, under new rules, in a new spirit. And the effort must be remorseless.

So, while we cannot yet control the sources of conflict, we can perhaps, in this new mood of humility and understanding, try to control the means of our annihilation.

Our national record in this field, I should say, has been a creditable one. President Truman first proposed a system of enforced disarmament to be administered by the United Nations in 1945. In 1946 and 1950 and 1951 his administration proposed plans for the world-wide control of atomic weapons. In 1953 President Eisenhower affirmed his support for this policy of enforced disarmament. And recently he has named a special assistant to prosecute the search for arms limitation.

All this has been in the right direction. But I wonder if we have yet spelled out clearly to the world that we know that mankind has crossed a great divide, that, compared with the stake of survival, every other interest is minor and every other preoccupation petty.

On this great issue, I fear we have too often been perfunctory where we should be passionate, more cynical than zealous, tepid and torpid where we should have dedicated our best energies and our highest purposes. And saber-rattling and bellicose speeches have all too frequently distorted and obscured America's peaceful purposes.

Let this phase be done with forever. Let us instead place effective arms control at the very core of our diplomacy and at the very heart of our communications with other lands. Surely if we could afford a crash program to build the hydrogen bomb, we can afford a crashing effort to control it.

And the opportunity may be at hand to boldly tackle once again this great unfinished business. I will not speculate on the more peaceful gestures from Moscow and Peiping which have excited our hopes this spring and which are the consequence of the power and patience of the great coalition of free nations which we helped so mightily to forge with aid to Greece and Turkey, the Marshall Plan, NATO, and all the rest. But there are significant and hopeful signs this fateful spring that the Soviet Union's stubborn attitude on arms control may be changing.

What are the chances that we may get somewhere at last in our efforts to prevent a hydrogen war? I don't know. While there are signs that patience and strength are paying off, I have no illusions that our search for peace will succeed easily. Yet, in all conscience, our great nation has no choice other than to use its day of leadership to work remorselessly for peace—to do its best to make sure that the epoch of American power produces, not the final earthly holocaust, but a world of justice, security, and freedom.

Faith, knowledge, and peace—these will be the cornerstones of such a world. And, of these, none will avail if peace is lacking, if an atom split in anger turns out to be mankind's last reality.

The Reputation of the Government

FOR ME to undertake a discussion of the subject of "Government and Private Reputation" seems, to me at least, peculiarly appropriate. My interest in government, involving as it has a double exposure to the popular franchise, has evaporated whatever pretensions I might once have had to the possession of private reputation.

I could, I suppose, provide an object lesson by showing my scars, for, as Professor Priest has said, in words that never occurred to Horace, *"Dura est ovicipitum via"*—or, the way of the egghead is hard.

So I can only wistfully suppose that there *are* people who still have reputations to protect and that, perhaps, I could help them most by saying merely: "Keep your necks well in and never run for office."

While I am patently beyond rehabilitation, I like to think that the law and the press continue to provide ports of refuge for the normal individual, and recognize the opportunities that daily fall in their paths to formulate sound and sensible principles for the protection of at least private reputations.

I will not attempt to define the dimensions of the problem in terms of the irreparable injury done to reputations by reckless or malicious assaults. I should like, instead, to suggest that there is some value in the exploration of this problem in terms of the reputation of the government, as distinct from that of the individual. The condition of the government's reputation at any particular point in time may have, it seems to me, a great deal to do with the bringing of the evil into being and, once the evil begins to manifest itself, there is too little appreciation of the wounds which government itself receives when the private reputations of its citizens are insecure against official attack. This latter aspect especially has too much sub-

From an address at the Association of American Law Schools, Chicago, December 28, 1953.

stance to be overlooked in any multi-sided discussion of the problem.

Government exists for all of us as a very real and ever-present force, and one with which we are in continuous, albeit sometimes shadowy, contact. We know that we owe it certain duties and marks of respect, and yet we also have a sharp, if inarticulate, sense that our obligations to render them are affected by countervailing responsibilities owed to us by government. Certainly the alacrity, enthusiasm, and effectiveness with which we discharge our part of the bargain is heavily conditioned by the degree to which we think our government is living up to its.

Let me give you an example of what I mean. During the election of 1952 corruption in government was one (and, I hasten to add, only one!) of the issues which appeared to contribute to the idea that it was time for a change. Now I think it fair to say that the particular instances disclosed were not, certainly as we have known governmental corruption in the past, markedly sensational. They did not reach to as high places as before, nor were they an improbable sequel to depression, war, boom, social dislocation—and the vast expansions of government and public spending.

The electorate did not, so far as I was able to observe, see the issue in the unsophisticated terms of one candidate's being for corruption in government and the other against, nor did I see much evidence of the naïve error of distinguishing between Republicans and Democrats on the basis of moral virtues inherently peculiar to either. Why, then, did the issue have any significance? In large part I find the answer in what seems at first blush to be a wholly disparate and unrelated issue, namely, the Korean War.

To me the Korean War is, and I suspect always shall be, the supreme example in my lifetime of the essential need for mutual trust and confidence between the ordinary citizen and his government. Coming as it did upon the heels of the prolonged and exhausting struggle of World War II; involving as it did a far-off unfamiliar country and people and no immediate and visible interest of our own; becoming as it did a costly stalemate with victory, in the guise it has always come to us before, nowhere to be seen or felt—surely no government was ever obliged to ask its citizens to put forth greater efforts in reliance for the most part on bare official assurance that the long-range national interest required it.

Our people, with that sixth sense which is at once the inner grace and outward shield of democracy, seemed to know, however imperfectly, that they were being summoned to the highest kind of duty; and they met the challenge in the face of confusions, provocations, falsehoods, and frustrations beyond description because of their respect for the right of government to ask the ultimate in sacrifice for aims judged by government to be necessary.

Under such extraordinary circumstances what were they entitled to expect of government? Not that while its leaders were asking for sacrifice, some of its hangers-on should be fixing tax cases or selling influence. When it was suggested that such things might be going on simultaneously, the resentment was, I suspect, wholly out of proportion to what might have been generated in more normal times. Warren Harding's government, you will recall, never had to ask the people to do anything except relax and watch taxes go down. And, as the 1924 election indicated, such a government is not held to account by the most exacting standards.

It seems not unlikely, however, that the job of being President of the United States will never again be as pleasant as Calvin Coolidge presumably found it; and that future administrations will all find a return to normalcy, whatever that may be, an inadequate and impossible objective. The preservation of the free world, the staving off of atomic disaster, the accommodation and adjustment of new forces in ferment in our own society and about the globe—all will combine to subject government to the most rigorous tests of strength and statesmanship. And the demands upon it will, of necessity, magnify its demands upon us. The concern of government thus must be to create such a relationship between itself and its citizens that the response of the latter in time of crisis is prompt, trustful, and generous.

Leadership to be greatly served must be cloaked in greatness. Idealism at the center must not be frayed around the edges.

But the reputation of government is, of course, damaged by

other kinds of disloyalty than the familiar problem of corruption. The disloyalty of the occasional Communists, or subversives of any stripe, who creep into government service, is destructive, too, and I suspect our people feel an almost personal affront about some of these disloyalties in government. While the sophisticated analysis of this problem, in terms of the disease being so much less dangerous than the cure, is probably true, it does not make me at all certain that the analysts know what the real danger was, or is. That danger never was that a small group of people could exercise any major influence over American foreign policy or deliver the government into the hands of either Communism or bankruptcy. The plan for reducing Germany to a pastoral state which has been ascribed to Harry Dexter White, for example, was not only rejected by the Truman administration which helped to rebuild Germany industrially, but so far as I can discover, it was also rejected by Stalin, who wanted German goods to rehabilitate the wrecked Russian economy. A danger greater than disloyal influence or espionage was that they hurt the reputation of government in the eyes of the people, and thereby loosen dangerously the magic bonds which tie a democracy together.

So as we seek for ways to protect private reputations against governmental attack, let us realize that the only time we have a problem at all is when the most vital reputation in the world —that of our government—itself is impaired.

It is the part of realistic wisdom to recognize that the vast majority of people in this country are not going to be too concerned about the private reputations of anybody if they sense a threat to the essential reputation of their government. This admittedly has its ugly side, but there is something also of the mysterious essence of democracy in the surviving desire of a people to rise up and strike out against a threat which is more damaging to the ideal of government they cherish than to the policies of the treasury of that government.

There is always, however, the other side of the coin of democracy. If we expect government to observe high standards of loyalty and honesty, we expect it no less to maintain the highest standards of freedom and liberty. One disloyal or dishonest person in government weakens democracy dangerously;

no less, and perhaps even more, does one tyrant, arrayed in the panoply of authority and heedless of those who fall in his way.

The tyrants, and the political opportunists who use them, do the same kind of damage as the dishonest and the disloyal. They chip away at the pride which American citizens have in their government—a pride which is a corollary of devotion to the principles of decent, effective, fair government.

For greatness in a government is not to be found in money honesty alone, in wisdom and vision in the formulation of primary policy, or even in unfailing expertness in spy-catching. There must be, beyond all these, a quality of what, if you please, I can only call justness—the meeting of the popular expectation that government is a protector of the basic equities, with a compassionate eye and a strong arm to see that each individual, no matter how weak or unappealing, is dealt with fairly and justly.

With this capstone virtue, government can command ". . . that loyalty on the part of the citizen which never fails to arise from the confidence that justice will always be done." Without it, to quote again, ". . . government writes its own epitaph. . . ." And in these trying times, no government—and certainly not one that bears the fateful responsibilities of the government of the United States—can afford to jeopardize that loyalty. For the price tags on peace and freedom which the government must collect from its citizens are forbearance and sacrifice and effort—and these are not eagerly given by the disillusioned.

Americans have, I am confident, a strongly developed sense of fair play. It is a rock against which many tides of racial and religious intolerance have beaten in the past, dangerously but vainly. At the moment there are mounting currents of repression and conformity, set in motion by our deep distaste for Communism and our frustration about the stubborn world, and swelled by impure springs of political expediency. But these, too, will recede in time, if the rock is not riven by other forces.

This natural instinct for justice focuses upon government. In large measure it is either realized or disappointed by governmental attitude or act. We had a notable instance of this in the case of the young lieutenant in Michigan who, although of proven loyalty himself, was about to be expelled from the Air Force as a security risk because he was related by blood to persons of allegedly doubtful loyalty. Well, "the government" did do the right thing, and our faith that "the government" would never let itself be guilty of such an outrage bore fruit.

The Air Force that day armed itself with a kind of weapon which, in the long run, is more damaging to our enemies than all of the atomic bombs now stored at the ready.

For the morality of government is, like the law, a seamless garment, and it cannot be rent in one small place without endangering the whole fabric. It is always a lamentable thing when the good name of an individual citizen is unfairly taken from him by anyone, but when the filching is done by government or with its connivance, government does immeasurable harm to itself and the effects on the world we live in are calamitous. The cause of freedom, of human decency, does not advance in measured tread. There are times of retreat and times of enduring advances. It may be given to our time to recognize that the reputation of our government, of surpassing importance in the affairs of men, reflects in no small measure the extent of its concern for justice, honesty, and restraint in dealing with all its citizens at all times and under all circumstances.

And let me say also that government, to the man in the street, is frequently as all-inclusive as it is ill-defined. He is not much given to speculation about the separation of powers; and the executive, the legislative, and the judicial often manage to get hopelessly intermingled in his mind. He does not distinguish too sharply between a cabinet member, a district judge, or a Congressional committee chairman. He simplifies and personifies, and government takes its coloration for him from the acts of all. All have, therefore, a responsibility for the picture that emerges. Anyone can deface it.

The short of the matter is that the survival of our freedom, individual and collective, is closely linked to the good name, the private reputation, if you please, of our government. Its preservation is necessary to evoke the loyalties, both at home and abroad, upon which government must make heavy drafts.

A New Year's Message

As 1955 APPROACHES, it is appropriate that we measure the progress made in the old year and adjust our sights higher for the new one. It is, in fact, a time for resolutions.

The killing has stopped in Indo-China, but large parts of the world remain divided into hostile camps—with ancient hatreds and young ambitions struggling for supremacy. Hunger still stalks the greater portion of the globe and fear shadows our troubled earth like an atomic cloud.

We in America are committed by history to a fighting faith in the power and destiny of free men in a free world. Our strength lies in the creativity of men and women brought together by common dedication to the majesty of liberty and to the dignity of man.

We believe that man is made in the image of God and that to trample on man is to trample on God. Our future depends on living up to that faith and instilling it in others; for we know that just as no man is an island unto himself—so no nation can isolate itself from its responsibilities to fellow men everywhere.

What more can Americans do—indeed, what must we do so that the nations of the world can live in peace and devote their full efforts to the greater welfare and happiness of their people?

I would say that first we must have the confidence and courage to believe that we can ultimately achieve genuine peace—for to lose the faith and the will is to court destruction.

Peace in our time also requires patience and power; patience with our friends and foes—firm, intelligent, and persistent understanding of their needs and desires; and power to withstand the multiple assaults on human liberties. It will require all of our political, economic, military, and moral resources

Broadcast over CBS, January 2, 1955.

to sustain the strength and the will to resist among free peoples and to fulfill the promise of delivery to enslaved millions.

We have the power, the courage, and the magnanimity to create the world of our dreams. As the American poet, Archibald MacLeish, once said: "We have the moment of creation in our hands."

The Educated Citizen

I AM INFORMED that this senior class banquet is being held at the expense of your accumulated reserves. I suggest that inviting me here is a very perilous thing to do because certainly within a few hours the Republicans will ask for equivalent time.

I was delighted to witness a moment ago your emphatic approval of my program for Princeton some thirty-two years ago—unlimited cuts, non-compulsory Chapel, and student firing of the Dean. I always considered that it was wise in politics to have—shall we say—a popular program. The trouble is that when I went into politics it appears that I changed my views.

I feel as though I were opening the hunting season on college seniors. From now until mid-June, college seniors are fair game for all of us uplifters, viewers with alarm, Chautauqua-style orators, even for occasional unemployed politicians. From now until mid-June college seniors are to be repeatedly reminded how fortunate they are and what they should do with their hard-won educational disciplines; they are to be warned repeatedly that the old order is changing, that the sky is overcast, visibility low; and they are to be urged and goaded and implored to accept the challenge to remake the future.

Thirty-two years ago—and I might say quite a number of pounds and a good many inches around the waist ago—when I graduated I believe I listened to these same challenges flung down by orators whose names I have completely forgotten. Now it is my turn to be forgotten. In doing my homework this morning on this evening's oration, I not only let my mind run back to the state of the world thirty-two years ago when I

From an address at the Senior Class Banquet, Princeton University, March 22, 1954.

graduated from Princeton but I also glanced at the *Nassau Herald* of 1922 in the hope that I could find something about myself that would impress you. I discovered that when my senior class voted to bestow the sobriquet of "biggest politician" upon one of its members I received only eight votes—but when it voted on "*thinks* he is biggest politician" I won second place, and that was due to a conspiracy among my roommates.

Thirty-two years ago my classmates and I graduated into a world that was quite different from the one you enter in 1954. Before settling down to the business of trying to earn a living, I did some more traveling. It was a happier, more hopeful world than the one I saw on a recent journey around the globe. A terrible war to make the world safe for democracy had just ended victoriously. A noble concept, the League of Nations, had emerged from the chaotic aftermath of that elemental struggle. It was the twilight of kings, the dawn of world-wide democracy. Optimism was boundless and people proclaimed that we were on the threshold of the new era of universal and perpetual peace and prosperity.

It didn't turn out that way. It wasn't a threshold after all. Ernest Hemingway soon wrote: "I was always embarrassed by the words sacred, glorious, and sacrifice and the expression in vain. We had heard them, sometimes standing in the rain almost out of earshot, so that only the shouted words came through, and had read them, on proclamations that were slapped up by billposters over other proclamations, now for a long time, and I had seen nothing sacred, and the sacrifices were like the stockyards at Chicago if nothing was done with the meat except to bury it."

But I don't need to tell you, a generation that was born and nurtured in the depths of depression and came to consciousness in war and to maturity in the confusion of world revolution— I don't need to tell you that your elders have made something of a mess of things. Things didn't turn out as we had thought they would in 1922, and somehow the hope and easy confidence we felt dissolved as more and more the articulate and vocal among us doubted their beliefs and believed their doubts.

Nor do I need to enumerate for you in sepulchral tone the problems that you face. You know them only too well. Perhaps

173

you can solve them. I would not presume to tell you how to do it. This university has given you the tools with which to try. Moreover, even if I would guide you, I could not. What a man knows at fifty that he did not know at twenty is, for the most part, incommunicable. The laws, the aphorisms, the generalizations, the universal truths, the parables and the old saws—all of the observations about life which can be communicated handily in ready, verbal packages—are as well known to a man at twenty who has been attentive as to a man at fifty. He has been told them all, he has read them all, and he has probably repeated them all before he graduates from college; but he has not lived them all.

What he knows at fifty that he did not know at twenty boils down to something like this: The knowledge he has acquired with age is not the knowledge of formulas, or forms of words, but of people, places, actions—a knowledge not gained by words but by touch, sight, sound, victories, failures, sleeplessness, devotion, love—the human experiences and emotions of this earth and of oneself and other men; and perhaps, too, a little faith, and a little reverence for things you cannot see.

Nonetheless, I would speak to you not of the past, when my generation held its hopes so high, but rather of the future. And if I cannot advise you on how to solve the momentous problems of your future, perhaps I can venture to suggest some duties and, if you please, some rules of conduct that, it seems to me, devolve upon the educated man. I would speak, then, about the educated man and his government, and about the educated man and his university.

The political organization that goes by the name of the United States of America consists of no fewer than 155,000 governing units, school boards, conservation districts, municipalities, states, the nation, etc. It is operated by some one million elected officials, ranging from mosquito district trustee to President, and by some six million full-time employees. Our government is so large and so complicated that few understand it well and others barely understand it at all. Yet we must try to understand it and to make it function better.

For the power, for good or evil, of this American political organization is virtually beyond measurement. The decisions

174

which it makes, the uses to which it devotes its immense resources, the leadership which it provides on moral as well as material questions, all appear likely to determine the fate of the modern world.

All this is to say that your power is virtually beyond measurement. For it is to you, to your enlightened attention, that American government must look for the sources of its power. You dare not, if I may say so, withhold your attention. For if you do, if those young Americans who have the advantage of education, perspective, and self-discipline do not participate to the fullest extent of their ability, America will stumble, and if America stumbles the world falls.

You know that our record as citizens in recent years has been something less than perfect. Too often our citizens have ignored their duty to their government. Too often they have not even bothered to vote. But this is not all. Participating in government in a democracy does not mean merely casting a ballot on election day. It means much more than that. It means an attitude, a moral view, and a willingness to assume a day-to-day responsibility. How many good citizens do you know who constantly deplore waste, inefficiency, and corruption in government, and who also go out and ring doorbells for candidates they believe in? Not very many. Far more say, "Politics is dirty"—and that is about their only protest about the quality of government, and far more use the word "politician" as a term of opprobrium, disrespect, and dishonor—and this in the land of Washington, Jefferson, and Lincoln. How many respectable citizens do you know who protest loudly about the lawlessness and venality but don't hesitate to fix a traffic ticket? And then there are the unscrupulous for whom anything goes if it is within the letter of the law, or at least not too far outside; the numerous kind for whom legality and morality are synonyms. "The Fix" has become endemic in our political life.

I would remind you of an axiom of political science: People get the kind of government they deserve. Your public servants serve you right. Our American government may be defined, perhaps, as the government that really cares about the people. Just so, our government demands, it depends upon, the care and the devotion of the people.

Now it is sadly true that there are corrupt officials that don't get caught, if not as many perhaps as the cynical suspect. It is also true that there are at every level of our government able, patient, patriotic, devoted public servants, but all too often their reward is ingratitude, contumely, and lately even investigation. In years gone by we required only of our career servants, upon whom the successful operation of this huge mechanism of government depends, that they serve at a financial sacrifice and that they serve with little glory or public recognition. Increasingly, it appears, we also require them to run the risk of being branded as "subversive," "undesirable," as "security risks." It becomes increasingly hard to attract good men to government, and no wonder. Thoughtful men do not enjoy living in an atmosphere of constant guerrilla warfare and suspicion.

You who have spent four years on this campus know better than most people that your greatest satisfactions, your greatest rewards, resulted from the free interplay of ideas. You know that your most penetrating insights resulted from the exchange and the interchange and clash of ideas. And I would remind you that just as a great university cannot operate in any but an atmosphere of intellectual freedom, neither can a great government. It is the function of the democratic form of government to nurture freedom. No less does the democratic form of government require freedom as the condition in which it can function at all.

I would suggest, then, that it is the duty of an educated man in America today to work actively to put good men into public office—and to defend them there against abuse and the ugly inclination we as human beings have to believe the worst. I would suggest that it is not enough merely to vote but that we, all of us, have the further obligation to think, and to maintain steadfastly the rights of all men to think freely. It is always true that when the citizens of a democracy become apathetic, a power vacuum is created, and corrupt men, or incompetents or worse rush in to fill it. But today our situation is even more dangerous than that. In ordinary times the corrupt or the incompetent can be suffered for a while and then ejected. But these are no ordinary times. The world's fate now hangs upon how well or how ill we in America conduct our affairs. And if a bad man is elected trustee of a sanitary district, or if an able man in Washington is left to shift for himself in the face of unjustified attack, then our government is diminished by that much—and even more because others will lose heart from his example. So you as educated, privileged people have a broad responsibility to protect and improve what you have inherited and what you would die to preserve—the concept of government by consent of the governed as the only tolerable way of life.

We in our country have, indeed, placed all of our faith, we have placed all of our hopes, upon the education, the intelligence, and the understanding of our people. We have said that ours is a government conducted by its citizens, and from this it follows that the government will be better conducted if its citizens are educated. It's as simple as that. We believe that the people will find their way to the right solutions, given sufficient information. We believe with Lincoln, "Why should there not be a patient confidence in the ultimate justice of the people?" (although I must confess to having entertained certain private fleeting doubts upon occasion). We have bet all our chips, if you please, on the intellectual improvement of our people. This is a magnificent gamble—but it is a gamble, for it raises the question whether we have reached the awesome pinnacle of world power we now occupy too soon, before we have sufficiently elevated our national mind to lead the world wisely. Only the educated man entertains doubts, and doubt is the beginning of wisdom; but doubt is not wisdom's fulfillment, and in a time of crisis the man who doubts may fall prey to the strong dumb brute—to the man on horseback.

There is in the moiling masses of Asia a tremendous power, potentially the greatest power on earth, and today our enemies conspire to gain the mastery of this power. They have at their disposal, as we all know, a powerful weapon, for Communism is a perversion of the dream of justice. And while we see its leading attribute as the perversion, the illiterate, the toiling masses still have their eyes fixed on the dream.

We, too, have a powerful weapon, truth, and we gain our strength from our thoughtful citizenry, which seeks and holds the truth with both its heart and its mind. The question is, however, whether we have come to decisive responsibility too early, before we were ready, before we had matured sufficiently. No man can say with certainty. Personally I am optimistic and confident, but this question will not be answered tomorrow; it will be answered in your lifetime, and it will be answered in large part by you, the privileged American.

If I have made your tasks and your responsibilities sound formidable, which indeed they are, may I also remind you that this is what makes the prospects of your careers so exciting. There is a wonderful passage in Emerson—and happily I couldn't lay my hands on it—I'll spare you from it. I hope sometime you will read that essay. It says the time to live is not when everything is serene, but when all is tumult—when the old admits being compared with the new. This is the time of early morning, when it is fresh and exciting. I think this is your generation, I cannot be sure. Change is the order of life and difficulties its meat. You live in a time of historic change and of infinite difficulty. But do not let the difficulties distract you. Face the problems of your time you must, deal with them you must. But do not allow the alarms and excursions and partisanship of our political scene to distract you, do not let even the awful problems of the Atomic Age claim all your attention. Dare, rather, to live your lives fully, boldly; dare to study and to learn, to cultivate the mind and the spirit, even though it isn't fashionable in your community. For though our people become prosperous as never before and though our foreign policy triumphs, these things are but instruments of the proper purpose, the higher purpose, of Western man—the cultivation of the mind and of the spirit.

It would be presumptuous, and out of character, for me to lecture you about your spirit. That I must leave to wiser, and to better men. But perhaps you'll forgive me if I draw on what experiences I have had—I have not always been an unemployed politician, you know—to say a word about intelligence and experience as attributes of the good judgment you will need—the good sense, if you please.

Don't be afraid to learn; to read, to study, to work, to try to know, because at the very best you can know very little. And don't above all things be afraid to think for yourself. Nothing has been, in my judgment, more disheartening about the contemporary scene the last several years in America than the growth of the popularity of unreason—of anti-intellectualism. One thinks of those chanting, screaming crowds that walked over precipices in Germany—and not so long ago. The conformists abominate thought. Thinking implies disagreement and disagreement implies non-conformity and non-conformity implies heresy and heresy implies disloyalty. So obviously thinking must be stopped. This is the routine. But I say to you that bawling is not a substitute for thinking and that reason is not the subversion but the salvation of freedom. And don't be afraid of unpopular positions, of driving upstream. All progress has resulted from people who took unpopular positions. All change is the result of a change in the contemporary state of mind. Don't be afraid of being out of tune with your environment, and above all pray God that you are not afraid to live, to live hard and fast. To my way of thinking it is not the years in your life but the life in your years that count in the long run. You'll have more fun, you'll do more and you'll get more, you'll give more satisfaction the more you know, the more you have worked, and the more you have lived. For yours is a great adventure at a stirring time in the annals of men.

"University" is a proud, a noble and ancient word. Around it cluster all of the values and the traditions which civilized people have for centuries prized more highly. The idea which underlies this university—any university—is greater than any of its physical manifestations; its classrooms, its laboratories, its clubs, its athletic plant, even the particular groups of faculty and students who make up its human element as of any given time. What is this idea? It is that the highest condition of man in this mysterious universe is the freedom of the spirit. And it is only truth that can set the spirit free.

The function of a university is, then, the search for truth and its communication to succeeding generations. Only as that function is performed steadfastly, conscientiously, and without interference, does the university realize its underlying purpose. Only so does the university keep faith with the great humanist tradition of which it is a part. Only so does it merit the honorable name that it bears.

When you depart, think occasionally upon your university's inherent ideas and purposes, as its outward trappings recede. Don't forget that Princeton is a university, as well as *your* university; and that it has obligations to the whole of mankind not just to you—obligations which it can neither ignore nor shirk, and which cannot, consistently with its honorable name and its place in the community of scholarship, be sacrificed to passing passions and prejudices.

The right to the serene pursuit of truth did not descend like manna from heaven; it was won by hard fighting, and the fight goes on and on to the end of time—even as the struggle between good and evil. In this continuing battle for freedom, Princeton and her sister universities are at the farthest front, and so should you be who are Princeton's children. As the archive of the Western mind, as the keeper of Western culture, the university has an obligation to transmit from one generation to the next the heritage of freedom—for freedom is the foundation of Western culture. As graduates of this university, as individuals who have made in it an investment of the golden, irretrievable years of your lives, you have an obligation to oppose the efforts of anyone, for whatever reason or in the service of whatever interest, to divert Princeton or any sister institution from her classic objective. If you are to be true to your democratic traditions and realize your own best selves you cannot, I suggest, do less.

And I hope you will carry away with you some of the wise serenity of the timeless courage, the unhurried objectivity which is the atmosphere of Princeton and which represents the collective imprint of its founders, students, and teachers who have gone before you.

I came here last night in darkness, after an absence of four or five years. I came with an old friend, an old classmate. We drove a little through the campus, after dusk. It was soft, the air fresh with the beginning of spring. I thought of some words that I read here long ago, written by the English poet, Alfred Noyes, who stayed for a time on the Princeton campus. They went something like this if I am not mistaken:

> Now lamp-lit gardens in the blue dusk shine
> Through dog-wood red and white,

And round the gray quadrangles, line by line,
  The windows fill with light,
Where Princeton calls to Magdalen, tower to tower,
  Twin lanthorns of the law,
And those cream-white magnolia boughs embower
  The halls of old Nassau.*

Sentimental? Yes. Nostalgic? Perhaps. Yet beautiful, true. Your days are short here; this is the last of your springs. And now in the serenity and quiet of this lovely place, touch the depths of truth, feel the hem of Heaven. You will go away with old, good friends. And don't forget when you leave why you came.

* From *Collected Poems*, Volume III, by Alfred Noyes. Copyright, 1913, 1941, by Alfred Noyes. Reprinted by permission of Mr. Noyes and the publishers, J. B. Lippincott Company and William Blackwood & Sons.

Women, Husbands, and History

COUNTLESS commencement speakers are rising these days on countless platforms all over the world to tell thousands of helpless young captives how important they are—as citizens in a free society, as educated, rational, privileged participants in a great historic crisis. But for my part I want merely to tell you young ladies that I think there is much you can do about that crisis in the humble role of housewife—which, statistically, is what most of you are going to be whether you like the idea or not just now—and you'll like it!

To explain what I mean I must ask you to step a long way back and recall with me that over vast periods of history and over most of the globe the view has prevailed that man is no more than a unit in the social calculus. Tribal life—the way of life pursued by man for by far the longest period of his history, of which there are many remnants today in Africa—knows no individuals, only groups with disciplines and group sanctions. But then at a certain point in time and place there took place the most momentous revolution yet achieved by mankind—a revolution compared with which such achievements as the discovery of fire or the invention of the wheel seem modest. In the origins of our Western civilization, among two small peoples of the eastern Mediterranean, the Greeks and the Jews, the great Copernican revolution of politics began: the discovery that the state exists for man, not man for the state, and that the individual human personality, spirit, soul—call it what you will—contains within itself the meaning and measure of existence and carries as a result the full range of responsibility and choice.

Once the Greek vision of reason and the Jewish concept of moral choice had sent man forth onto the stage of history in

From an address at the Smith College Commencement, Northampton, Massachusetts, June 6, 1955.

this new guise of self-determination and responsibility, clearly only one form of society would provide a framework for the new energies and capacities that could now be released. That form of society is the free society upon which the peoples of the West have been engaged for the last two thousand years, with disasters and setbacks, with triumphs and tragedies, with long sweeps of history's pendulum between the extreme of freedom and tyranny, of individualism and collectivism, of rationalism and spiritualism.

The peoples of the West are still struggling with the problems of a free society and, just now, are in dire trouble. For to create a free society is at all times a precarious and audacious experiment. Its bedrock is the concept of man as an end in himself, as the ultimate reason for the whole apparatus of government, and the institutions of free society fulfill their task only in so far as this primary position of the free citizen— the *homo liber et legalis*—is not lost to sight. But violent pressures are constantly battering away at this concept, reducing man once again to subordinate status, limiting his range of choice, abrogating his responsibility, and returning him to his primitive status of anonymity in the social group. And it is to these pressures in their contemporary forms that I want to call your attention because I think you can be more helpful in identifying, isolating, and combating these pressures, this virus, than you girls perhaps today realize.

As you have learned here at Smith, science, among other things, arose out of the disintegration of feudal society and the rebirth of individualism in the Reformation and the Renaissance. As the individual mind was released from medieval bondage, as reason again became the test of faiths, the processes of free inquiry opened vast new fields of knowledge and human endeavor. There followed an almost explosive expansion of mental horizons. Science, born of freedom, and technology, born of science, grew by leaps and bounds into a giant of power and complexity. Certainly the material well-being of Western man was advanced with a speed and to an extent never before seen on earth. And there were great spiritual advances.

But, as always, history's pendulum swung too far, this time toward the extreme of social fragmentation, of individualism, of abstract intellectualism. And it seems to me that the very process which, in the name of individual liberty, disintegrated the old order—this very process has developed into a powerful drive toward the precise opposite of individualism, namely totalitarian collectivism.

Let me put it this way! Individualism promoted technological advances, technology promoted increased specialization, and specialization promoted an ever-closer economic interdependence between specialties. The more intense the specialization, the more complete the interdependence of the specialties—and this necessity of interdependence constitutes a powerful economic drive toward that extreme of a machine state in which individual freedom is wholly submerged.

As the old order disintegrated into this confederation of narrow specialties, each pulling in the direction of *its particular* interest, the individual person tended to become absorbed—literally—by *his particular* function in society. Having sacrificed wholeness of mind and breadth of outlook to the demands of their specialities, individuals no longer responded to social stimuli as total human beings: rather they reacted in partial ways as members of an economic class, or industry, or profession whose concern was with some limited self-interest.

Thus this typical Western man—or typical Western husband!—operates well in the realm of means, as the Romans did before him. But outside his specialty, in the realm of ends, he is apt to operate poorly or not at all. And this neglect of the cultivation of more mature values can only mean that his life, and the life of the society he determines, will lack valid purpose, however busy and even profitable it may be.

And here's where you come in: to restore valid, meaningful purpose to life in your home; to beware of instinctive group reaction to the forces which play upon you and yours; to watch for and arrest the constant gravitational pulls to which we are all exposed, your workaday husband especially, in our specialized, fragmented society that tends to widen the breach between reason and emotion, between means and ends.

And let me also remind you that you will live, most of you, in an environment in which "facts," the data of the senses, are

184

glorified, and value judgments are assigned inferior status as mere "matters of opinion." It is an environment in which art is often regarded as an adornment of civilization rather than a vital element of it, while philosophy is not only neglected but deemed faintly disreputable, because "it never gets you anywhere." Even religion, you will find, commands a lot of earnest allegiance that is more verbal than real, more formal than felt.

You may be hitched to one of these creatures we call "Western man," and I think part of your job is to keep him Western, to keep him truly purposeful, to keep him whole. In short—while I have had very little experience as a wife or mother—I think one of the biggest jobs for many of you will be to frustrate the crushing and corrupting effects of specialization, to integrate means and ends, to develop that balanced tension of mind and spirit which can be properly called "integrity."

This assignment for you, as wives and mothers, has great advantages. In the first place, it is home work—you can do it in the living room with a baby in your lap, or in the kitchen with a can opener in your hands. If you're really clever, maybe you can even practice your saving arts on that unsuspecting man while he's watching television. And, secondly, it is important work worthy of you, whoever you are, or your education, whatever it is—even Smith College—because we will defeat totalitarian, authoritarian ideas only by better ideas; we will frustrate the evils of vocational specialization only by the virtues of intellectual generalities. Since Western rationalism and Eastern spiritualism met in Athens and that mighty creative fire broke out, collectivism in various forms has collided with individualism time and again. This twentieth-century collision, this "crisis" we are forever talking about, will be won at last not on the battlefield but in the head and heart.

If the Colosseum at Rome is, as some say, the symbol of Roman failure to integrate mind and spirit, or means and ends, the hydrogen bomb, we might say, is the symbol of our own very similar self-betrayal. And one may hope that Hiroshima, like Rome's bloody arena, may be remembered at some distant day as a scene symbolizing a new beginning for mankind.

So you see, I have some rather large notions about you young ladies and what you have to do to rescue us wretched slaves of specialization and group thinking from further shrinkage and contraction of mind and spirit. But you will have to be alert or you may get caught yourself—even in the kitchen or the nursery—by the steady pressures with which you will be surrounded.

And now that I have dared to suggest what you should do about your husbands and friends, I am, recklessly, going to even make some suggestions about your children as well.

In the last fifty years, so much of our thinking has been in terms of institutional reform—reform of the economic system, social security, the use and misuse of government, international co-operation, etc. All this thinking has been necessary and salutary, but somewhere along the line the men and women whose personalities and potentialities will largely determine the spirit of such institutions have been lost to sight. Worse than that, we have even evolved theories that the paramount aim of education and character formation is to produce citizens who are "well adjusted" to their institutional environment, citizens who can fit painlessly into the social pattern.

While I am not in favor of maladjustment, I view this cultivation of neutrality, this breeding of mental neuters, this hostility to eccentricity and controversy, with grave misgiving. One looks back with dismay at the possibility of a Shakespeare perfectly adjusted to bourgeois life in Stratford, a Wesley contentedly administering a county parish, George Washington going to London to receive a barony from George III, or Abraham Lincoln prospering in Springfield with nary a concern for the preservation of the crumbling Union.

But in this decisive century it seems to me that we need not just "well-adjusted," "well-balanced" personalities, not just better groupers and conformers (to casually coin a couple of fine words) but more idiosyncratic, unpredictable characters (that rugged frontier word "ornery" occurs to me); people who take open eyes and open minds out with them into the society which they will share and help to transform.

But before any of you gallant girls swear any mighty oaths about fighting the shriveling corruptions and conformations of mind and spirit, before you adopt any rebellious resolutions for the future, make no mistake about it—it is much easier to get yourself and yours adjusted and to accept the conditioning

186

which so many social pressures will bring to bear upon you. After all tribal conformity and archaic dictatorship could not have lasted so long if they did not accord comfortably with basic human needs and desires. The modern dictators are reviving a very ancient and encrusted way of life. Hitler discovered this. The Fascists knew it. The Communists are busy brainwashing all over Asia. And what they are washing out is precisely independence of judgment and the moral courage with which to back such judgments. And there are, alas!, some leaders in our country who certainly have a brainwashing glint in their eye when they meet with an unfamiliar idea.

Now, as I have said, women, especially educated women such as you, have a unique opportunity to influence us, man and boy, and to play a direct part in the unfolding drama of our free society. But I am told that nowadays the young wife or mother is short of time for the subtle arts, that things are not what they used to be; that once immersed in the very pressing and particular problems of domesticity many women feel frustrated and far apart from the great issues and stirring debates for which their education has given them understanding and relish. Once they read Baudelaire. Now it is the *Consumers' Guide*. Once they wrote poetry. Now it's the laundry list. Once they discussed art and philosophy until late in the night. Now they are so tired they fall asleep as soon as the dishes are finished. There is, often, a sense of contraction, of closing horizons and lost opportunities. They had hoped to play their part in the crisis of the age. But what they do is wash the diapers.

Now, I hope I have not painted too depressing a view of your future, for the fact is that Western marriage and motherhood are yet another instance of the emergence of individual freedom in our Western society. Their basis is the recognition in women as well as men of the primacy of personality and individuality. I have just returned from Africa where the illiteracy of the mothers is an obstacle to child education and advancement and where polygamy and female labor is still the dominant system. The common sight on the road is an African striding along swinging his stick or his spear, while a few feet behind comes the wife with a load of firewood on her head, a baby on her back and dragging a couple more children by the hand.

The point is that whether we talk of Africa, Islam, or Asia, women "never had it so good" as you do. And in spite of the difficulties of domesticity you have a way to participate actively in the crisis in addition to keeping yourself and those about you straight on the difference between means and ends, mind and spirit, reason and emotion—not to mention keeping your man straight on the differences between Botticelli and Chianti.

In brief if one of the chief needs in these restless times is for a new quality of mind and heart, who is nearer to the care of this need, the cultivation of this quality, than parents, especially mothers, who educate and form the new generation?

So, add to all of your concerns for Western man, your very special responsibility for Western children. In a family based upon mutual respect, tolerance, and understanding affection, the new generation of children—the citizens of tomorrow—stand their best chance of growing up to recognize the fundamental principle of free society—the uniqueness and value and wholeness of each individual human being. For this recognition requires discipline and training. The first instinct of all our untutored egos is to smash and grab, to treat the boy next door as a means not an end when you pinch his air rifle, or deny the uniqueness of your small sister's personality when you punch her in the stomach and snatch her lollipop.

Perhaps this is merely to say that the basis of any tolerable society—from the small society of the family up to the great society of the State—depends upon its members learning to love. By that I do not mean sentimentality or possessive emotion. I mean the steady recognition of others' uniqueness and a sustained intention to seek their good. In this, freedom and charity go hand in hand and they both have to be learned. Where better than in the home? And by whom better than the parents, especially the mother?

In short, far from the vocation of marriage and motherhood leading you away from the great issues of our day, it brings you back to their very center and places upon you an infinitely deeper and more intimate responsibility than that borne by the majority of those who hit the headlines and make the news and live in such a turmoil of great issues that they end by being totally unable to distinguish which issues are really great.

Yet you may say that these functions of the home could have been as well fulfilled without your years of study, performed perhaps better by instinct and untroubled by those hints of broader horizons and more immortal longings which it is the purpose of a college education to instill.

Well, there are two things to say to that. The first, of course, is that in modern America the home is not the boundary of a woman's life. There are outside activities aplenty. But even more important is the fact, surely, that what you have learned here can fit you as nothing else can for the primary task of making homes and whole human beings in whom the rational values of freedom, tolerance, charity, and free inquiry can take root. You have learned discrimination. You have the tolerance which comes from the realization of man's infinite variety. Because you have learned from history the pathos and mutability of human affairs, you have a sense of pity. From literature you have learned the abiding values of the human heart and the discipline and sacrifice from which those values will flower in your own hearts and in the life of your families.

There can be no waste of any education that gives you these things. But you can waste them, or you can use them. I hope you'll use them. I hope you'll not be content to wring your hands, feed your family, and just echo all the group, the tribal ritual refrain. I hope you'll keep everlastingly at the job of seeing life steady and seeing it whole. And you can help others —husbands, children, friends—to do so too. You may, indeed you must, help to integrate a world that has been falling into bloody pieces. History's pendulum has swung dangerously far away from the individual, and you may, indeed you must, help to restore it to the vital center of its arc.

Long ago at the origins of our way of life it was written of a valiant woman in the Book of Proverbs:

Strength and beauty are her clothing; and she shall laugh in the latter day. She hath opened her mouth to wisdom and the law of clemency is on her tongue; she hath looked well to the paths of her house and hath not eaten her bread idle. Her children rose up and called her blessed; her husband and he praised her.

I could wish you no better vocation than that. I could wish a free society no better hope for the future. And I could wish you no greater riches and rewards.

FIVE

America and the World

Traveler's Report

FOR SIX months I have traveled across this vast and troubled world, for tens of thousands of miles—which were just as exhausting as the campaign, but I didn't encounter as much opposition! My mind is filled with recollections of people I talked with from Syngman Rhee and the Emperor of Japan, to Pope Pius and Queen Elizabeth; of the sights I've seen, moving and beautiful, sordid and sickening; of the rugged front in ravaged Korea where, pray God, the strife has stopped for keeps; of the ugly war in the wet, green rice paddies of Indo-China where Communism, masquerading as nationalism, imperils the whole of southeast Asia; and of millions of refugees huddled in squalid camps and hovels stretching from Korea across Asia to western Europe—remnants of many more victims of the wars, revolutions, intolerance and savagery that have cursed our time on earth.

A trip like mine is a sobering experience. It is more than a privilege, it is a responsibility to be an American in this world. It isn't one world; it's more like three worlds—the allied world, the Communist world, and the uncommitted world. Almost a billion people live along the route I took in 1953. Most of them live in Asia and most of the so-called uncommitted peoples live in Asia. They don't belong to the white minority of the human race, and tragically many of them are poor, undernourished, and illiterate.

Asia is in revolution. Civilizations are very old, but political independence is very young. In the new states the economies are shaky, public administration is weak; and they are hungry and poor, sensitive and proud. Nationalism is rampant. And the West, identified with the hated colonialism, is suspect.

From an address at the Civic Opera House, Chicago, September 15, 1953.

193

Utterly preoccupied with their own overwhelming problems, they see little of the world conflict and don't appreciate America's global responsibilities. They know from experience a lot about feudalism, landlords, money lenders, and oppressors, and the theories of Karl Marx sound pretty good to many of them, who know surprisingly little about the ugly realities of Communism in practice. Nor is there the perception one would expect of the menace of international Communism as a new imperialism.

There is little tradition of democracy in these new states, but independence, won at long last, is a passion, which partly accounts in some quarters for their opaque view of Communist China where to many Asians it appears that the foreigners have been thrown out and the ignominy of centuries erased by Asians. There is reverent admiration for the ideas of the American Revolution, the Bill of Rights, and the great utterances of human freedom. But they think they see contradictions in waves of conformity and fear here at home, and hypocrisy in our alliances with the colonial powers and professed devotion to freedom and self-determination.

The ideological conflict in the world doesn't mean much to the masses. Anti-Communist preaching wins few hearts. They want to know what we are for, not just what we are against. And in nations like India, Indonesia, and Burma they don't accept the thesis that everyone has to choose sides, that they have to be for us or against us. Nor do I believe that we should press alliances on unwilling allies. After all, we had a long record of neutrality and non-involvement ourselves, and the important thing is that such nations keep their independence and don't join the hostile coalition.

But in spite of all their doubts and difficulties I was impressed by the devotion of the leaders of Asia to the democratic idea of government by consent rather than force, and by the decisive manner in which so many of the new countries of Asia have dealt with violent Communist insurrections and conspiracies. Their revolutions have not produced Utopia and they are struggling with infinite difficulties to raise living standards and satisfy the rising tide of expectations. They want rice and respect, and they want to believe in wondrous America that sends friendly, earnest people to help them, and that believes in them, and the aspirations of all God's children for peace, dignity, and freedom.

We are on the eve of great decisions in Asia. Korea is the first step. Personally I have been skeptical of Red China's intentions, but when we search for settlements we have to *search,* and when we negotiate we have to have something to negotiate *with* as well as *for.* Many of our friends think China wants peace and trade above all, as they themselves do. With so much at stake in Asia—the unification of Korea, Formosa, peace and security in Indo-China—it would seem to me that we owe it to ourselves as well as to our friends at least to find out, if we can, what Communist China's ultimate intentions are.

If I may risk a prophecy, the hostile world is going to pay more and more attention to Asia, especially huge, uncommitted India. And I suspect that as Europe's Eastern empires shrink, there will be left to us more of the burden of defense and of helping to guide the great forces which great changes have unleashed in Asia.

The Middle East is largely a power and defense vacuum, except for doughty little Israel and tough, strong Turkey. Peace is imperative in the Middle East—peace between the Arab states and Israel, which is engaged in an historic effort to provide refuge and new hope to oppressed people.

In Europe, the recovery since the war is spectacular. In western Germany it looks ironically as though the vanquished were better off than the victors. In France the progress has not kept pace; there is grave social unrest and political frustration which can be remedied and will be, pray Heaven, by heroic measures. Among Frenchmen the conviction is growing that France can no longer maintain the defense effort in Europe, fight Communism in Indo-China with weapons and at home with larger social and economic expenditures, all at the same time. We should bear in mind that many Frenchmen vote Communist not from conviction, but in protest. Hence the increasing clamor to get out of Indo-China altogether and spend more on housing, industrial development, and social betterment at home.

The most urgent problem in Europe today is, of course, Germany: how to channel its developing strength and resources into paths that will benefit both Europe and the world, how to resolve the age-old rivalries of France and Germany, and how to satisfy the intense German desire for reunification, whetted by the gallant workers' revolt of June, 1953, in the Soviet Zone, which exhilarated the whole free world.

In short, the difficulties are many and the hazards great everywhere. But things are better. There is hope in the air, born of America's postwar policy of assistance and resistance, of growing strength and self-confidence, and of Stalin's death followed by shifting winds from Moscow, truce in Korea, rebellion in eastern Europe, troubles behind the iron curtain.

But the world is weary; there is universal anxiety and impatience to ease the tensions, to explore every possibility of settlements by conference and negotiation. The Soviet will exploit discord in our ranks at every opportunity in order to divide and enfeeble the grand alliance of the free. There is uncertainty abroad about America and our objective. Is our objective to discover through negotiation ways to relax tensions, or is it intensification of the cold war; is it coexistence or extermination of Communist power?

Some of the misunderstandings may seem incredible to us, but it is well to try to see ourselves as others see us. Many think we are intemperate, inflexible, and frightened. And people who have lived in insecurity for centuries don't understand how there can be insecurity and fear in America which has never been bombed or lived in thralldom. Also, like ourselves, proud nations resent any real or suspected interference in their domestic affairs. Nor can they reconcile our exhortations about the peril with deep cuts in our defense budget. And everywhere people think they recognize the dominant mood of America in what is called "McCarthyism," now a world-wide word. Inquisitions, purges, book-burning, repression, and fear have obscured the bright vision of the land of the free and the home of the brave.

Most of our friends want and need trade, not aid. There is an uneasy feeling that the United States is showing signs of economic nationalism, of a drift toward no trade and no aid. But our friends must trade to live, and not many are going to go hungry, I suspect, to prove to us just how anti-Communist they are.

196

Just as there are many misconceptions about us, we have many illusions about others, and one of them is that irritations, doubts, and disagreements are symbols of ingratitude or anti-Americanism. Some hostile feeling is inevitable, particularly in occupied areas, but I found surprisingly little. Misgivings about our wisdom, unity, and clear purpose, yes, but also widespread admiration and gratitude for our faith and fortitude, and prayerful hopes for the sobriety, good judgment, and moral vitality of American leadership. At my journey's end Winston Churchill said to me with emotion: "America has saved the world."

Our foreign assistance programs have succeeded, especially in Europe. They have cost us dearly, but I bless the day when President Truman went to the aid of Greece and Turkey and commenced the Marshall Plan. Stronger, more self-reliant, our friends are feeling more independent of Washington, and are talking back to us now, which seems to me a healthy sign.

I think we are winning the cold war step by step. The spread of Communism has been arrested. And while Moscow has military potency, the Communist idea has diminishing appeal, at least in Europe.

But though the imminent danger has receded, this is no time to wobble or lower our guards, not with the hydrogen bomb and no certain evidence that the seductive music from Moscow reflects any basic change in the Soviet design of world dominion. And it is no time for arrogance, petulance, or inflexibility either.

If I am not mistaken, holding our allies together is going to be an ever-harder job which will tax mightily our patience, resolve, and statesmanship. For we can't "go it alone." Unilateralism is but the new face of isolationism and it spells disaster.

Looking to the future, it seemed to me clearer than ever that the economic, military, and political integration of Europe is the best hope for balancing Soviet power and for enabling the states of Europe to exercise a powerful, positive, and peaceful influence in the modern world. We have already invested years of effort and encouragement and billions of dollars toward this bold and imaginative end.

We must surmount a thicket of difficulty; we must bring the discussion back to the level where once again it challenges the imagination and the hopes of all Europe.

We must now think afresh; and, I believe, in terms of a European system of durable assurances of non-aggression—for Russia, as well as for France, Germany and the rest of us. But whatever commitments we make to our European allies to buttress such assurances we must be prepared to make on a long-term basis. For there is anxiety lest the shaping of our policy may be slipping from the respected hands of President Eisenhower into the hands of men less concerned with strengthening our alliances abroad than with appeasing our isolationists at home.

And at this moment a new fact confers a grim and pressing urgency on the international situation—the hydrogen bomb. For some years efforts toward the limitation and control of armaments have been stalemated. Once more, I think, we should fix our sights high, as we did in 1947, and resume the initiative in re-exploring the possibility of disarmament. The alternative to safety through an effective plan for arms limitation is safety through more massive military spending and more frightening weapons development.

As it is, we seem now to be taking the initiative in unilateral disarmament. We've tried that before, and I am as opposed to unilateralism in our disarmament policy as I am in our foreign policy.

In the past, new initiatives have had little impact on the Kremlin. I do not know that they would have any more today. But conditions have changed. The Soviet threat has aroused the massed military power of the free peoples. Russia learned in Korea that the West has the will to meet force with force. The death of Stalin and revolt in the satellites altered the situation inside the Soviet Union.

In these circumstances we should press forward—not under any foolish illusion that one grand conference would yield security, but rather with realistic recognition that the foundations of stability must be laid, stone by stone, with patient persistence. We owe it to ourselves and our anxious, weary friends to expose Communist intentions if we can; to confer when we can; to reduce tensions and restore hope where we

198

can. The door to the conference room is the door to peace. Let it never be said that America was reluctant to enter.

Under our Constitution, foreign policy is the responsibility of the Executive. The Democrats in Congress have shown that they are eager to help the President carry out an effective foreign policy, restore the leadership of America, and give fresh inspiration and confidence to the great alliance which is indispensable to our security. If it brings the President great personal success we will all rejoice, because the nation and the free world will be the beneficiaries.

And, finally, we must bear in mind that the world's troubles do not all spring from aggressive Communism. Many of them would be here anyway, and always will be. The quest for peace and tranquillity isn't a day's work, it is everlasting. We will have to learn to think of the responsibility of leadership not as a passing annoyance but as a status in an interdependent world that we Americans, Democrats and Republicans alike, must live in, trade in, work in, and pray for, in the accents of mercy, justice, and faith in a power greater than ours or any man's.

We may be approaching the end of the first phase of this era—stopping the spread and influence of Communism. Will strength and perseverance prevail in the second phase and the great threat wither? We haven't the resources to remedy all the ills of man. And we can't remake the world in our image and likeness. But we have erected here in the United States man's happiest home. Respect for our own principles and the courage to live by them, at home and abroad, will be a potent force in the world, and, in the long run, our greatest contribution to a world in which peace is a prayer.

War, Weakness, and Ourselves

WHAT, I am asked, are the greatest perils for America today? By "America," I suppose we all think of not *just* the real estate or inhabitants of the United States, but also of the idea that we who live here share and cherish in common—the concept of government by the free consent of the governed as the only tolerable system of management of human affairs. When we think of dangers to America, I suppose we think not alone of our lives and fortunes, but also of freedom to choose and change our political structure, our economic structure, and our rulers as we, the people, collectively, see fit; freedom under our laws to give and think and speak as we, the people, individually see fit; in short—freedom.

For *that* America, it seems to me, the greatest perils today are war, weakness, and ourselves.

I say *war* because it is the everlasting and ever more destructive curse of mankind. I say *weakness* because these are dangerous times; the world is in revolution, and we of the West and our democratic ideas are besieged. I say *ourselves* because of an ebbing of the essential quality of self-confidence in American life which has brought us to the first period of self-doubt in all our history.

First, the peril of war: There seem to be three kinds or intensities of war nowadays—total war with atom, hydrogen, or even cobalt bombs; total war without the use of weapons of mass extermination; and, finally, the regional or local war with which we have become familiar in China, Greece, Korea, and Indo-China.

In our divided world, hearts are cold, tempers hot, mistrust profound, and power delicately balanced. In this situation, any

Article in Look *Magazine, November, 1954.*

little war may rapidly grow to encompass the world. Indeed, the doctrine of "massive retaliation" solemnly proclaimed by our own Secretary of State and Vice-President seemed to put the United States in the position of renouncing little wars in favor of big wars without restriction to scope or weapons.

Manifestly, such foolish talk did not frighten our enemies, who promptly increased their pressure in Indo-China, but the suggestion of devastating war by remote control from the United States certainly appalled our friends, who would be the first victims of massive *counter*-retaliation.

The fact is that since Russia exploded her first atomic bomb in 1949, any real security in our monopoly of such weapons has vanished. Nor is there much security in a vast superiority of nuclear weapons, assuming we have such superiority and can maintain it. For as long as the enemy can deliver *any* atomic blows to our country by aircraft, agent, or submarine, he can do us grievous injury—injury which could not be healed by the heavier blows we might strike in retaliation. And, of course, the damage Russia could do our allies, who are not thousands of miles across the Arctic, but next door, is obvious and is one of the reasons for the dread of Europeans that a rash America may drag them into another global conflict.

Maybe, with superior bombs and planes, we could knock out the enemy first, but how much of the world would become uninhabitable as a result? The massive use of nuclear weapons may well prove as dangerous to the victor as to the victim. Large quantities of radioactive elements loose in the world won't respect boundaries or distinguish between friend and foe.

Surely, no physical peril greater than atomic war has confronted mortal man since the Flood. And surely, too, it is foolish to think that a few well-placed mass-extermination bombs could be the swift and certain ambassadors of peace and tranquillity—especially when dispatched to an enemy having the same instruments of genocide.

But just because of the frightfulness and futility of trading atomic blows, even unequal blows, it seems probable that we will reach, perhaps we already have reached, an effectual atomic stalemate. The fears of friend and foe to the contrary notwithstanding, the United States will never be an aggressor and will not launch preventive war. Someone else will have to start it, so is it not likely that ambitious foes will carefully count the cost of precipitating mass extermination with all the grim and lingering consequences to animal and vegetable life on this planet? The malign weapons of bacterial and chemical warfare were not used in the last world war by tacit agreement. So now, it seems not unlikely that today's much greater threats to the human race may likewise not be used. But after what we have seen of the ravenous appetite of Communist imperialism, how can we be sure what the enemy will do? Which is precisely what *they* are saying about us, abetted by the belligerent pronouncements of some of our louder and lighter leaders.

Yet the possibility, as well as the prayer, that the weapons of ultimate catastrophe may not be used brings me to the peril of general war without such weapons, whether by mutual forbearance or by atomic disarmament, which seems the only sensible course for all of us. After the last two wars, it is incredible that we can talk about them with a sense of comparative relief, indeed nostalgia, for the good old-fashioned way. We call it war with "conventional" weapons. But we— and the enemy likewise, we must assume—have been busily developing guided missiles, atomic cannon and submarines and all manner of new weapons in addition to atom and hydrogen bombs. The next "conventional" world war would not be conventional at all in terms of the last one, even as the last one was unlike the previous one. It is well to remember our horror and revulsion when the Nazis opened the last war with the new methods of the blitz and mass murder. And it ended with far more devastating bombings of the cities of Germany and Japan, where they are still sweeping up the rubble nine years later.

It would seem, then, that "total war" is but a delicate euphemism for total destruction, and that it makes little difference, except in the degree of totality and the rapidity of incineration, whether it is done by conventional or nuclear means.

And, finally, we must all have learned, even the tyrants, that in another total war—with or without unleashing all the demons locked in the atom—there can be no victors, only survivors.

But in local limited warfare, apparently, there still can be victories after a fashion. The guerrillas from within or without who tried to deliver Greece and the eastern Mediterranean to the Communists were crushed at long last. In Korea, cynical aggression was repulsed by the United States and United Nations forces. And Ho Chi Minh and the Communists have scored a great victory at the expense of the new state of Vietnam and the free non-Communist world.

We cannot yet accurately measure the cost of the defeat in Indo-China. At first, the President said he "could conceive of no greater tragedy" than for us to get involved there. But a little later, when our government was considering armed intervention and calling for "united action," our officials described Vietnam as of "transcendent importance," and its loss as the "prelude to the loss of all southeast Asia." Two months later, however, when "united action" had failed and Dien Bien Phu had fallen, official language changed again, Vietnam became more expendable and the loss was minimized.

The fact is, of course, that the loss of rice-rich Tonkin and some eleven million people dangerously enfeebles the rest of Vietnam and thrusts an advanced base for aggressive Communism well into southeast Asia. But there is little point in speculating on the magnitude of the disaster in Indo-China. If it increases Asian awareness that Communism is the new imperialism and the real menace to their new-found freedoms, if it serves to accelerate Asian realism and defensive solidarity, it will not have been a total misfortune by any means. The reason for mentioning its implications is that they illustrate the peril for us in small wars as well as big ones. We can be nibbled to death as well as blown to death.

Just as war in any dimension is a danger to us, so is *weakness*. We know from long historical experience that only the strong can be free, and that a military vacuum offers a tempting target. And we have seen in China, and latterly in Indo-China, where the French and Vietnamese forces far outnumbered the Vietminh, that a country which lacks inner cohesion and the will to protect itself is vulnerable, regardless of its statistical military strength.

Measured by any such standards as military power, economic strength, and the will to defend ourselves, the United States is strong, perhaps stronger than ever before in peacetime. Why, then, do I list weakness as one of our greatest perils? Because Communism and nationalism, the two immense facts of this age, are world-wide, and therefore our means of dealing with these explosive forces must be measured in global dimensions. They must be measured in broader terms than America's muscle and money, for our strength and influence are compounded of other ingredients too—of vision, diplomatic skill, magnanimity, confidence, and, most of all, endurance in the long contest with tyranny which we call the cold war.

After the last war, the old empires of the West in Asia and the Middle East crumbled before the irresistible forces of nationalism, anti-colonialism, and independence. We Americans, who are the children of a nationalist revolution against a colonial master, should be the first to rejoice at the new freedom that has come to many people while others were losing theirs in eastern Europe. But I must also mention at least a few of the less joyous realities about the new independence. More and weaker national units have replaced the older, larger concentrations of power in the non-Communist world. Free Asians don't fully perceive that the real enemy is not the hated European imperialism of the past, but the new Communist imperialism of China and Russia.

The patronizing white man has several strikes on him in Asia, and, whatever our illusions, even we Americans are not universally loved or trusted. The appalling difficulties of these poor, proud peoples only enhance their respect for Russia's dramatic achievements in quickly industrializing a backward country. To many of them, it seems sensible to follow America's historical example and keep neutral while they try feverishly to change for the better, and overnight, conditions that have hardly changed for centuries.

Whether the new and undeveloped countries of the world with meager capital, skills, and experience can lift the level of their economies and satisfy the rising expectations of their

204

people by democratic, voluntary means is perhaps the most important issue of our times. For if they can't, they may turn to force, to totalitarianism, as the only answer.

I have not mentioned the bitterness in the Arab world, or the restiveness in Africa and the rumblings in South America. But I think it is clear that the Communists are fishing in vast and troubled waters. Everywhere, they exploit poverty, ignorance, discontent, and injustice, real or fancied. So it must be clear why in this weary, unheroic, endless competition, strength cannot be measured just by military power and money. Failure to understand and sympathize with this great revolution of rising expectations would be a mistake with incalculable consequences to America. We, the descendants of the first modern revolution for political freedom, must not let totalitarianism beat us in a contest of ideas among people who won their freedom more than a hundred and sixty years later.

To wean the uncommitted peoples from their democratic convictions is not, however, the only objective of our tireless foes. They intend to divide and destroy the coalition of the anti-Communist states by generating disunity, hoping to deal with us separately, and hoping to set one against another. To us, the preservation of our coalition is imperative, and it is facing severe strains these days.

In Germany, there is growing agitation for reunification even at the price of neutrality. Issues regarding Red China—the problems of trade, admission to the U.N., and China's status in international relations—are sources of conflict between us and our allies. They believe that it is possible to recognize a mortal enemy and yet negotiate with him, but that it is impossible to ignore, as we did at Geneva, the existence of a country numbering nearly a quarter of mankind and casting a shadow over half of us.

Many factors have contributed to a decline of late in confidence in American judgment and leadership. As a technique associated with totalitarianism, "McCarthyism" has deeply shocked our democratic friends. Coupled with the long series of empty slogans—"liberation," "unleashing Chiang," "seizing the initiative," "massive retaliation," the "new look"—the bluster and tough talk of some of our public figures suggest to our friends either that domestic politics has a priority over international responsibility, or that there is substance to the Russian propaganda that the United States is the real "aggressive" power. The talk about "trade, not aid," followed by tariff increases does not help. And large numbers of American servicemen with their families and high pay in many lands create inevitable tensions. No one acts as frightened of the Communists as we do. And it is irritating to British parents with a son fighting in the Malay jungle or to French parents with a son buried in Indo-China to be constantly told by Americans that they don't appreciate the Communist menace.

Confusion, inconsistency, and ineptitude have certainly not strengthened the coalition of late or enhanced respect for American leadership or partnership. The voice of authority in the United States is indistinct. Congressional leaders contradict administration leaders and the latter have contradicted each other. While rattling the saber and talking tough about rolling back the enemy, our government was cutting the military budget, disengaging American forces, and reducing taxes. The bluff in Indo-China didn't work. After all the bold, brash words and gestures, when the showdown came, America was impotent. Unable to fight, unable to negotiate, unable even to speak, the United States sat mute at the Geneva conference while the Moscow-Peiping axis called the tunes.

If the fabric of international security has unraveled a little, we are not, however, alone responsible. France has rejected EDC, on which we had banked so heavily—too heavily— and the hope for European integration has suffered a setback. Now the Russians and their collaborators will try to block any other plan to incorporate Germany in a western European framework. Whether due to misgivings about us, to the softer winds from Moscow, to weariness or what not, a mood of relief and complacency not unlike that of Munich seems to be emerging since the armistice in Indo-China. Some Europeans thought after Munich that Hitler could be trusted. Pray Heaven they have no such illusions today about Mao and Malenkov. While we pray for peace, real peace, there is no evidence yet that "peaceful coexistence" means to them any interruption in the cold war. Until that evidence is forthcoming in deeds as well as words, we dare not relax, lower our guard, or reduce our vigilance. Quite the contrary. Yet such seems to be the spirit and mood of some British leaders, and also of the neutralists and all the collaborators, conscious and unconscious. The short-term result can only be to sharpen and prolong dissension in the free world. The long-term result of false counsels and wishful thinking could be disastrous.

To meet the overwhelming demands of the nationalist revolution and to withstand the Communist imperialism will require great strength of mind and body and spirit. America dare not default, and that's why I say that weakness is one of our great perils.

Perhaps, in discussing the dangers of war and weakness, I have suggested the other peril that seems to plague us—self-doubt. The quality that is missing from our national life is self-confidence, the ebullient spirit that sustained us when, as a handful of colonials, we stood up to the greatest empire on earth and fought for our independence; when we hammered together on the forge of civil war a federal union dedicated to the rights of man; when we rolled back the frontier to unlock the mighty continent; when our sweat and genius earned the young republic first place among nations in the dawning industrial age; when twice we deployed our troops around the globe to halt the march of a tyrant's faceless armies.

In fact, we were successful for so long that we may have developed some unworthy, arrogant illusions that we are always right about everything and that we and our ideas must, of course, inevitably prevail.

Perhaps, in short, we are ill-prepared for adversity. But in our world, security, let alone victory, is not going to be cheap and easy. It is going to take years of patience, endurance, and understanding; of standing firm sometimes, of negotiating sometimes, of giving something to gain more, of fighting if we must, but, above all, of never, never—even under the most trying and frustrating conditions—losing faith or yielding to the counsels of impatience.

We who have been nourished on the blithe myth of invincibility, who have never been invaded in modern times, never lost a war, who have watched, from generation to generation, our curves of production and standards of living constantly rise, are suddenly waking to the fact that today we are not on the offensive, but the defensive—that we are no longer invincible or omnipotent—maybe not even omniscient. No wonder our confidence is shaken.

But will we who have never known national adversity lose our confidence and our way in these trying and troubled times? Are we in fact, as Professor Arnold Toynbee suggests, beginning the decline that has marked the course of all prior civilizations?

It would be fairly easy to make a case in support of such a thesis. One could point to the deterioration of our foreign relations; to irreconcilable political conflicts that inhibit formation of consistent long-term policy; to excessive partisanship, shameless demagoguery, and political expediency; to the cynical exploitation of fear for political advantage; to unawareness of the deep-cutting currents of change running everywhere in the world; and to a kind of schizophrenia that causes some rational Americans to turn away from the grave dangers without, while they chip away at our civil liberties within. Even conformity—thought control—has reappeared in our land just at a time when we are exhorting the world to stand fast against the tyrannies of Soviet Fascism. And it looks as though we were in more danger nowadays of exploitation of the mind than the body, of becoming mental robots than economic slaves, thanks to the new techniques of mass communication and mass manipulation.

But America's greatest contribution to human society has not been material, but rather the originality and diversity of her ideas—the moral sentiments of human liberty and human welfare written into the Declaration of Independence and the Bill of Rights by the grand original non-conformists.

The great weapon of democracy, of freedom, has been that it could hold its own in a free contest of ideas. Are we now trying to close the lists? We cannot, I submit, let anyone within our sovereign body persuade us that in order to protect our institutions we should abandon them. We cannot lose confidence in ourselves and keep the world's confidence.

It is, of course, a dangerous time to be alive. For it is a time of revolution, of transition from something known to something as yet unknown that may be very bad or very good. And over it all hangs the fearsome cloud of an atom split in anger. But these are facts of life that cannot be disposed of by querulous bickering over whose fault it is.

Can we meet the tests of this difficult time? Can we resolve the conflict between security and liberty? Can we challenge the dogmatic, rigid ideas of Communism with the flexible, liberal ideas of democracy? Can we halt the flight from freedom, head off the holocaust?

Of course we can, but not as fugitives from freedom, not by following the counsel of fearful men who seek certainties in an uncertain world, and panic when they cannot find them; who see change not as a challenge but as a threat; who seek salvation in a futile effort to hold back the hands of the clock of history; who dream of yesterday rather than tomorrow.

These men are not numerous, and never were; but they are persuasive—paticularly so when the people are weary after great exertions and anxious in the presence of new and un-familiar dangers.

But it is incredible that we should falter now, and take counsel of the fainthearted. Surely the spirit which met and mastered all the monstrous problems of our great and rapid growth will not today quail before any external threat. In times of crisis, it has always been our spiritual resources that have given us the courage to mobilize our material resources. "In God We Trust" is not just a slogan stamped on our media of material exchange, but the great affirmation of faith that has wrought the miracle of America.

No thoughtful man can ignore the drive of the belly, but no wise leader will make material self-interest paramount to the demands of the spirit—not here in America, where, time after time, we have pursued an ideal without measuring the cost to ourselves. As Elmer Davis said: "This republic was not estab-lished by cowards; and cowards will not preserve it."

Strong words, perhaps, but worth pondering by anyone who is reluctant to call upon Americans to face up to the con-tinuing perils of our times—and who therefore runs the far greater risk of seeing our world end, in T. S. Eliot's phrase, "not with a bang, but a whimper."

Israel and the Arabs:
Ancient Glory and New Opportunity

IT WAS just ten years ago when I was on a war mission in Europe that I dined alone one night with Dr. Chaim Weizmann in war-shattered London. It was the time of the V-2 rockets and the Nazis' last convulsion of violence. Victory in the West was drawing close. The blackout still lay heavy on London but the darkness was full of new hope. For hours I sat spellbound in his modest hotel rooms listening to a tired old man quietly recount exciting fragments from the past and dream vividly of the future of Zion. It was the year of his seventieth birthday and the year of the beginning of the concept of what is now called the Weizmann Institute. He talked of how applied science could help new settlers in a new homeland earn a living; how the absorptive capacity of Palestine could be enlarged to accommodate many more by the development of new opportunities in industry and agriculture. But he also talked of the spirit that would unite the ingathered outcasts of the world— the spirit of freedom, of intellectual liberty.

The free pursuit of knowledge, the free exercise of the mind, the free exploration of the riddles of nature and of human nature—these are the prerequisites of every other kind of freedom. And I think I understand better now, since I have been to Israel, what Dr. Weizmann was dreaming aloud that night in war-hushed London—that it was inconceivable that the Jewish people who had upheld their intellectual traditions in spite of centuries of bondage, humiliation, and discrimination should now submit to the most destructive tyranny of all— voluntary ignorance.

Almost nine years later I visited the Weizmann Institute at

From an address before the American Committee for the Weizmann Institute, New York, December 2, 1954.

Rehovoth during a visit to Israel and there I met and talked with the Institute's scientists, including Dr. Anna Weizmann, his sister, and herself a scientist. And nearby I visited his widow in her lovely home amid the green and gold orange groves of Rehovoth.

I had come to Israel from a journey around the world. In some places I had felt the rise of hope. One saw it in men's eyes; one heard it in men's voices. I had seen construction and reconstruction in war-shattered regions and underdeveloped areas. Yet I had also seen despair and human misery on a monstrous scale. But, paradoxically, I felt both hopeful *and* despairing in the purposeful halls of the Weizmann Institute.

The Institute is a place of hope, of light, of rationality, of dedicated toil and search for truth. It is a symbol of mankind at its best. It points the way to the peaks of human attainment. Already man has such knowledge that he could abolish the grosser forms of human misery. He can reduce disease and ignorance and approach nearer than ever before to paradise on earth. Yet, over and over, he turns aside to maim and murder; to enslave; to smother truth and freedom; and to prepare, with mighty exertion, the means to make this planet, earth, as cold and lifeless as the moon.

The pity of all this was the greater to me because there, in tiny Israel, one was the more keenly aware of the somber pathos of humanity, for while the scientists in this remarkable institution sought to improve the condition of mankind, their brethren, rifles in hand, maintained everlasting vigil on the watchtowers. And there through ancient Rehovoth marched the ghostly hosts of Philistines, Hebrews, Romans, Arabs, Crusaders, and all the others who have passed that way before leaving desolation in their wake.

Who profited from those ancient wars? Who remembered even the causes of those faraway, lethal disputes? And if it was madness for the ancients to destroy one another and scorch the earth that gave them life, was it not now wicked madness for neighbors to endure one another only with hatred, or to die in conflict to no discernible end?

Asking such questions there at Rehovoth on the ancient border of Judea and Philistia one could recall how Sancho Panza once addressed himself at length to his donkey. "And," said Cervantes in a moving evocation of human loneliness, "the donkey did not answer."

Ours is an age of technology. Yet in the vast reaches of the Middle East with its more than fifty million people and its huge actual and potential wealth, the Weizmann Institute is about the only scientific research group. But it is not an instrumentality of the Israeli government. Deriving its financial support from private sources, the Institute is independent, flexible, and unhampered by bureaucracy or the shifting courses of politics.

Yet it is not these things that make the Institute worthy of our attention and generosity. It is important to the people of Israel, but it is also important to the free world. For science is civilized man's primary tool for gaining ascendancy over his material environment by bending the resources of nature to his needs and so bringing himself to a higher estate. It enables men to overcome the lack of many natural resources by creating them in a laboratory, or by producing what might be wrested from nature only at prohibitive cost.

As the Weizmann Institute is an instrument for changing the physical face of Israel, it is also clear that science can make great changes in much of the Middle East. Many of the physical problems of Israel are those of her neighbors. Thus, for example, the Institute is trying to solve the problem of commercial desalting of sea water. And certainly the Institute could be enormously helpful to its neighbor as a regional school and experimental laboratory, an inspired and enduring Point 4, and a light against darkness. But this fruitful consummation awaits, of course, genuine peace between the Arab States and Israel.

Men of good will everywhere would welcome the coming of such a fruitful relationship and a mutually enriching collaboration. These peoples are neighbors. They will continue to be neighbors. They are ethnic kin. They have similar problems of agriculture and industry. They are peoples, moreover, who centuries ago shared the highest adventures of the mind and spirit. They once jointly brought to a still largely crude western Europe, medicine, astronomy, mathematics, philosophy, and a prose and poetic literature. I suggest that nowadays they

212

might jointly bring about a renaissance of the Middle East; a revival of some of its ancient glories of learning and the arts, and the economic well-being of its people through the application of modern techniques to agriculture and industry.

And since the peoples involved are ancient peoples who have seen the passing of many centuries and the death of many kings, and have known the exaltation of victory and the disillusion of defeat, they are admirably equipped by time and experience to resolve their difficulties in the name of a common good.

As for us in the United States, we must ask ourselves whether the problem of the defense of the Middle East is one of rifles or of bread—or of both; whether the enemies, despair and poverty, within are not as menacing as the common enemies without. And I have noticed of late with great satisfaction what appears to be some change of emphasis by our government from the military aspects of security to long-range economic development, at least in Asia.

As a friend of Israel since its inception, permit me to counsel patience and a broad perspective. In all fairness, one must see the Israel-Arab conflict in the context of the whole Middle East and Far East security program. One must, I think, accept the over-all assumption that an Arab world with a friendly orientation to the West is better for Israel than an Arab world with a friendly orientation in the other direction. One cannot, in good faith, take issue with the striving of our officials and other Western nations to improve relations, co-operation, and confidence in the Arab world. This would be a major goal of any administration in Washington.

But let me return from this distant excursion to the Weizmann Institute named in honor of one of the great men of our times—Chaim Weizmann, linguist, scientist, statesman, visionary—and first President of Israel. Already one of the most effective research complexes in the world, the Institute has come far within a short time. And there is every reason to believe it will go farther in the future, that it will make greater and greater contributions to Israel and to human understanding. And perhaps it will also help to point the way for the "know-why" of ethics to catch up and unite with the "know-how" of science, which is the greatest challenge to human understanding of all.

While there are larger research institutions, the promise of the Weizmann Institute is very great, and I think there may be something prophetic about the fact that its scholars are working on that soil where once the small David went out to meet the giant Goliath.

The Formosa Crisis:
A Peaceful Solution

MY FELLOW COUNTRYMEN:

I have not spoken to you for more than four months. And I do so tonight only because I have been deeply disturbed by the recent course of events in the Far East and because many of you have asked me for my views. I have waited until the first excitement about the islands, Quemoy and Matsu, has subsided and we can more calmly examine our situation in the Straits of Formosa and in Asia. In matters of national security emotion is no substitute for intelligence, nor rigidity for prudence. To act coolly, intelligently, and prudently in perilous circumstances is the test of a man—and also a nation.

Our common determination, Republicans and Democrats alike, is to avoid atomic war and achieve a just and lasting peace. We all agree on that, I think, but not on the ways and means to that end. And that's what I want to talk about—war, and ways and means to a peaceful solution in the present crisis in the Straits of Formosa.

On this April evening, I remember vividly that it was in April just ten years ago that the largest conference in all diplomatic history met at San Francisco to write the Charter of the United Nations—a charter of liberation for the peoples of the earth from the scourge of war and want.

The spirit of San Francisco was one of optimism and boundless hope. The long night was lifting; Hitler's armies were on the eve of collapse; the war lords of Japan were tottering. Our hearts were high in that bright blue dawn of a new day—just ten years ago.

But tonight, despite the uneasy truces in Korea and Indo-China, our country once again confronts the iron face of war—war that may be unlike anything that man has seen since the

Radio Speech, Chicago, April 11, 1955.

creation of the world, for the weapons man created can destroy not only his present but his future as well. With the invention of the hydrogen bomb and all the frightful spawn of fission and fusion, the human race has crossed one of the great watersheds of history, and mankind stands in new territory, in uncharted lands.

The tragedy is that the possibility of war just now seems to hinge upon Quemoy and Matsu, small islands that lie almost as close to the coast of China as Staten Island does to New York —islands which, presumably have been fortified by the Chinese Nationalists with our approval and assistance.

Having loudly hinted at American intervention in Indo-China just a year ago, and then backed away; having forced General Chiang Kai-shek to evacuate the Tachen islands when the Communists made menacing gestures just a couple of months ago, we now face the bitter consequences of our government's Far Eastern policy once again: either another damaging and humiliating retreat, or else the hazard of war, modern war, unleashed not by necessity, not by strategic judgment, not by the honor of allies or for the defense of frontiers, but by a policy based more on political difficulties here at home than the realities of our situation in Asia.

Given these unhappy choices it appears that President Eisenhower will decide what to do if and when the attack comes, depending on whether in his judgment it is just an attack on these islands or a prelude to an assault on Formosa. While our President has great military experience, perhaps it is not improper to ask whether any man can read the mind of an enemy within a few hours of such an attack and determine whether, at some later date, the enemy plans to go further and invade Formosa. Is it wise to allow the dread question of modern war to hinge upon such a guess?

Many of the President's most influential associates—including the Republican leader in the Senate and the Chairman of the Republican Policy Committee—have been insisting that he pledge us to the defense of these islands. They say that another bluff and backdown, another retreat in Asia, would add substance to what the Chinese Communists say about the U.S. being a "paper tiger."

216

Those who demand a pledge to go to war also say that having gone this far with Chiang Kai-shek to let him down now, when he is reinforcing these islands and preparing an all-out stand, would deal a heavy blow to the morale of his forces and endanger the defenses of Formosa itself.

Now there is undeniable merit to these and other arguments, but I must say in all candor that they seem to me overborne by the counter-arguments, and I have the greatest misgivings about risking a third World War in defense of these little islands in which we would have neither the same legal justification nor the same support as in the defense of Formosa. They are different from Formosa. They have always belonged to China. But Formosa belonged to Japan and was ceded by the Japanese peace treaty. We have as much right to be there as anybody, except perhaps the real Formosans.

But, of course, the President's judgment must be final. He asked for and got from Congress the sole responsibility for making this decision. His word is our law, and, as Senator Lyndon Johnson, the majority leader, has said: "We are not going to take the responsibility out of the hands of the constitutional leader and try to arrogate it to ourselves." So the ultimate decision must rest with the constitutional leader, the President, and he will have my prayers for his wisdom and fortitude in making this critical decision, if he must and when he must. I only hope that the inflammatory voices in his party and his administration do not unbalance his consideration of these critical questions:

Are the offshore islands essential to the security of the U.S.?

Are they, indeed, even essential to the defense of Formosa—which all Americans have been agreed upon since President Truman sent the Seventh Fleet there five years ago?

Or is it, as the Secretary of Defense says, that the loss of Quemoy and Matsu would make no significant military difference?

Can they be defended without resort to nuclear weapons?

If not, while I know we now have the means to incinerate, to burn up, much of living China, and quickly, are we prepared to use such weapons to defend islands so tenuously related to American security?

Finally, are we prepared to shock and alienate not alone our traditional allies but most of the major non-Communist powers of Asia by going to war over islands to which the United States has no color of claim and which are of questionable value to the defense of Formosa?

Are we, in short, prepared to face the prospect of war in the morass of China, possibly global war, standing almost alone in a sullen or hostile world?

These are the questions that must be answered, this time I hope with more concern for realities in Asia and for unity with our allies, than for fantasies in Formosa and for placating implacable extremists in America.

At this late date there may be no wholly satisfactory way of resolving the dilemma. But if we learn something from this experience, then perhaps we can turn our present difficulties to good account and devise an approach more in keeping with the realities of Asia and of the Hydrogen Age.

And that causes me to say that the division of our coalition over these offshore islands, the weakening of the Grand Alliance of free nations pledged to stand together to defend themselves, is in my judgment a greater peril to enduring peace than the islands themselves.

I know some politicians tell us that we don't need allies. Life would certainly be much simpler if that were so, for our friends can be highly irritating. But it is not so. We need allies because we have only 6 per cent of the world's population. We need them because the overseas air bases essential to our own security are on their territory. We need allies because they are the source of indispensable strategic materials. We need, above all, the moral strength that the solidarity of the world community alone can bring to our cause. Let us never underestimate the weight of moral opinion. It can be more penetrating than bullets, more durable than steel. It was a great general, Napoleon, who wrote that: "In war, moral considerations are three-quarters of the battle."

Should we be plunged into another great war, the maintenance of our alliances and the respect and good will of the uncommitted nations of Asia will be far more important to us than the possession of these offshore islands by General Chiang Kai-shek ever could be. Moreover, the maintenance of a united front is of vital importance to the defense of Formosa itself, since, in addition to the material and military support our friends might contribute, their moral support, and the knowledge by the Communist leaders that they would be facing a united free world, would be a much more effective deterrent to an assault on Formosa than is our present lonely and irresolute position.

How shall we mend the walls of our coalition? How shall we frustrate the supreme aim of the Moscow-Peiping axis— to drive a wedge between America and her allies? And is there any hope of a peaceful solution of the offshore island question?

I think so. Senator George, the Chairman of the Foreign Relations Committee, has recently pointed the way: "We nations of the free world," he said, "must understand each other and reach a measure of unity before any hopeful approach can be made to a re-examination of . . . our Far Eastern problems."

And Governor Harriman of New York, long familiar with the problems of maintaining a coalition, warned us the other day that in Asia "the whole world is a party at interest," and that it has been not only illogical but deadly dangerous, he said, "to arrogate to ourselves the sole responsibility for decisions which involve the future of many people."

So I would urge our government to promptly consult our friends, yes, and the uncommitted states too, and ask them all to join with us in an open declaration condemning the use of force in the Formosa Strait, and agreeing to stand with us in the defense of Formosa against any aggression, pending some final settlement of its status—by independence, neutralization, trusteeship, plebiscite, or whatever is wisest.

Nor do I see any reason why we should not invite Soviet Russia, which is united by treaty with Red China, to declare its position, to indicate whether it prefers the possibility of ultimate settlement by agreement to an unpredictable, perhaps limitless conflict, started by an arrogant, foolhardy Communist China, either by miscalculation or by design.

Fortified by such an international declaration denouncing the use of force; with the assurance of such collective support for the defense of Formosa; and with the addition, thereby, of moral solidarity to military strength, I should think Quemoy and Matsu would have little further importance to the Nationalists, let alone to us—and that they could then be relinquished, before we stumble any farther down the dismal road to war that nobody wants.

Diplomacy prescribes no rigid formula for accomplishing our objectives, and another major avenue in the quest for a peaceful solution in the Far East remains unexplored: the United Nations. I should think that the United States, together with friends and allies in Europe and Asia, could submit a resolution to the United Nations General Assembly, calling upon the Assembly likewise to condemn any effort to alter the present status of Formosa by force. And I think we could afford to go further and call upon the United Nations Assembly to seek a formula for the permanent future of Formosa, consistent with the wishes of its people, with international law, and with world security.

One of the weaknesses of our position is that we have been making Formosa policy as we thought best regardless of others. We have not made it clear that we are helping to hold Formosa not as an offensive but as a purely defensive measure. We have not made it clear because the administration has not been clear itself. But we can't expect other nations to support policies they disagree with, let alone ambiguous and dangerous policies.

Joint action along the lines I've indicated would put Formosa policy on a much broader and more comprehensible basis. In the eyes of the Asian nations we would thereby achieve a consistent and morally unquestionable position in providing for the protection of the Formosans according to the principles and ideals of international law. In the eyes of our European friends we would once more have asserted our full belief in the value, indeed in the indispensability, of maintaining the alliance of the free world against the slave world. And in the eyes of our Nationalist friends on Formosa, surely the understanding and support of the bulk of the non-Communist world is a much stronger defense of Formosa than these islands can possibly be.

But, if the Chinese Communists refuse; if they insist on force and reject any peaceful solution, then at least it would be clear to everyone who the aggressors were. And, clearly, if the Chinese are so bent on violence, so intoxicated by their success,

220

so indifferent to the grisly realities of modern war, then we have no alternative but to meet force with force. But let us at least meet it with our allies beside us and the blame placed squarely where it belongs—not on America's fantasies and inflexibility, but on the unteachable and unquenchable ambition and the indifference to human life of China's Communist regime.

To profit from this unhappy experience we might ask ourselves how we ever got in this position, how the prestige and honor of the great United States, not to mention the peace of the world, could be staked on some little islands within the very shadow of the China coast in which we have no claim or interest.

The answer, of course, lies partly in the fact that domestic political considerations have influenced our Formosa policy lately. Domestic politics should not enter our foreign affairs, least of all factional conflict between the two wings of the President's party, but they have, and too often our hot and cold, vacillating behavior has reflected efforts to please both of the views that divide our government and the Republican party, especially on Far Eastern policy.

And, while I do not belittle some recent achievements in the foreign field, for the same reasons too much of our foreign policy of late has disclosed a yawning gap between what we say and what we do—between our words and deeds.

For example, you recall that just a year ago as the Communist pressure rose in Indo-China, so did our warlike, menacing words. The Vice-President of the United States even talked of sending American soldiers to fight on the mainland of Asia. But what happened? Nothing.

Likewise all the bold, brave talk about liberation that raised such vain hopes among the peoples behind the iron curtain has long since evaporated, with the loss of half of Vietnam and much of our prestige and influence.

So also we hear no more of last year's dire threats of instantaneous and massive atomic retaliation. Instead, the President has spoken lately of pinpoint retaliation with tactical weapons. I fear, however, that the psychological effect of the use of atomic weapons, large or small, will be most unfortunate.

But there has been plenty of massive verbal retaliation, and the administration's policy of extravagant words has alarmed our friends a good deal more than it has deterred the aggressors. For our allies assumed that the great United States meant what it said.

Now let me be clear. I am not criticizing the administration for abandoning these extravagant positions; I am criticizing it for taking such positions, for making threats which it is not prepared to back up, and thereby undermining faith in the United States. Theodore Roosevelt said: "Never draw unless you intend to shoot," and I fear this wordy warfare has made more friends in Asia for China than for us.

Another example of these winged words, as we have seen, was President Eisenhower's dramatic announcement two years ago that he was unleashing Chiang Kai-shek, taking the wraps off him, presumably for an attack on the mainland to reconquer China. However, it was apparent to everyone else, if not to us, that such an invasion across a hundred miles of water by a small, overage, underequipped army against perhaps the largest army and the largest nation on earth could not possibly succeed without all-out support from the United States.

Since it seemed incredible to sober, thoughtful people that the government of the United States could be bluffing on such a matter, the President's unleashing policy has caused widespread anxiety that we planned to support a major war with China which might involve the Soviet Union. Hence we find ourselves where we are today—on Quemoy and Matsu—alone.

What, then, are the lessons to be drawn from the past two years?

In the first place, I think we should abandon, once and for all, the policy of wishful thinking and wishful talking, the policy of big words and little deeds.

We must renounce go-it-aloneism.

We shall have to face the fact that General Chiang's army cannot invade the mainland unless we are prepared to accept enormous burdens and risks—alone.

The world will respect us for recognizing mistakes and correcting them. But if our present posture in the offshore islands, for example, is a wrong one, who will respect us for stubbornly persisting in it? If we cease to deceive ourselves over the hard realities of power in the Formosa situation, we shall have taken the first step toward our first essential—the restoration of unity of purpose and action between ourselves and our allies in the free world. But our friends have made it clear that so long as fantasy, rigidity, and domestic politics seem to stand in the way of peaceful Formosa settlement, they will not support us if, in spite of our endeavors, a conflict should break out.

So, finally, let us face the fact that keeping friends these days calls for more statesmanship than challenging enemies, and the cause of world peace transcends any domestic political considerations.

But, preoccupied as we all are these days with the immediate problem of these islands, we must try to keep things in perspective somehow, and not lose sight of our main objectives. For beyond Quemoy and Matsu, and even Formosa, lie the urgent and larger problems of Asia—the growing attraction of enormous, reawakened China, the struggle of the underdeveloped countries to improve their condition and keep their independence, and the grave misgivings about America.

If the best hope for today's world is a kind of atomic balance, the decisive battle in the struggle against aggression may be fought not on battlefields but in the minds of men, and the area of decision may well be out there among the uncommitted peoples of Asia and Africa who look and listen and who must, in the main, judge us by what we say and do.

It is not only over the offshore islands crisis that we need a new sense of direction and to mend our fences. Too often of late we have turned to the world a face of stern military power. Too often the sound they hear from Washington is the call to arms, the rattling of the saber. Too often our constructive, helpful economic programs have been obscured, our good done by stealth. Thus have we Americans, the most peaceful and generous people on earth been made to appear hard, belligerent, and careless of those very qualities of humanity which, in fact, we value most. The picture of America—the kindly, generous, deeply pacific people who are really America—has been clouded in the world, to the comfort of the aggressors and the dismay of our friends.

As best we can, let us correct this distorted impression, for we will win no hearts and minds in the new Asia by uttering louder threats and brandishing bigger swords. The fact is that we have not created excess military strength. The fact is that compared to freedom's enemies we have created if anything too little; the trouble is that we have tried to cover our deficiencies with bold words and have thus obscured our peaceful purposes and our ultimate reliance on quiet firmness, rather than bluster and vacillation, on wisdom rather than warnings, on forbearance rather than dictation.

We will be welcome to the sensitive people of Asia, more as engineers and doctors and agricultural experts, coming to build, to help, to heal than as soldiers. Point Four was an idea far more stirring, far more powerful, than all the empty slogans about liberation and retaliation and unleashing rolled together. So I say, let us present once more the true face of America— warm and modest and friendly, dedicated to the welfare of all mankind, and demanding nothing except a chance for all to live and let live, to grow and govern as they wish, free from interference, free from intimidation, free from fear.

Let this be the American mission in the Hydrogen Age. Let us stop slandering ourselves and appear before the world once again—as we really are—as friends, not as masters; as apostles of principle, not of power; in humility, not arrogance; as champions of peace, not as harbingers of war. For our strength lies, not alone in our proving grounds and our stockpiles, but in our ideals, our goals, and their universal appeal to all men who are struggling to breathe free.

Partnership and Independence

BETWEEN winter and fall, the world has seen Communist diplomacy swing from storm to fair, while opinion among the free nations has swung as widely from apprehension to hope.

These, however, are surface changes, and underneath there is reason to suspect that very little has really changed. For one thing, the "spirit of Geneva" was certainly Russia's objective as well as ours, and while our anxiety has since diminished and tensions have relaxed, it has been in spite of the fact that no major Soviet policy has been modified to speak of. We can and should hope for better things as a result of the approaching Foreign Ministers' meetings, but hope must not become a substitute for proof, nor must our faith outstrip their works.

But there is another and deeper reason for avoiding excessive euphoria about the international shape of things to come. Some of us have become so obsessed with the Communist menace, so hypnotized by the division of the globe into two camps, that one sight of Marshal Bulganin with a smile on his face, or Mr. Khrushchev and Mr. Bohlen in the same rowboat, has a suddenly relaxing effect—a warm and welcome feeling that the division of mankind may really be coming to an end and with it all the evils that have plagued us for the last half-century.

But of course it isn't so. Communism feeds on but does not create all the frictions and conflicts of our small world. Communism did not prevent the long breach between Russia and Yugoslavia. Communism has not reconciled East German workers to their "norms." Communism cannot decide whether Russia or China should dominate the North Korean satellite. Communism does not change a Chinese rice deficit into a surplus. And so it goes.

And Communism did not cause the great revolution of

Address at Queen's University, Kingston, Ontario. October 15, 1955.

225

independence that has swept the postwar world and brought so many great new nation states into existence with all their new problems and the accompanying fragmentation of power in the world. The rights and claims of nation states, the divisions among diverse racial and religious groups, the hard clash of competing economic interests—all these preceded Communism and exist today independently of it. This is the tough, rough substance of international relations, and although Communism, the cold or cool war and the division of the world, may make the working over of this raw material more difficult and explosive, they do not alter the basic fact that the power relations of sovereign states are perhaps the most unpromising material conceivable for the good life on earth.

And so when two national communities, Canada and the United States, living side by side—as Poland has lived beside Russia or Belgium by Germany—continue through a period of history that has seen more and worse wars than any other in man's homicidal career—when two such communities contrive to keep the peace, maintain friendly relations, and steadily increase their economic interdependence and common well-being, the matter is not one simply for mutual congratulation. It is rather a matter for thoughtful and thankful investigation, and of deep interest and ultimate hope that in the relations between the United States and Canada some clue can be found to the international good life in an atomic world. For this, much more than Communism, is, I believe, the riddle which we must solve. I was going to say "which we must solve, or perish." But in the afterglow of Geneva such dread words are not yet fashionable again. And, moreover, it seems to me probable, if paradoxical, that the final extinction of our heedless species has become less likely as its means of self-annihilation have become more lethal.

The political foundation of the successful relationship between Canada and the United States has unfortunately become something of a cliché. "The unguarded frontier" we either take for granted or use. But it is worth noting that we can make those excursions back and forth almost without the usual genuflections to the national rituals of customs, visas, currency inspections, and so forth, which harass so much of the world.

But the greater significance of this frontier is, of course, that we have long since given up the idea of using force and have accepted in our relations with one another the rule of law, of mediation, of peaceful adjustment. And the result is at least one working model of an international society in which force is not the final arbiter. There can be no more vital contribution to the atomic age.

And now let me suggest a moral from this story of our happy coexistence and contiguous existence. Few nations have entirely complementary economies. Certainly between the United States and Canada there are economic interests at issue which, in other states and other epochs, would have led to bitter hostility and conflict. The most obvious is the contrast in economic power and scale and the fear, in the smaller neighbor, that the economic giant next door may overlay its economic independence. Such fears are rampant in the world today as the less developed nations—in Asia, Africa, and Middle East—look passionately for the means of increasing their supplies of capital and developing their resources. Yet they fear almost as passionately that assistance from abroad, particularly assistance from the capitalist West, will endanger their newly gained and fearfully prized independence. Ideologically and politically, this may well be the greatest single obstacle in the way of a general mobilization of resources to aid the underdeveloped areas.

Looking back over the last four hundred years, the nations are not irrational in their fears. Western trade and Western capital were, historically, the opening wedge of Western imperial control. But need they look only backward to their own experience? Surely between Canada and the United States, between a small and, in the physical sense, not yet fully developed nation and its giant neighbor—giant in terms of developed resources—a relationship is growing which is more typical of modern Western thought and practice than the mercantilism and colonialism of Europe in centuries gone by. Nine billion dollars of American capital are invested in Canada, and three hundred American business enterprises are established on Canadian soil. But in return the expansion of Canadian prosperity has enabled Canadians to invest nearly two billions in the United States. Thus, in terms of per capita investment,

227

Canada's stake in the United States is actually higher than that of the United States in Canada.

There is no trace here of the "imperialism" the underdeveloped areas of the world regard with such infinite distaste. At no time, probably, has the American government been so aware of the lively independence of Canada's policy makers, and, as Canadian prosperity has grown in the last decade with so rare a combination of momentum and stability, at no time have Canadians in general been more conscious of their separate and effective nationhood. Economic co-operation with a powerful neighbor has brought no lessening of political independence. On the contrary, the prosperity it has helped to foster has increased Canadian self-confidence.

Here, surely, is a lesson and an encouragement for any nation that fears the effects of Western capital assistance in the development of its native resources. And one could cite other instances in which economic co-operation beneficial to both countries has taken the place of the more habitual struggles for resources between rival states. Wars have been fought for the control of great waterways and harbors—the Rhine, the Danube, the Dardanelles—indeed Tsarist Russia's favorite excuse for southward expansion was its need for a "warmwater port." More recently we have seen rivalries between Rotterdam and Antwerp cause friction within the promising Benelux experiment. In Asia, Pakistan and India are struggling to find a compromise in the use and division of the great rivers of the Punjab.

But today, in North America, a chain of lakes and waterways more mighty than any of these is—after prolonged Canadian pressure, I may say, and say gratefully—to be developed in peaceful co-operation by both the nations concerned. The St. Lawrence Seaway is, no doubt, taken for granted as a symbol of creative, functional co-operation between nation states—but that is to underestimate its significance. By any historical comparison, it would have been more normal to have fought for the control of the lakes than to have developed them jointly. In fact, the very success of our peaceful experiments tends to lessen the impact they should have in the world at large as examples and portents of a new and better method of handling international relations.

I repeat that our achievements in economic co-operation have not been accomplished against a background of natural and effortless economic harmony. On the contrary, over a wide area, the two economies are strictly competitive. Both are manufacturing nations, each trying to penetrate the other's market. And both are massive exporters of foodstuffs at a time when surpluses of their biggest bulk exports are piling up on both sides of the border and when the disposal of these surpluses has become the most urgent of agricultural problems.

While our countries have both joined the Wheat Agreement and have had a reciprocal trade agreement for twenty years, broadly speaking, I suppose, we must admit that we have not so far made any very spectacular joint contribution to the easing of trade problems, save in so far as postwar prosperity has expanded the market for all our goods.

Our trading relations have been bedeviled by all the familiar restrictive devices of international commerce—tariffs on both sides, imperial preference in Canada, quotas and "peril points" and shifting criteria on the part of the United States.

Yet here, our two nations have taken a step away from the frictions of the past. The Joint Economic Board established now makes it the concern and duty of our governments to meet, discuss, and work out joint solutions and not settle back to a mutual process of vigorous throat-slitting. This principle of joint consultation was, incidentally, the main reason for the success achieved under the Marshall Plan, and it should be regarded not as a temporary postwar expedient, but as a settled procedure of the Western economic community, even as such consultative arrangements have been established between our countries and between all the Western nations for our mutual defense.

But I do not want for one moment to suggest that Canada has made its distinguished contribution simply as partner and co-worker with the United States. On the contrary, I believe that the Canadian people have achievements to their credit of incalculable importance in this new age in which the nations of the world are being jostled into compulsory neighborliness. Nations are continuing entities. Neither Communism nor any other "ism" is going to blur the clear frontiers of established communities. Science may bring nations closer in space, but, of itself, it creates no greater closeness of understanding. In the United States, unique conditions have enabled a combination of federalism and assimilation to produce a melting pot of peoples and out of them to build a new nation. But these special American conditions do not apply in Europe. No melting pot yet conceived is hot enough to melt and fuse its many nationalities. Nor do American conditions apply in large parts of Asia, even where, as in India, a federal structure has been built up.

But in Canada, we can witness as it were a triumph of internal coexistence in the peaceful integration of the French provinces in a wider Canadian Commonwealth. There has been no loss of entity—of language, culture, or religion. But the divergence has made for richness, not division and strife. It has created a pattern which, in its preservation of national identity and the merging of it in a greater whole, may prove the finest example that the New World can give the Old, and the best proof that the fratricidal national rivalries of the past can be resolved without surrender or those rugged ruptures of violence that are so long in healing—as we Americans well know from our Civil War experience.

Nor do I think this achievement would have been possible without another outstanding and admirable feature of Canadian political life—I mean its stability, its tolerance, and its good sense. This national temper has served well through many crises in which, to be frank, the behavior of neighbors to the south has sometimes shown to less advantage. One might recall the speed and efficiency with which Canadians handled the issue of Communist espionage and kept it rigidly and beneficently apart from the tangle of party politics. More recently, we could applaud the quiet skill with which government and public alike tackled the distribution of the Salk vaccine.

But these incidents, handled so differently in our two countries, are simply the by-products of Canada's settled political system and of a mature public opinion which give public life a good sense and a restraint valuable indeed in all domestic matters, but without price in the angry, uncertain world of hot, cold, and cooling wars.

It is no coincidence, I am sure, that Canada has earned in the councils of the British Commonwealth, of NATO, and of

230

the United Nations, a weight and influence which numbers alone could never give. It is the recognition the nations extend to the still, small voice of reason, conciliation, and compromise. And upon the world's willingness to heed such voices our ultimate hope of peaceful coexistence must depend.

The Road Away from Revolution

WE CAN SEE NOW a painful but just irony in the designation "Armistice Day." For November 11, 1918, brought only an armistice; it did not bring peace. Instead, the years since 1918 have been a parody of peace, a series of intervals between wars; and war itself has grown more ghastly and more appalling. The crisis in human history which Wilson perceived with such clarity thirty-five years ago is now upon us with redoubled urgency. In an age when total war threatens not just a setback to civilization, but its total destruction, it will profit us Americans to revisit Woodrow Wilson and reconsider his contributions to the struggle for peace.

When one thinks of Wilson and the peace, one thinks of the League of Nations—and rightly so. Yet, I doubt if the concept of the League, noble as it was, exhausted Wilson's search for peace. If I have any thesis here tonight, it is that Wilson's war against war depended only in part on the creation of new international mechanisms. It depended even more, in my judgment, on the creation of a new international spirit. And he deeply believed that the new international spirit could emerge only from new values in our own social and economic life. Wilson knew that his crusade for peace could never succeed unless the world was committed equally to a crusade for justice.

One must not forget that President Wilson first came upon the national scene, not as a student of world affairs, but as the eloquent exponent of the gospel of the New Freedom in our domestic affairs. The rise of industry and business, he felt, had transformed the economic order. There was need for a new liberation—"for the emancipation of the generous energies of a people." His mission was to work for liberation; to

From an Armistice Day address at the University of Virginia, Woodrow Wilson Centennial, November 11, 1955.

work for social justice; to establish public policy on the basis of the welfare of all, not on the welfare of a narrow group.

Let us remember the context of the times. The last years of the nineteenth century had seen an ominous concentration of wealth, and with it of political power, in a few hands. And the economic system, left to itself, would not reverse a process which it had, in fact, set in motion. *Laissez faire* could not cure what *laissez faire* had helped to start. Only one agency commanded enough authority to redress this dangerous unbalance, and this was the national government. It should use its great powers, derived from the popular vote—from "the just consent of the governed"—to restore equilibrium in the community and ensure that all interests shared in the expansion and enrichment of American life.

This was Wilson's greatest undertaking. And his central effort was to establish, as the standard of public policy, at the very core of his party's faith, the concept of the common good. As he once said: "In a self-governed country, there is one rule for everybody and that is the common interest." Wilson was by no means the first or only American politician to devote his political career to the advancement of the general welfare. But what Wilson achieved was to translate this dedication into the terms of the new industrial society.

Of course, lamentations and predictions of catastrophe ushered in such Wilsonian reforms as the Federal Reserve System, the income tax, the Federal Trade Commission, the Clayton Antitrust Act, and the rest. Reforms are always frightening to some, and his enduring achievement lay in introducing, lastingly and indelibly, the principle of the common good into the welter of confusion and conflict of the modern economy. Wilson's concept was based on the rights and interests of *all* sections of the community. He knew, as Lincoln did, that government *for* the people had to be government *by* and *of* the people.

What Wilson sought was a new birth of freedom, based on equality of rights and social justice. What he feared was government by a single interest. Wilson saw the public good in the co-operation and balance of the various sectors of the community; farmers, workers, businessmen—all must be considered. "We shall not act either justly or wisely if we attack established interests as public enemies," he wrote. And all had a right to be represented in the processes of governmental decision. Nor—may I add, in this university town which knew Wilson as well as Jefferson—nor did he propose to banish experts and even professors from the operation of government! Once, indeed, in his retirement he wrote to another great Southern statesman, Cordell Hull: "I am not afraid of making ours a 'highbrow' party, for highbrows at least think and comprehend the standards of high conduct."

In the years since Wilson, we have enlarged much of his original program. Public control of credit policy has become more effective, a more progressive income tax has helped widen the distribution of wealth, the first steps toward federal protection for the worker have been expanded into a general system of social security, the farmers have been helped not only by soil conservation and credit but by the underpinning of prices. These measures have extended the spirit of the New Freedom. Far from acting as shackles upon the independence of the economy, they have helped create a stability of purchasing power, a width of consumption and a scale of market of which business could hardly have dreamed in Wilson's day.

Nor has the business community suffered from the rising political and economic power of the other sectors. On the contrary, the intervening years have vindicated triumphantly his concept of the common good, of the government's role in securing it, and of the realizable harmony of diverse economic interests within an expanding democratic community. If you require a monument to his achievement, I would ask you to look round at the American economy of which he laid so many secure foundations.

The Wilsonian reforms thus helped produce the vast material abundance we have today. But, more important still, they contributed to a renewal of the American moral purpose. They gave meaning in a world of affairs to the fact that we are, in the words of Paul, members, one of another; they reminded us that the vital community depends on integrity, upon generosity and decency in human relationships, and on equality in human opportunities.

What Wilson saw in the nation he came to see even more

urgently in the world. In the international anarchy of his day—an anarchy which plunged Europe into war within eighteen months of his election—he had the vision, all over again, of the strife, the bitterness, the disaster which must follow if uncontrolled forces are allowed to struggle with each other with no restraints imposed by the community as a whole. The philosophy behind the League of Nations, indeed, was Wilson's guiding idea of the common good applied to international society.

As we all know, he failed to convey this vision to his people, or at least to a sufficient number of their leaders. Our nation took no part in the world's first experiment in international order. But, looking back today with the hindsight of over thirty years, we also know that his vision of a community of nations under law was—and is—the only road to lasting peace. The dream of 1919 has become the reality of the United Nations.

And so, once again, if we look for monuments to the work of Wilson, we can find them built into the very foundations of our postwar world.

This does not mean that, for Wilson, the League then—or the United Nations today—would constitute the whole of a strategy of peace. The grounds of the universal unrest and perturbation lie deeper; they lie, Wilson himself suggested, "at the sources of the spiritual life of our time." Underneath the recriminations of diplomats and the conflicts of nation-states, there boiled up then—as there boils up today—the hopes, resentments, and aspirations not just of leaders but of great masses of people seeking for themselves and their children the rights and privileges which, Wilson said, "all normal men desire and must have if they are to be contented and within reach of happiness."

This, it seems to me, is the heart of the matter—and the heart not only of democracy and of freedom but of peace itself. Violence is, after all, the confession that mutual relations of respect and good will have broken down and the web of common life has been torn apart. The most urgent task before any society, domestic or world-wide, is to check grievances, clashes, blind oppositions of interest, long before they reach the flashpoint of war.

235

These subterranean pressures rising round the world—of dire need, of hunger and disease, of awakened hope, of nationalism, of envy, of impatience to make up for lost centuries—these are the explosive stuff of international life. And this Woodrow Wilson knew, just as he knew that poverty and underprivilege and the gulfs between rich and poor were fire hazards in America's basement. In one of his last public utterances, he discussed the phenomenon which so threatens and alarms us today—the rise of Communism.

"The sum of the whole matter is this," Wilson said, "that our civilization cannot survive materially unless it is redeemed spiritually." What we require, he said, must include "sympathy and helpfulness and a willingness to forego self-interest in order to promote the welfare, happiness, and contentment of others and of the community as a whole." This, he said, thinking of the terror of the Communist alternative—this "was the road away from revolution."

I would suggest that Wilson still has much to say to us today. And that what he has to say is that we must wage more fiercely than ever the same twofold struggle of a generation ago: the war against want and oppression, and the war against war itself.

We have made a start in the war against poverty and oppression. But our world is not moving by the action of some inscrutable "hidden hand" toward spreading prosperity, rising standards, and the extension of freedom. On the contrary, the drift is the other way, to population outstripping resources in backward lands, to wealth accumulating in the already wealthy West, and to the Communists' propaganda and infiltration. If they succeed in capturing the revolution of the underdeveloped areas—the uncommitted third of the world—as they have already captured the revolutions of Russia and China, the circle of freedom on earth will dangerously shrink.

Yet anti-Communism and self-interest should not be our only motive in offering a helping hand to people struggling for dignity and independence. Unselfishness and magnanimity are also part of the American record. And there is much we can do to help reverse the fatality in less fortunate lands whereby poverty breeds ever more poverty and hatred breeds ever more hatred. We can set our overwhelming resources of wealth and skill to work to improve the productivity and standards of life. We can furnish more of our brain power for activity abroad and widen the opportunities for giving education and training to our foreign friends here in the United States. And we can convince the peoples of the world that we do this not just to check Communism or to impose Americanism or to perpetuate colonialism, but because we believe that the dream of a fearless, free, and equal society, first cherished within these shores, is more potent than ever and can be spread around the world.

But perhaps the most urgent struggle of all is the war against war itself. Our past failures to control war caused great wreckage in the world and took many lives, but they did not destroy the world itself. Total war in the nuclear epoch will not let civilization off so lightly.

What humanity now demands is a great leap ahead in our thinking and in our action. We talk of "limiting" war. But that is not enough. War in the Hydrogen Age resists limitation: one cannot keep a chain reaction on a leash. So the ultimate goal is not limitation, it is not an uneasy balance of weapons, or of terror, but the abolition of war by the abolition of the means of war.

The difficulties in the way of achieving an enforceable system of disarmament are immense. Maybe the problem is insoluble now as it has been in the past. But it seems to me that the urgency is such that we can settle for nothing less than a sustained and dogged search for effective disarmament with the best brains we can muster, and that we have no greater foreign policy objective.

That we must move ahead creatively and decisively along all the world's fronts in the struggle for the common good of freedom becomes more imperative every day. Each day's news is another plea for sober realism. For now that the rosy mists around last summer's meeting at the summit are rising we see all about us signs of the disintegration of our whole security system. The fabric is unraveling. Most recently Arab-Israel hostility has risen to a new pitch of intensity along the Egyptian frontier, just as the Soviet design to split the Arab world from the West becomes more apparent.

It is interesting and relevant to recall that Wilson believed in encouraging Jewish settlement in Palestine and took an active part in making the Balfour Declaration a vital part of the Palestine mandate under the League of Nations. Since then the state of Israel has become a fact, and, unhappily, so also has the bitter hostility of its Arab neighbors. For five years violence along the armistice lines has been mounting. Unless these clashes cease there is danger of all-out war developing while we debate which side was the aggressor.

A major effort of statesmanship is required if we are to avert a political disaster in this troubled area. We have shown little initiative within or outside the United Nations in devising measures to prevent these border clashes. After years of experience it would seem evident that the only way to avoid bloodshed and violence along the border is to keep the troops of these antagonists apart. And I wonder if United Nations guards could not undertake patrol duties in the areas of tension and collision. Certainly both sides would respect United Nations patrols where they do not trust each other.

In this country we have been dismayed by the arms deal between Egypt and Russia. Of course there should be an equitable balance of armed strength so that neither side feels that it lives by the grace of its none-too-kindly neighbor. We must help, if need be, to counteract any Soviet attempt to upset such a balance, and we must make it emphatically clear that the status quo shall not be changed by force. But we do not want to see an arms race in this area where the principles of Woodrow Wilson's fourteen points once shone like a lighthouse after centuries of dark oppression.

The Middle East has long been an area of Russian ambition. And we trust our friends there have neither overlooked the fate of nations which have listened to the siren songs of Moscow, nor forgotten that the Soviet Foreign Minister told the Nazi Foreign Minister in 1940 that one of the conditions of a Nazi-Soviet agreement was that the Persian Gulf was to be a sphere of Soviet influence.

The contagious flames of undeclared war between Israel and her neighbors have smoldered too long. We applaud the peaceful efforts of the Secretary General of the United Nations and we must bestir ourselves to help create conditions which will work toward peace, not conflict, in this troubled area. The United States does not choose sides when it chooses peace.

Let us, I say, not deceive ourselves. The Soviets have sharply altered their tactics and stepped boldly forth from the shadows of conspiracy and secrecy. To our dismay they are now competing openly and directly with the West. We must take care lest the illusions of the new charm policy further weaken our defenses, moral and physical. And we must take care, too, lest a rigid military-security diplomacy hobble our foreign policy. We cannot meet each new problem in the war against war and the war against want just in terms of air bases, military alliances, and nuclear stockpiles. If we do, our influence will steadily ebb away in those crucial areas of the world where progress and peace are the major concerns.

So, let us keep our powder dry, our minds supple, our hearts warm, and our spirits high as the great contest of our times moves forward into a new, even more perilous phase.

As Woodrow Wilson devised new methods to promote the common good among men and among nations, so must we devise new methods to meet the challenges of our times. Surely this is what the spirit of Wilson has to say to us today. And it commits us to the institutions for world understanding and for peace which Wilson tried so nobly to establish.

It commits us to labor relentlessly against the causes of war and against the means of war—a labor which must go on and on until men everywhere can live in the sunlight without oppression and fear.

This image from the greatness of America's bright past commits us most of all to enliven the new international spirit without which Wilson knew that neither institutions nor material programs could succeed. It is the spirit that recognizes that justice transcends victory, that "humanity is above all nations," that "every man beareth the stamp of the human condition," that in the words of our Illinois poet:

There is only one man in the world and his name is All Men.
There is only one woman in the world and her name is All Women.

239

There is only one child in the world and the child's name is All Children.*

Let us take this occasion to consecrate ourselves to these purposes, until at last Wilson's words will no longer mock us—until at last the world will be truly safe for democracy.

* From *Names* by Carl Sandburg. Copyright 1953 by Carl Sandburg. Reprinted by permission of the author.